Also by the author
Flat-Tops and Fledglings:
A History of American Aircraft Carriers

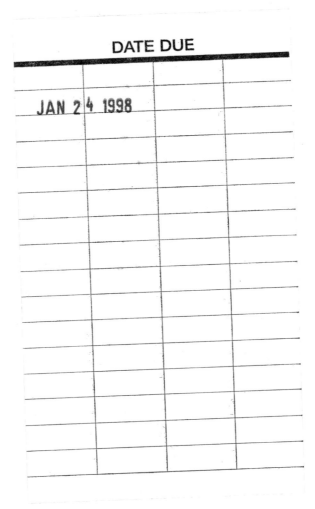

HOW THEY BECAME THE

BEATLES

A Definitive History of the Early Years: 1960–1964

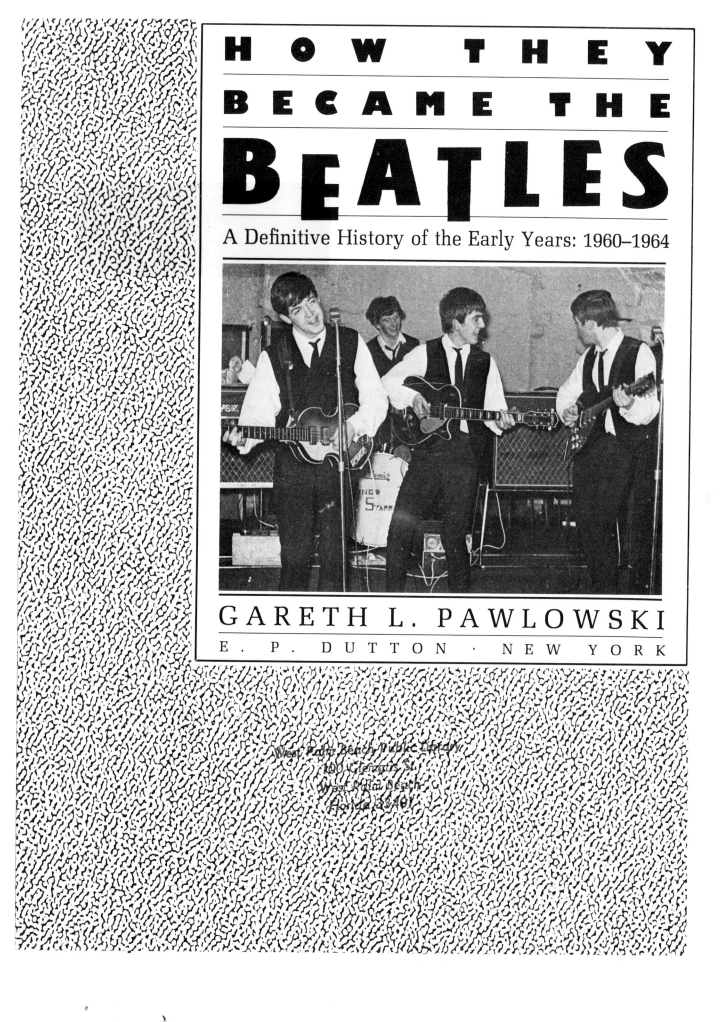

GARETH L. PAWLOWSKI

E. P. DUTTON · NEW YORK

Published in the United States by E. P. Dutton, a division of
Penguin Books USA Inc., 2 Park Avenue, New York, N.Y.
10016.

Published simultaneously in Canada by Fitzhenry and
Whiteside, Limited, Toronto.

Library of Congress Cataloging-in-Publication Data

Pawlowski, Gareth L.
How they became the Beatles: a definitive history of the
early years: 1960–1964 / Gareth L. Pawlowski. — 1st ed.
p. cm.
ISBN 0-525-24823-4
1. Beatles. 2. Rock musicians—England—Biography.
I. Title.
ML421.B4P38 1989
782.4166'092'2—dc20
[B]   89-32060
          CIP
          MN

Designed by Jackie Schuman

10 9 8 7 6 5 4 3 2 1

First Edition

ILLUSTRATION CREDITS

The author and publishers wish to thank the following for per-
mission to use photographs in *How They Became the Beatles*:
The British Broadcasting Corporation: pp. 152 (both), 153, and
264 (top)—photographs copyright © by BBC.
Peter Kaye Photography: pp. 99 (both), 100 (both), 101 (bottom),
103 (both), and 104 (top)—photographs copyright © by Peter
Kaye Photography.
Gareth L. Pawlowski: all photos on pp. 13–22 and 47–56 copy-
right © by Gareth L. Pawlowski.
Alan Swerdlow: all photographs on pp. 65–78.
All color photographs are from the private collection of Thomas
J. Meenach III.
The remaining illustrations are all from the private collection
of the author.

For my Rusty

ACKNOWLEDGMENTS

Many people provided me with original material and in-depth interviews to make this history as definitive as possible. I would like to acknowledge everyone who helped, and, in particular, all those who provided me with much of the material that made this book possible.

For allowing me into their homes I wish to thank: Pete Best, Clive Epstein, Queenie Epstein, Allan Williams, Cheniston K. Roland, Albert Marrion, Bill and Virginia Harry, Pete Kaye, Bill Connel, Les Chadwick, Val Whitaker, Bob Wooler, and Alan Swerdlow. For personal interviews, correspondence, and many telephone conversations, I wish to thank: Tony Sheridan, Jurgen Vollmer, Dick James, Randy Wood, Bernadette Farrell, Brian Kelly, Valerie Keene, Bel Baker, Tony Saunders, John Stump, Bob Steele Photography, Lori, and Robin.

C O N T E N T S

Since the first published accounts of the Beatles began to appear, the history of their early years has been marred by misconceptions. I believe an author should be held accountable for what is presented to readers.

Unfortunately, this has not been the case with most of the Beatles' biographers because the authors consistently fail in one major area—original research. Having read most of the Beatles histories that have been published since 1964, I discovered that many books offered the same erroneous data that had appeared in previously published accounts. Not one writer had bothered to challenge what had already been published.

How They Became the Beatles is a concise, accurate depiction of the Beatles' early years (1960–1964). Major events in the boys' rise to fame have been corrected and differ from previously published accounts. In reconstructing the events that make up their early history, I have worked primarily from original documents and photographs, and from private interviews conducted during my research in England.

My interest in collecting original printed material and first-issue recordings began in 1954. Although I had enjoyed the talents of Joni James, Hank Williams, Hank Snow, Eddie Fisher, and Frankie Laine during my early teen years, I did not become a devout fan of any particular artist until the summer of 1954. It happened during a visit to Memphis, my hometown. While growing up in Memphis I had listened to the true country music styles of Roy Acuff, Red Foley, and T. Texas Tyler. During my visit to Memphis in 1954, I happened to hear a new song by a new singer named Elvis Presley. The two country music radio stations played "Blue Moon of Kentucky" at least ten times a day. The song impressed me so much that whenever it aired I frantically searched for my brother so that he could hear this exciting new singer. When he finally heard the song about three days later, he too was hooked.

The disc jockey said that Elvis Presley would appear at the Slim Whitman Country Jamboree on Friday night, July 30, 1954. Bob Neal, who would become Elvis's second manager, hosted this event at the Overton Park Shell.

Hearing Elvis sing live eleven days after the release of his first Sun single ("Blue Moon of Kentucky"/"That's All Right," [Sun 209]) is a memory forever embedded in my mind. Elvis also sang "Good Rockin' Tonight"—six weeks before he recorded the song.

It was not only the voice of Elvis that was different; Scotty Moore's lead guitar and the bass-slapping humor of Bill Black made the trio an unbeatable act. Terms such as "rock-a-billy," and "rock 'n' roll" did not yet exist, but the music was new and exciting on that hot July night. Another unusual thing occurred that evening that was just as memorable as Elvis's performance— the crowd's response. Teenage girls and older women screamed hysterically as Elvis sang and moved on the stage.

During 1955, Elvis, Scotty, and Bill were advertised as Elvis Presley and his Blue Moon Boys, because "Blue Moon of Kentucky" was played a lot more than the record's flip side. I began collecting Elvis records and material from that moment. By the time the first Beatles records were issued in America, I had been collecting original first-issue recordings of rock 'n' roll, and rhythm & blues for nine years.

The first time I heard the Beatles occurred on another hot July night, this time in 1963 in Los Angeles.

The KRLA Top 50 during one week in July had "Don't Think Twice" by Peter, Paul and Mary at the Number 1 position, while the Beatles song, "From Me to You," debuted at Number 42.

The author (at right) with brother and grandmother, Friday, July 30, 1954, a mere four hours before hearing nineteen-year-old Elvis Presley sing "Good Rockin' Tonight" at the Overton Park Shell—six weeks before he recorded it on his first Sun single. You should have been there!

Although Del Shannon had a Top 100 hit of the same song, the Beatles version was getting a lot of airplay by popular demand in Los Angeles, San Francisco, Phoenix, and other large cities across America.

Suddenly, Elvis had a rival for my loyalty. Yet it would be about five months before this new quartet from Liverpool would become popular with America's youth.

I began collecting data and first-issue records by the Beatles in July 1963. The first books published in 1964 were excellent in providing a skeleton background of the Beatles' early years (1960–1964), but there were vast discrepancies in the descriptions of key events. I began doing my own research.

As a researcher I have never accepted as gospel any published accounts of an event presented by newspapers or writers who are under deadline pressure. The results may be journalistic sensations, but they frequently establish gross inaccuracies and misconceptions. Usually this is attributed to the fact that the reporters themselves have relied on previously published information rather than undertaking time-consuming private research.

When I decided to do this book I went to England to learn about the Beatles. In many instances I was able to acquire original negatives from people who took photographs of the boys and their shows. These people also provided firsthand information regarding key events.

For example, every book that describes the Beatles' audition for Larry Parnes in May 1960 mentions three of the groups that were present, then includes other groups that were not even there! I was able to find the photographer who took the pictures at this event. I obtained his original negatives, which show all five bands in sequence. His personal account of what occurred during the audition is supported by the photographic record.

Research also disproved a long held belief that "How Do You Do It" was recorded November 26, 1962. While visiting EMI in London I made photocopies of the original Abbey Road handwritten log for the Beatles recording sessions. The log shows that "How Do You Do It" was the first song the boys recorded during their first Parlophone recording session on September 4, 1962.

In the authorized biography of the Beatles, published in 1968, the author writes that when George Martin listened to the January 1, 1962, audition tapes from Decca Records, he was impressed by Paul's voice on "Hello Little Girl." In 1968, there was no one to dispute this because no one but those present at the audition knew who sang any of the songs. In 1975, the Decca audition tapes of the Beatles surfaced in bootleg form. Clearly, it was John who sang "Hello Little Girl," not Paul. Yet many books published after this information became known still have George Martin being "impressed with Paul's voice" on the song.

How They Became the Beatles will not be the last book published about the Beatles. And, no doubt, future authors and fans will find new information. However, it is my hope that future historians, as well as fans of the Beatles, will now have some basis for separating fact from fiction. Why print the legend when the truth is available?

Burbank, California, 1989

HOW THEY BECAME THE BEATLES

I N T R O D U C T I O N

Liverpool is an ancient metropolis surviving in a modern world, a city devoid of sparkling glass-faced skyscrapers and sprawling freeways. Situated two hundred miles northwest of London, this bustling seaport still reflects the Victorian architecture of the nineteenth century, with monuments and structures that appeared when Liverpool became a city by royal charter in 1880.

Liverpool has played host to numerous firsts in historical achievements. In 1840 the Cunard Steamship Line launched the world's first steamships to distant ports. One decade earlier the world's first passenger railroad was inaugurated and was involved in the world's first train accident the same year.

Before 1939 the city held the distinction of being the second largest seaport in the United Kingdom, and was among the leading European import markets for cotton, grain, and cattle.

After World War II, during which Liverpool was severely damaged by relentless bombing, the cotton industry began to wane and the city has never matched the prosperity of the prewar era.

Among Liverpool's interesting accomplishments are the two-mile-long Mersey Vehicular Tunnel between Liverpool and Birkenhead. The Catholic cathedral is second in size only to St. Peter's in Rome. In the center of Liverpool is St. George's Hall, renowned for its Greco-Roman architecture. Completed in 1854, it contains a large public hall, law courts, and a concert hall. The Pier Head, featuring the Royal Liver Building, stands as the most prominent attraction. And a special landmark today is a small coffee bar on Slater Street known as the Jacaranda Club.

Liverpool is no longer remembered for its great shipping and railroad centers. Unemployment there has reached the highest level in England. Robberies are double the national average. One-fifth of the city is a maze of demoralizing slums, and Liverpool leads the world's death rate for lung cancer.

Despite these grim statistics, Liverpool is known today as the birthplace of four individuals who never represented it in Parliament and never became star athletes on its famous soccer teams. Instead, they created a new movement in popular music, established novel dress and hairstyles for young people everywhere, and became famous all over the world by their first names: John, Paul, George, and Ringo.

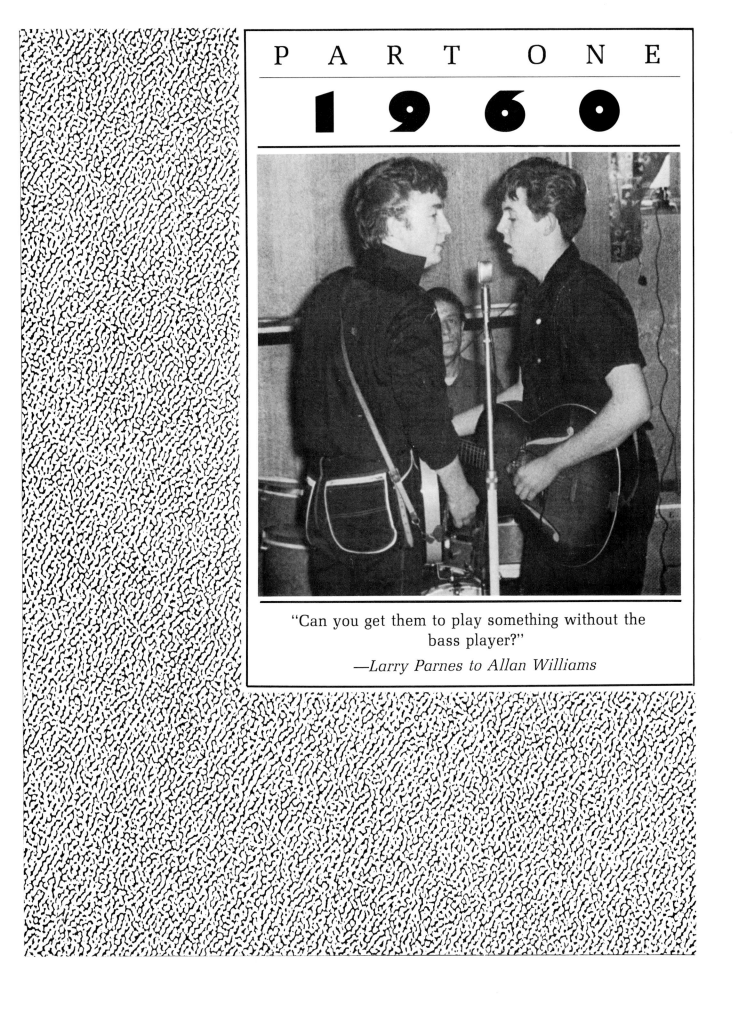

P A R T   O N E

1 9 6 0

"Can you get them to play something without the
bass player?"

—*Larry Parnes to Allan Williams*

If the term "jack-of-all-trades" had to be applied to one individual, Allan Williams would be the first to claim the title. In his efforts to hustle a buck the Liverpool Welshman has been involved in just about everything.

In September 1958, Williams—then a plumber—came up with an idea that would, he hoped, increase his bank account. He leased a store at 23 Slater Street and christened it the Jacaranda Club.

"I remember walking down Slater Street," says Williams, "and I saw a For Lease sign above Owens Watch Repair Shop. The thought occurred to me that I could draw a lot of the local people if I opened a coffee bar."

Many coffee bars were sprouting up all over Liverpool. These were small clubs, commonly with bamboo and rubber plant decor, where customers drank espresso coffee and listened to contemporary music performed live.

"I gathered some people," continues Williams, "to help paint the walls and decorate the dull surroundings. As we worked, several names were suggested before a chap named Bill Coward said we should call it the Jacaranda. We liked the sound of it and everyone agreed it was a good name."

The Jacaranda Club opened its doors to the public with as much fanfare as one might expect from a former watch repair shop.

Cheniston K. Roland worked as a photographer at the club and remembers it well. "The Jacaranda was very austere. By the name, you would get visions of a great club but it was just a shop with newly painted walls. There were bench seats and a trelliswork ceiling that had been dropped, and it had fish nets over it with hanging colored balls. If you had set out to build a nightclub, it wouldn't have had the effect of the Jacaranda."

People came to the club as Allan Williams had envisioned, but even his fertile imagination could not have predicted the types of customers who would be flowing through its doors.

Cheniston recalls that "the people who came to the Jac during the day were ten million miles removed from those who came at night. The day people were businessmen, reporters, the town prosecutor, a publisher, and the like. Back then, Slater was a two-way street and you could always see a bull-nose Morris or Rolls-Royce pull up.

"Nighttime was another story. Liverpool's youth became the customers. They were attracted to the club because Williams would let rock 'n' roll

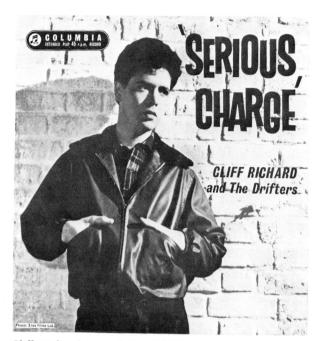

Cliff Richard topped the British music charts in 1960 when the Beatles began to chart their course to success.

groups perform in the basement of the coffee bar. As a result, the Jac became *the* meeting place for rock groups."

The various beat groups dreamed of playing the fancy clubs but were shunned since these places hired only professional musicians—mostly jazz bands—and catered to a higher class of clientele. Beat groups and their audiences were working class and their amateur sound was not acceptable to the managers or customers of elite establishments.

In the beginning the popular group at the Jac was Lord Woodbine and His All-Steel Caribbean Band. Later, Woodbine himself opened a club off Parliament Street but his band continued to play at the Jac as the Royal Steel Caribbean Band. Other bands that played regularly at the club were Rory Storm and the Hurricanes and Derry and the Seniors.

Sometime during October 1959 four young men started coming to the Jacaranda. Their names were John Lennon, Paul McCartney, George Harrison, and Stuart Sutcliffe. They called themselves the Quarry Men and told Williams they were interested in playing at the Jacaranda. Williams said they could practice in the basement. His gesture was particularly generous since their primitive music was little more than noise. They were in fact

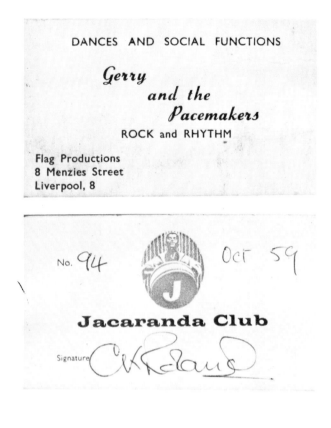

Top: Business card of Gerry and the Pacemakers. *Above:* Photographer Cheniston K. Roland's membership card for the Jacaranda Club. *Right:* Allan Williams with Janice the stripper outside the Jac.

just learning how to play their instruments. Paul and Stuart were trying to become bass players while John struggled to provide rhythm for George's guitar. The group had no drummer.

Early in 1956 "Heartbreak Hotel" by Elvis Presley had topped the music charts in fourteen countries. Before Elvis, John Lennon was influenced by two other singers. Bill Haley's "Rock Around the Clock" hit England in 1955, and one year later Lonnie Donegan caused a lot of excitement with "Rock Island Line."

Elvis Presley was the most popular new sound to come along. Teenagers all over the world were mesmerized by this exciting new singer in America. And John Lennon was caught up in this wave. The most striking thing about this new music was the instrument used to produce it—the guitar. John knew that no formal musical training was neces-

sary, because anyone could teach himself to play a few chords on a guitar.

John lived with his aunt, Mimi Smith, who did not approve of his choice of music, nor could she understand his obsession with the guitar. She repeatedly told him that "you'll never earn your living by it." So John visited his mother, Julia, and talked her into buying him a used guitar.

But John—age fifteen—wasn't thinking about music as a career. He was seeking a little fun and formed a skiffle group. Actually, it was simply a duo consisting of John and his schoolmate, Pete Shotton.

John named the two-man band the Quarry Men, after their school, the Quarry Bank High School.

No complete list exists naming all the boys who joined and left the Quarry Men. Paul McCartney became a member during October 1957. By early 1958 the group had grown to a quintet with John

The Jacaranda crowd liked to have a good time. Allan Williams, in white shirt and tie, is in the back.

Right: The first flyer Williams printed up for the Liverpool Stadium event. Eddie Cochran died in a car accident and was unceremoniously scratched off the flyers. *Far right:* A second hastily printed flyer for the first Liverpool rock show to feature local groups, May 3, 1960.

MAY 1960

JACARANDA ENTERPRISES
.... BY ARRANGEMENT WITH LARRY PARNES

THE GREATEST SHOW EVER TO BE STAGED

LIVERPOOL STADIUM

Tuesday, May 3rd at 8 p.m.

(THREE HOUR PROGRAMME)

BY SENSATIONAL DEMAND   RETURN OF
Gene Vincent   ~~Eddie Cochran~~

Sensational Added Attraction from U. S. A.
Davy Jones
ITALY'S NERO AND HIS GLADIATORS

Peter Wynne   **Lance Fortune**

The Viscounts

Colin Green   **Billy Raymond**
AND THE BEAT BOYS   YOUR HOST & COMPERE

PLUS Liverpool's CASS AND THE CASSANOVAS
RORY STORM AND THE HURRICANES
& OTHER LEADING LIVERPOOL ROCK GROUPS

PRICES: — 10/- — 7/6d. — 5/- — 3/6d.
Tickets available from Lewis's, Cranes, Rushworth's, Beaver Radio. Frank Hessy, The Stadium. Top Hat Record Bar. Dale St., and the Jacaranda Coffee Bar.

IN ENGLAND

LIVERPOOL STADIUM

Tuesday, May 3rd at 8 p.m.

(THREE HOUR PROGRAMME)   DOORS OPEN 7-30 P.M.

GENE VINCENT

Davy Jones

ITALY'S NERO AND HIS GLADIATORS
with the fabulous NEW SOUND from Italy

Lance Fortune PYE HIT PARADE, "BE MINE"

Peter Wynne   **Julian X**

The Viscounts

Colin Green   **Billy Raymond**
AND THE BEAT BOYS   YOUR HOST & COMPERE

PLUS Liverpool's CASS AND THE CASSANOVAS
RORY STORM AND THE HURRICANES
JERRY AND THE PACEMAKERS
MAL PERRY AND RICKY LEA
& OTHER LEADING LIVERPOOL ROCK GROUPS

Gene Vincent, the first American rock star to perform in Liverpool, headlined the Stadium show and gave the crowd their money's worth. Vincent's professionalism and sophisticated performance left the crowd in a frenzy. "Woman Love" silenced the awestruck audience.

and Paul, plus Eric Griffiths (guitars), Len Garry (bass), and Colin Hanton (drums). George Harrison joined as another guitarist in March 1958.

By January 1960 the Quarry Men had evolved into a quartet consisting of John, Paul, George, and Stuart Sutcliffe.

Paul McCartney had been impressed by Bill Haley and His Comets, but he was not really awestruck until Elvis came along. He bought a guitar but had a difficult time getting any decent sounds from it. Finally, he realized the difficulty came from being left-handed and he had the guitar altered.

George Harrison was fourteen years old when he became interested in music. He had not been affected by American singers such as Frankie Laine and Johnnie Ray, but was impressed when he heard "Rock Island Line" by Lonnie Donegan's skiffle group. When Elvis arrived, he began teaching himself to play the guitar.

While Paul and George were attending the Liverpool Institute, Stuart Sutcliffe met John Lennon at the Liverpool College of Art. Stu, who couldn't play any instrument and was ignorant of popular music, was awed when he heard John, Paul, and George playing together. Stu was encouraged to buy a bass guitar and join the trio, who said they would teach him to play it. Stu eventually learned a few chords but his contribution as a musician was nil.

Although Elvis was everyone's idol, John, Paul, and George were also inspired by other American singers such as Gene Vincent, Buddy Holly, Little

After the show, Johnny Gentle (left) and Rory Storm mingle with Liverpool fans.

Richard, Jerry Lee Lewis, and Chuck Berry. Only two English singers had made names for themselves—Tommy Steele and Cliff Richard—and even they were unknown beyond Britain's shores.

Cheniston Roland came to the Jacaranda one day and had his ears bombarded with an unusual musical cacophony. "What's all that bloody racket in the basement?"

"It's one of my groups, the Quarry Men," answered Williams. "You're not the first to complain, but they've got a sense of direction and I promised to get them some bookings when they improve."

Williams knew the four youngsters had some-

Local star Rory Storm belts out a number while Richard (Ringo) Starkey, clean-shaven and wearing sunglasses, pounds the beat as the Hurricanes perform. This is the earliest known picture of Ringo performing.

Billy Fury was the first Liverpool rocker to make it. His first 10″ Decca LP featured Andy White—who would later stand in for Ringo on "P.S. I Love You"—on drums. *The Sound of Fury* projected what at the time seemed an aggressive rebel image to the young fans in England.

thing but their sound was shallow and unpolished.

"They kept asking me to find gigs for them," says Williams, "but I just told them to keep practicing."

When the Quarry Men weren't busy trying to improve their technique they would sit in the audience at the club, drink tea, and admire the music of Rory Storm and the Hurricanes—the number-one rock band in Liverpool. The group's drummer was a young man named Ringo Starr.

About this time, Williams was inspired with yet another enterprise that would interest local teenagers. After reading a London advertisement for the Chelsea Arts Ball, he decided he could sponsor the same type of affair locally. There had never been anything like it in Liverpool.

"You couldn't even find Liverpool on the tourist maps," says Williams. "There was no place where I could promote the local rock groups. So I decided to rent St. George's Hall. And that's how the first Liverpool Arts Festival was conceived."

It would also be the last.

The festival was scheduled to take place over a weekend. Cheniston adds: "the Liverpool Arts Festival gave rise to local talent that had been congregating in the clubs. It became a sort of focal point for all activities in the town, including sculptors, painters, pop groups, singers, and comics who were knocking around the clubs.

"I had an exhibition of photography. The displays were in the Everymans Theatre in the daytime and concerts were held in the evenings. In addition to the singers and other groups, political discussions were held along with poetry reading. Most of the people who ever amounted to anything from Liverpool got their start at the arts festival."

The Quarry Men were not allowed to perform at the festival because Allan Williams did not consider their musical ability worthy of exhibition. However, John, Paul, and George did contribute by constructing floats and assembling the artwork.

During the festival Cheniston befriended Stu Sutcliffe, the neophyte bass player. "He was more levelheaded," says Cheniston, "and a successful art student. Lennon was a failure at art school. Stuart would come over to my shop and talk about pictures and composition."

The arts festival was killed, recalls Cheniston, when "some local college kids went up to the galleries and threw flour and foam from fire extinguishers onto the floor below. Things got out of hand and a big melee broke out. Of course, the Liverpool council wasn't too pleased and made sure it would not happen again."

Throughout the early months of 1960 the spirits

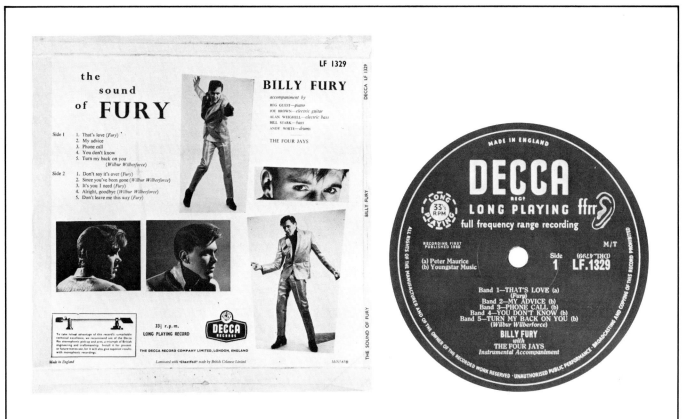

of all the local rock groups were at a low ebb. Their days were spent sulking at the Jacaranda Club, where discussion centered on the ill-fated festival. They had been given a taste of performing on stage to excited audiences. Now it was all over. They went to Williams with pleas for him to find them some engagements. Williams had begun to let the boys perform in the evenings at the Jacaranda. Their music, however, was still amateurish, and audiences were not responsive.

Then Allan Williams heard about a rock show at the Liverpool Empire produced by London talent agent Larry Parnes. "The show starred Gene Vincent," says Williams. "I wanted to see what the reaction would be from the teenagers, so I bought a ticket and went inside. When Gene Vincent came on stage the girls in the audience screamed and went wild. I said to myself that I could put on a bigger show and give the local bands a chance to be on stage with known rock 'n' roll groups."

Williams began organizing the "Greatest Show Ever to Be Staged" in Liverpool, produced under the banner of "Jacaranda Enterprises, by arrangement with Larry Parnes." The three-hour program would star Gene Vincent and Eddie Cochran and feature local bands.

Although listed at the bottom of the bill, Rory

Storm and the Hurricanes, Cass and the Cassanovas, and other Liverpool groups would get their first chance to appear in a big rock show.

Once again, however, John, Paul, George, and Stu were excluded. Owing to the response (or nonresponse) from customers at the Jacaranda, Williams did not feel confident of their ability and thought their playing was still too unpolished for the paying public. He told them to keep practicing.

Two weeks before the show Larry Parnes called Williams from London with tragic news. Eddie Cochran had just been killed in an auto accident. Although Gene Vincent had also been in the car and had suffered a leg injury, he agreed to perform. Parnes suggested that the show be canceled. Williams disagreed, explaining that the kids in his bands were all keyed up and he didn't want to disappoint them. The show would go on as scheduled.

On May 3 the big event took place in Liverpool Stadium. This time it was Larry Parnes's turn to sit in the audience watching an Allan Williams production.

John, Paul, George, and Stu were also watching.

Afterward, Parnes had a long talk with Williams and expressed his admiration for the groups from Liverpool. He wanted to hire a couple of bands to back one of his artists for a tour in Scotland.

Three days later a letter from Mark Forster, one of Parnes's assistants, arrived at the Jacaranda Club. The letter stated that "Duffy Power will be touring Scotland from June 2nd to 11th inclusive . . . and Johnny Gentle will be touring Scotland from June 16th to 25th. For these two periods, as agreed, we are willing to pay your groups £120.0d plus the fares from Liverpool. . . . Should you agree to these suggestions we will arrange for both Duffy and Johnny, who incidentally is a Liverpool boy, to travel up to Liverpool to rehearse with your groups towards the end of May."

The letter continued: "We will make arrangements for Mr. Parnes to come and audition your groups to select the most suitable. He will also bring Billy Fury as Billy will want one of these four groups for his own personal use. Incidentally, the idea of Billy wanting a group from his own hometown will provide several interesting press stories and publicity tie-ups."

The groups chosen by Williams to compete for this tour were Gerry and the Pacemakers, Cass and the Cassanovas, Cliff Roberts and the Rockers, Derry and the Seniors . . . and the newly renamed Silver Beatles. At last, Williams felt that the boys were ready to demonstrate their musical abilities.

Lennon was very excited because Billy Fury was a local boy who had made it big, and the possibility of backing him dominated John's thoughts.

The Silver Beatles practiced every day. Although they had no drummer, the problem was solved by arranging for a stand-in at the audition.

When the big day came the boys were very tense. This could prove to be their first big break or a monumental disappointment.

The Jacaranda was not large enough to hold the auditions but this presented no problem to Williams. He had recently leased the Wyvern Social Club at 108 Seel Street and was having it converted into his latest venture, the Blue Angel Club.

May 10 was a beautiful sunny morning as the bands wandered into the Wyvern Club. The musicians wore stylish suits, carried expensive instruments, and were well known locally. Suddenly, the Silver Beatles felt out of place in their jeans, sweaters, and tennis shoes. Their distressed mood, however, was overshadowed by a more serious dilemma. The drummer they had hired wasn't there.

Upon the arrival of Billy Fury, Larry Parnes, and Mark Forster, the auditions got under way. Parnes and Fury watched with little enthusiasm as each band—first Cass and the Cassanovas, then Derry and the Seniors, then Gerry and the Pacemakers—played several rock classics. During a break in the auditions, John Lennon, spellbound from being in the presence of a star, approached Fury with a slip of paper and asked for an autograph.

Cheniston Roland says: "I aimed my camera at Fury. I didn't recall Lennon next to Billy until I developed the negative. Fury was the big man and I took the photo because of him and not Lennon. That's why Lennon is only in the upper right portion. Of course, today it would be the other way around." Clearly visible on the paper Fury signed are sketches John had made at art school a few days earlier.

After the break, Cliff Roberts and the Rockers had their turn. Finally, it was time for the Silver Beatles. When Parnes learned that their drummer had failed to show up, Johnny Hutchinson, drummer for Cass and the Cassanovas, reluctantly agreed to sit in. Hutchinson was one of the most talented drummers among the Merseyside bands. The fact that he would help the Silver Beatles must have come from some irrepressible urge to do a good deed, because he openly regarded the boys as slovenly dressed unknowns whose musical talents "weren't worth a carrot."

Mark Forster looked at Lennon and asked for the group's name.

"Silver Beatles," answered John. This was the first time they'd ever had a chance to use it.

John, Paul, and George went into a rowdy number while Stu stood with his back to the judges. The routine drum beat from Hutchinson made him look like a computer-programmed robot.

Parnes and Fury immediately noticed the difference in style from the previous contestants. When John sang an Elvis song, Williams became annoyed at workmen who were banging away and ordered them to stop until the auditions were finished.

After they had performed a couple of songs, their rent-a-drummer, Tommy Moore, arrived. Moore had been collecting his drum kit from another club on the other side of town.

When the boys had completed their repertoire, Billy Fury looked at Parnes and said, "This is the group, the Silver Beatles."

Parnes agreed that they were the most interest-

The Larry Parnes/Billy Fury audition, May 1960 (through p. 22). *Top left:* The first group to audition was Cass and the Cassanovas, with Johnny Hutchinson on drums. *Top right:* The second group was Derry and the Seniors. *Above:* While Derry (Derek Wilkie) poses, Howie Casey does his bit on the saxophone.

Top: Gerry and the Pacemakers were third. *Left:* Gerry Marsden solos at the microphone. *Facing page, left and top right:* Up fourth were Cliff Roberts and the Rockers.

Right: An historic moment: During a break in the auditions, Billy Fury graciously signs his autograph for John Lennon (right).

When Cheniston Roland snapped frame 14, he took the first photograph ever of the Silver Beatles. From left, Stu Sutcliffe, John Lennon, Paul McCartney, substitute drummer Johnny Hutchinson, and George Harrison.

(This frame, alone among the audition photos, should be recognizable to fans. Shortly after the audition, Roland sent a print of this negative to Allan Williams along with a bill. Williams never paid, so Roland never printed any of the others. In 1963, Williams sold this picture to a London newspaper, and that second-generation copy, in its cropped form, has been reproduced repeatedly over the years.)

ing of the groups, but noticed that Stu Sutcliffe had been trying to hide his lack of ability. Parnes turned to Williams. "Allan, can you get them to play something without the bass player?"

A lump suddenly formed in Williams's throat. He was not prepared for this, but a request from Larry Parnes could not be denied. Williams asked the boys to do a number without Stu.

Lennon objected. "We're a group, all or none. That's the way it is."

Parnes was not anxious to provoke an argument and did not pursue the matter. He told Williams the group would be accepted if they changed their minds about the bass player.

The Silver Beatles stood by Stu.

When the auditions were over, Williams, Parnes, and the others went to the Jacaranda to celebrate. Williams wanted a memento to mark this one and only historic visit of Larry Parnes and Billy Fury to a Liverpool audition. He asked Cheniston to take a picture. Besides Williams, the photo included his wife, Beryl, Parnes, and Fury in front of the Jacaranda Club about two hours after the Wyvern auditions.

Williams's identity as a former plumber emerged later on the back of this photo. Printed in bold letters is a message: *Allan urgent fix water pipe in the basement—fan to repair in alcove.* And at the bottom: *Gas jet to radiators to secure gas leaks.*

Never a dull moment at the Jac.

Allan Williams was aware that the Silver Beatles were sounding better every day. And they kept pestering him for gigs.

"I decided to become their manager," says Williams, "but first I had to find a drummer.... I asked Brian Cassar [Cass of Cass and the Cassanovas] if he knew a good drummer. He suggested Tommy Moore, who had played with the boys at the Wyvern audition. He said that Tommy worked at the Garston Bottle Works. I went and found him at the bottle company and offered him a job with the Silver Beatles. He climbed down from the forklift and accepted."

Conflict arose from the start between John Lennon and Tommy Moore. They did not like each other. Tommy, at thirty-six, was much older than nineteen-year-old John. As weeks passed John kept up a continual stream of caustic remarks aimed at Tommy and threatened to dampen the team spirit of the group.

Williams had been sending some of his groups on the road and now he felt the Silver Beatles were ready. He arranged for them to back Johnny Gentle on the Scotland tour, the dates of which had been moved up to May 20–28.

Before setting off for their first professional tour the boys had to get excused from their daily routines. Lennon and Sutcliffe concluded that the art college wouldn't miss them and decided simply to skip classes. Harrison had already quit school to work as an apprentice electrician and was able to get his vacation early. McCartney, always a politician, slick-talked his father into believing that the Liverpool Institute had granted all students a two-week holiday to prepare for exams.

Tommy Moore faced the most difficult task—that of persuading his girlfriend that he'd come back with a lot more money than his paycheck from the bottle works.

Johnny Gentle was shocked upon meeting the Silver Beatles. They wore black jeans and black T-shirts and appeared as if they had been sleeping in them for weeks. Also, they had no amplifiers for their electric guitars.

While driving to Scotland, with Gentle at the wheel, the van hit an automobile. The Silver Beatles were shaken but uninjured—except for the drummer. Tommy Moore had been struck in the mouth by an instrument case and lost his front teeth. He was taken to a local hospital while the group continued onward to their first engagement.

Top: While the Silver Beatles began to perform, Roland turned and captured Billy Fury and Larry Parnes watching and listening (Cliff Roberts is on Fury's left). This is the first recorded image of "audience" reaction to the Beatles. *Above:* Are they aware that Stu Sutcliffe's back is turned on purpose?

The manager at the club inquired about the drummer's absence and was told about the accident. He was sympathetic but insisted on a drummer.

John went back to the hospital and ordered Tommy to get out of bed and fulfill his obligation.

Left: Paul McCartney sings while Tommy Moore, since arrived, plays drums—this is the only shot of the Silver Beatles in which Moore is clearly visible. *Below:* Some of the equipment was borrowed from the Pressmen. *Below right:* Stu Sutcliffe with his back toward those watching the audition.

The injured drummer finally agreed but was in pain throughout the tour. Lennon took advantage of this in a cruel manner by relentlessly tormenting Tommy while onstage.

When the tour was completed Tommy had suffered enough physical pain from his injury along with the constant abuse from Lennon. He returned to his job at the bottle works.

The Silver Beatles found another drummer, a man named Norman Chapman.

The Scotland tour had been the Silver Beatles' baptism in show biz and they had been elated to see their name, although in small print, on advertising posters.

After returning to Liverpool, however, they were back at square one. Most of their time was spent loafing at local coffee bars and they were lucky if they got two gigs a week.

On May 20, while the boys were in Scotland, Allan Williams had met with Les Dodd, head of Paramount Enterprises. Dodd arranged for the Silver Beatles to appear with Gerry and the Pacemakers on June 6 at Grosvenor Hall. They received £10; £1 went to Williams as their manager and £1 to the bouncer, leaving each member of the band with about $4.50 U.S.

Four days earlier the Silver Beatles had appeared at the Neston Institute in Wirral, but they were called the Beatles in a review by the *Heswell and Neston News and Advertiser.*

When Norman Chapman put on an army uniform for two years of required national service, the group was once again without a drummer. Many times they tried to lure Tommy Moore back for their occasional engagements. One evening, while Tommy was working the night shift, they stopped at the bottle works on their way to a gig. Tommy completely ignored their pleas. Another time they

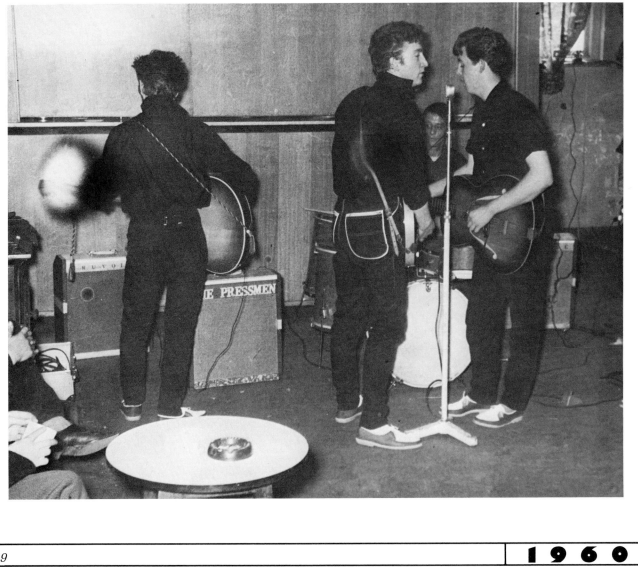

went to his apartment, but had to cope with Tommy's girlfriend. She was still losing sleep over the paltry pay he had earned for the Scotland tour and was absolutely livid about the bill from Tommy's orthodontist. She had two words for the group: "Piss off!"

During this desolate time the Silver Beatles' only regular job was playing background music for a stripper named Janice in a club partly owned by Allan Williams. The boys were paid ten shillings per week to provide sultry guitar chords as Janice wiggled and writhed for an audience of drunken sailors and panting businessmen.

And there they might have stayed if one of Williams's other acts—a steel band—hadn't run out on him. "I went to the Jacaranda one evening," says Williams, "to see if the Caribbean Steel Band was [still] there. I had received letters from other [club owners] asking me to let them perform in their clubs, but refused. Steel bands were very scarce in England at the time. Well, to my surprise, the steel band was gone!"

A few days later, Williams received a letter from the band, who had skipped town and gone to Hamburg in West Germany. "They told me how great it was and that I should open a club there. I wondered what Hamburg had to offer so I went there and paid a visit to several clubs. The bands were German rock groups and were lousy. I knew my Liverpool bands were better and the people would go wild over them.

"When I got back to Liverpool I found out that Derry and the Seniors were unhappy with their payment on various gigs and had gone to London to get even with their promoter. I went along to make sure they didn't get into trouble. While there I went to the Two I's Bar in Soho and ran into Bruno Koschmider, a Hamburg nightclub owner. I reminded him about my group. We agreed on terms and drew up a contract. The first band I ever sent to Hamburg was Derry and the Seniors."

The Silver Beatles were constantly asking Williams about going to Hamburg. "I finally decided they were good enough," says Williams, "but again faced a never ending problem. No drummer. And this is when Pete Best became a Beatle."

Pete Best was born in Madras, India. His father, John, was a successful boxing promoter who had enlisted during World War II and had been sent to India as a physical training instructor.

In Delhi, John met and married a pretty Red Cross worker named Mona, who had been born there of English parents. When Pete was eleven he began calling her Mo, which was short for mother.

After the war ended in 1945 the Bests moved to

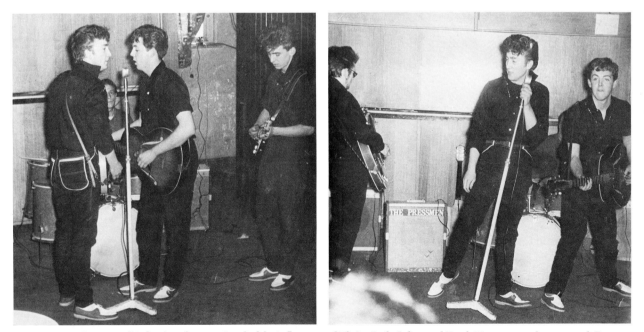

Facing page: Lennon displaying the unmistakable influence of Elvis. *Left:* John and Paul, Tommy on drums, and George Harrison playing lead guitar. *Right:* The final shot taken of the audition itself.

Top: Rory Storm appeared at the audition for only one reason—to have his picture taken with Billy Fury, a picture he intended to plaster Liverpool with. Rory succeeded, but Parnes was furious and threatened never to audition another Liverpool band if Williams had the photo printed. This was the final photo taken at the Wyvern Social Club that day. *Above:* Parnes, Beryl Williams, Allan Williams, and Fury outside the Jacaranda after the audition.

Liverpool. The family moved frequently before settling down in a huge Victorian house in the suburb of West Derby at 8 Hayman's Green.

Pete went to Blackmoor Park School, then to junior high, and finally to Collegiate High School, where he won a scholarship when he was seventeen.

"My early influences in music," says Pete, "came from Gene Krupa and, later, Joe Morello. I started playing the drums and would practice in the basement of my house. Most homes have one cellar but our house was overendowed with them and consisted of seven adjoining basement rooms. My mother decided to turn the cellar into a coffee club."

All of the work of converting the cellars into a club was done voluntarily by Pete's friends, who labored daily for six months before the doors opened in August 1959.

It was Pete's mom who named the club. The Casbah, derived from the 1938 film *Algiers,* one of her favorite Hollywood movies, which starred Charles Boyer and Hedy Lamarr.

"Mo sat at a table in the foyer where the tickets were issued and the shillings changed hands," says Pete. "On sale were coffee, Coke, hot dogs, and crisps in a room set aside as a bar with tables, a fireplace, and espresso coffee machines. The club was open all week but live groups appeared only on weekends. During the week people danced to music from the jukebox. Everywhere there was music and happiness. Everyone came to enjoy themselves, the musicians as well as the members. Eventually, the club would grow to more than two thousand members."

One of the first groups to appear at The Casbah in the fall of 1959 was the Quarry Men, which at the time consisted of John Lennon, Paul McCartney, George Harrison, and Ken Brown, with other musicians coming and going. From time to time Pete would sit in on drums because the group had no regular drummer.

"One night," explains Pete, "Ken Brown, a guitarist, wasn't well enough to play, but when the time came to settle up, Mo included him in the Quarry Men's payout anyway. They became extremely annoyed and protested that they should share Ken's money. This resulted in Ken quitting the Quarry Men and suggesting to me that we should form a group of our own, with Ken on rhythm guitar, Charlie Newby as lead guitarist, and Billy Barlow on bass and myself on drums.

RORY STORM
and the
Hurricanes

Presented by:-
DOWNBEAT
PROMOTIONS

54 BROADGREEN ROAD
Liverpool 13
STOneycroft 3324.

*PLEASE SEND
BY PHOTOS to
Entertainments Staff
TO BUTLINS HOLIDAY
CAMP
PLLWHELI
NORTH WALES
I'll send you ... Rory Storm ... when ... great*

When Rory Storm and the Hurricanes played at Butlin's, a summer resort, later in 1960, Storm wrote directly to Cheniston Roland on the back of the group's business card, requesting copies of the photo of Fury and himself. *Left:* An ad for Butlin's, summer 1960. *Above:* Front and back of card.

That's how the Blackjacks were born. We had no intention of competing with the bands that were more experienced and trying to make a living out of music.

"One evening in August 1960," continues Pete, "the phone rang and my mother answered it. The caller was Paul McCartney, who asked to speak to me. My mother told him that I was not in but would take a message. When I came home I saw the note in which Paul said the Beatles had been promised a trip to Hamburg, but would have to get a permanent drummer. I called Paul and said I would like to join the group and he told me to meet him at the Jacaranda for an audition."

Pete Best auditioned and became a member of the Beatles (who had deleted "Silver" from their name) on August 15. He was twenty.

"I became the group's drummer on the spot," says Pete. "I had a Blue Pearl Premiere drum kit and was very proud of it. We played two gigs at the Jacaranda before going to Hamburg."

The first contract was drawn up on August 17 between Bruno Koschmider and Jacaranda Enterprises. The Beatles would be paid 30 Deutsch marks (DM) per person each day of work, beginning August 17 until October 16. Additional clauses listed certain restrictions and assured that

if the Beatles violated the agreement they would compensate Mr. Koschmider in full. Koschmider was responsible for getting work permits for the group, but he never did.

"Prior to the trip," says Williams, "I got an old cream-and-green-colored van. It was dented but had a roof rack to store the equipment. The Beatles were flat broke so I drew up an I.O.U. stating that they had received £15 from me as part payment of the engagement in Hamburg, to be deducted. Stuart Sutcliffe and Paul McCartney signed on behalf of the Beatles."

The group departed Liverpool about ten o'clock on the morning of August 16. Eight people, including Williams, his wife, and a Liverpool club owner named Lord Woodbine, were crammed into the van headed for Hamburg via the hook of Holland.

"We pulled into New Haven just in time to make the night ferry," says Williams. "The dockworkers were not very happy with the bundle atop the van and asked about its contents. The problem was whether they could get it on the crane. Lennon, always the leader, said, 'Come on, mates, you can do it.' And they did."

Rolling through the flatlands of Holland the group sang songs to pass the time and arrived in Hamburg that evening.

Before World War II Hamburg was Germany's leading seaport, and the third largest port in the world after London and New York. Situated on the Elbe River, the city is built around the mouth of the little Alster River.

Although it is an old city, only a few of its older buildings survived the heavy bombing of the Allies. The worst attacks came during July and August 1944, leaving Hamburg a mass of ruins with nearly 60,000 dead.

The city's sole contribution to music came from two famous composers who were born there, Johannes Brahms and Felix Mendelssohn.

When the Beatles arrived fifteen years after World War II had ended, Hamburg was a depraved sintown whose criminal and sexual activities were known all over Europe. After the Berlin Wall went up, gang wars erupted when East German villains streamed into the city from Berlin. Violent clashes between these undesirables involved the numerous nightclubs, which employed more bouncers than waiters.

The Beatles were expecting Hamburg to be like Liverpool but were knocked for a loop upon arrival.

"We could only gape in sheer wonder when we hit the Reeperbahn," says Pete. "It was a jungle of neon and sex, where every other door seemed to lead to a place where girls were taking off their clothes, and other bizarre things, like lady mud wrestlers."

As Allan Williams steered the van along the exotic sights, John smiled and said, "This is a bit of all right, lads."

"I think we're going to like it here," Paul replied cheerfully.

Williams drove to the Kaiserkeller, where the boys met Bruno Koschmider, a heavyset, broad-shouldered man with bushy eyebrows and no neck.

"The Kaiserkeller was bright and lively and throbbing to the music of Derry and the Seniors," says Pete. "The booze was flowing and people were having a good time."

The Beatles thought they would be playing at this fun palace, but Koschmider quickly burst that bubble by taking them down the street to his other club, the Indra. It was dark and sleazy, with only two customers.

"Is it open?" Pete asked cheerfully.

"No one comes to the Indra," Koschmider as-

Top: Original letter from Paramount Enterprises setting up the Silver "Beetles'" Grosvenor Ballroom performance for June 6, 1960. *Above:* The agreement, dated May 20, 1960, for the performance, which also featured Gerry and the Pacemakers.

sured them, "but you'll make it into another Kaiserkeller."

The boys were disappointed but were more interested in sleep after their long journey from Liverpool. A comfortable hotel bed and a hot bath occupied their thoughts. Koschmider, however, wasn't about to provide any such luxury. He had arranged for them to sleep at the Bambi Kino, a cinema that specialized in B Westerns and sex films. At the Bambi, the boys were led along a gloomy hallway to a small room containing two beds and a dilapidated couch.

"You could just about swing a cat in here," Paul said, "providing it's got no tail!"

John and Stu immediately claimed the beds while Koschmider took Paul and Pete to two smaller rooms without windows. Paul called them "dungeons." The rooms were next to the cinema's rest rooms and the Beatles had to wash and shave with cold water from the urinals.

On opening night at the Indra a small crowd was on hand to see the new rock group from Liverpool. The Beatles were really depressed as they ambled onto the stage, but Koschmider was in the audience yelling for them to "make show!"

And that's what they did.

"We went from one extreme to the other," says Pete. "John and Paul were the looniest. John did his best to imitate Gene Vincent, grabbing the microphone as if he were going to lay into the audience, leaping around like a maniac. Stu remained a puppet, quiet and cool. Paul screamed like Little Richard and George was real serious, and tried to keep the act from becoming too ridiculous. There wasn't much I could do from behind the drums, other than stand up or hop around with a tom-tom under my arm."

As the nights of bedlam passed, an act began to develop. They were "making show" and the audiences loved it, as these four buffoons stomped across the stage, half-crazed, for hours at a time.

"The songs were exclusively American," says Pete. "Fats Domino, Carl Perkins, along with Elvis and Little Richard. The Germans really loved the Ray Charles classic 'What'd I Say,' because they could participate by echoing the lyrics and banging their beer bottles on the tables. By this time we were drinking more than our fair share of Hamburg's booze. You couldn't help it. They'd be sending us drinks all the time. It came by the crate and we drank onstage. The Germans realized that 'making show' could create an enormous thirst."

The crowds began to grow as more people on the street heard about the crazed Beatles at the Indra. The shows were soon extended from 12:30 until 2:00 in the morning.

On October 3 the police closed the Indra because the neighbors were constantly complaining about the noise. It was the end of showtime at the Indra, but not the end for the Beatles in Hamburg. Although their contract called for a two-month engagement, it could be extended verbally. Bruno Koschmider contacted Williams, who had returned to Liverpool, and asked for an extension. An agreement was made for their continued appearances at the Kaiserkeller—but not for long.

On October 4 the Beatles began playing at the Kaiserkeller. Also appearing was Rory Storm and the Hurricanes, with Ringo Starr on drums. At this time Ringo knew the Beatles only slightly.

During the first Hamburg tour the most popular members of the Beatles were Stu Sutcliffe and Pete Best. Stu wore dark glasses and sported a James Dean look; Pete appeared sullen and withdrawn while pounding out a steady beat on his drums. Although Paul and John did their share of shouting and yelling, their rapport with the audience was overshadowed by Pete Best, the man in back on the drums, a mysterious figure.

The Beatles were drawing increasingly large crowds and their sound was improving every day. During their free time they went to the Top Ten Club to hear Tony Sheridan, a top-notch singer and guitarist who captivated audiences. Impressed with Tony's professionalism, they began to see him socially. Occasionally, they would even go onstage and back him. The crowds went crazy.

During this time the Beatles met Astrid Kirchherr, a twenty-two-year-old Hamburg girl from a reputable family. She had studied art at a private school and was now employed as a photographer's assistant. Astrid's boyfriend was Klaus Voorman, a talented illustrator she had met at art school. Klaus, the son of a physician, also rented a room at the Kirchherr family residence.

One evening Astrid and Klaus quarreled and Klaus went to a movie. Afterward, he wandered in the St. Pauli area and became intrigued by the rock 'n' roll music coming from the Kaiserkeller. Curiosity lured him inside, where he sat down at a table and nervously eyed the rough Reeperbahn crowd. This strange new world fascinated Klaus, who had

Telephone No.
ROYAL 6544

JACARANDA ENTERPRISES

23, Slater Street,
Liverpool 1.

An Agreement made the 17th day of August 1960

between Mr. Bruno Koschmider hereinafter called the Management

of the one part, and Jacaranda Enterprises hereinafter called the Artiste

of the other part Witnesseth that the Management hereby engages the Artiste

and the Artiste

accepts an engagement to present The Beatles

appear 5 musicians

(or in his usual entertainment) at the stated place of entertainment, and for

the dates for the periods and at the salaries stated in the Schedule hereto

The Artiste agrees to appear at one Evening Performance

none Matinee.

at a salary of D.M. 30.— per person per day of work

(commencing Wednesday 17.8. SCHEDULE (play
till Sunday. 16.Oct. 1960
inclusive)

The Artiste shall not, without the

appear in any place of public entertainment

the place of entertainment mentioned

and 30 weeks after this

Bill matter, programme

to be sent to

not later than day

ADDITIONAL CLAUSES.
a prompt start is required
£ 10 starling to be paid
to Mr. A.R. Williams per week

Return pass to England to be paid

A. R. Williams

jacaranda enterprises

23 SLATER STREET LIVERPOOL 1 / ROYAL 6544

Recieved from Allen Williams the
sum of £15 part payment of
proposed engagement in
Hamburg To be deducted.
    S.F. Sutcliffe
    J.P. McCartney
15-8-1960   on behalf of
    A.R. Williams   the 'Beatles'

Antrag

auf Erteilung eines Sichtvermerks zur Einreise nach — zur Durchreise durch — Deutschland
Application for a Visa to enter — to travel through — Germany
Demande de délivrance d'un visa d'entrée en — de transit par — l'Allemagne

An d. Botschaft — Gesandtschaft	— Generalkonsulat der Bundesrepublik Deutschland
To the Embassy — Legation	— Consulate-General of the Federal Republic of Germany
Ambassade — Légation	— Consulat Général de la République fédérale d'Allemagne

in / in / à

1. Familien- und Vornamen
Surname and Christian names
Nom de famille et prénoms

SUTCLIFFE
Stuart Fergusson Victor

2. Geburtstag und Geburtsort
Date and place of birth
Date et lieu de naissance

geboren am 23/6/40
Born on
in Edinburgh, Scotland.

3. Wohnsitz oder dauernder Aufenthaltsort
Domicile or permanent residence
Domicile ou lieu de résidence permanente

53. Ullet Rd.
Liverpool 8.
Lancashire

4. Familienstand
Marital Status
Situation de famille

ledig Single.
Single
célibataire

verheiratet, verwitwet, geschieden seit
Married, widowed, divorced since
marié, veuf, divorcé depuis

5. Staatsangehörigkeit
Nationality
Nationalité

jetzige
Present nationality British
actuelle

frühere
Former nationality
d'origine

6. Beruf
Trade or profession
Profession

Musician.

---

7. Was für einen Paß besitzen Sie?
What type of passport do you possess?
Quel passeport possédez-vous?

British   Paß-Nr. L0268031
ausgestellt durch Foreign Office: Branch Passport Office.
Issued by
in Liverpool
am 13th August 1960.
gültig bis zum 13th Aug. 1965
Valid until

8. Reiseweg, Reiseziel, Reisezweck
Itinerary, destination, purpose of travel
Itinéraire, destination, but du voyage

Hamburg (St. Pauli).
Musical Entertainment.

9. Voraussichtlicher Zeitpunkt der Einreise und Dauer des Aufenthalts in Deutschland
Prospective date of entry and duration of stay in Germany

Einreise etwa am March 15th.
Entry on about
Aufenthaltsdauer (3) three months.
Duration of stay

10. Begleitende Kinder
Accompanying children

11. Art des beantragten Sichtvermerks
Type of visa applied for
Nature du visa demandé

Entry.

12. Bemerkungen
Notes
Remarques

Die vorstehenden Angaben entsprechen der Wahrheit. Mir ist bekannt, daß ich mich durch wissentlich falsche Angaben strafbar mache.

The above statements are true. I know that I am liable to a penalty if I knowingly make a false statement.

Liverpool   S.F. Sutcliffe
(Ort und Datum)   (Eigenhändige Unterschrift)
(Place and date)   (Signature)

Preparations for Hamburg. *Clockwise from bottom left:* The I.O.U. handwritten by Stu Sutcliffe and cosigned by J. P. (Paul) McCartney for money Williams advanced to the boys for the Hamburg trip (Williams says, "The boys never paid me back"). The contract (partially destroyed by fire) for the Beatles' first Hamburg engagement, arranged by Allan Williams. Stu Sutcliffe's German visa.

never been to a nightclub. He was thrilled by the crazy antics of Rory Storm and the Hurricanes, who were playing onstage.

The Beatles were taking a break at a table next to Klaus. He kept glancing at their gray-and-white-checked coats, black shirts, and greased hair.

When the Beatles began "making show" Klaus was very impressed and did not leave until they had completed their act four hours later. Klaus excitedly told Astrid about his great adventure that night and begged her to go with him. She scolded him for wasting time at such a sordid place. Nice girls never went to the St. Pauli district.

Klaus kept going back to the Kaiserkeller. He wanted to meet the Beatles but was shy and also embarrassed by his halting English. He soon overcame his shyness and showed John and Stu a record cover he had designed. John wasn't impressed but Stu was more receptive to a fellow artist.

Eventually, Klaus persuaded Astrid to join him at the club and she immediately fell in love with Stu Sutcliffe.

"He was so tiny but perfect," says Astrid. "So pale, but very, very beautiful."

"She was a striking lady," says Pete, "wearing a black leather jacket, which contrasted with her blond hair and pallid skin. Although she was attracted to Stu she became a regular at our table along with Klaus. We all got along fine, even though she knew no English and Klaus had to play interpreter."

Astrid and Klaus raved about the Beatles to their circle of friends, who also started going to the Kaiserkeller. It soon became a strange mixture of arty types and the usual Reeperbahn rockers.

During the next few weeks Astrid was never without her camera and she took many pictures of the Beatles at the club and other Hamburg locations. She took them home to meet her mother, who gave them tea. It was the first home in Germany the boys had visited. They were soon eating dinner there every night, after which Astrid would drive them to the Kaiserkeller in her car. She also had Klaus tutor her in English. "He nearly went out of his mind trying to explain things to me," says Astrid. "I just couldn't learn it." She began a tortuous regime of studying a German-English dictionary.

Two months later Astrid and Stu announced their engagement and bought rings for each other, according to the German custom.

Miraculously, Klaus remained a good friend of

Astrid as well as of the Beatles and would later move to England and design the cover for their *Revolver* album.

Unknown to the Beatles, all of the managers of Hamburg clubs were watchful of their performers and did their best to prevent them from wandering to other establishments. Koschmider had a spy named George Stenner planted in the Top Ten Club.

One evening while the Beatles were onstage with Tony Sheridan, Koschmider's faithful informant quickly departed and reported that the Beatles had broken their contract agreement "not to appear in any place of public entertainment within a radius of twenty-five miles of the place of entertainment mentioned for 30 weeks before and 30 weeks after this engagement."

Tony Sheridan had originally played at the Kaiserkeller and had been lured away by Peter Eckhorn, manager of the Top Ten Club.

The Beatles admitted their contract violation but didn't believe they had committed a sin, since Koschmider had not lived up to his part of the agreement with Allan Williams.

Koschmider flew into a rage and felt very brave with his rough-looking henchmen behind him. "If you leave me you won't ever play the Top Ten!" he screamed. "You can take that any way you like. My boys know how to create trouble!"

"Get stuffed," replied Lennon, as the Beatles stood their ground.

Pete says: "By this time we were as mad as Koschmider. At the very least he promised we would end up with broken fingers, but we knew he wasn't crazy enough to send us back to Liverpool in a coffin."

Suddenly, everything started to go wrong. A few days later the Beatles got into a fight with George Stenner, the informer. Someone called the police, who rapidly took an interest in George Harrison upon learning that he was only seventeen.

"They sent him back to Liverpool," says Pete, "for being underage in St. Pauli. But nothing could stop the rest of us from going to the Top Ten."

On December 14 a small fire broke out at the Kaiserkeller. It wasn't dangerous but gave Koschmider an opportunity to harass the boys. He called the police and accused the Beatles of arson.

Paul and Pete were awakened in their room by plainclothesmen who roughly hauled them to the station and put them into a cell. John was not taken and Stu had moved to Astrid's house.

John Lennon, who at the time rarely allowed himself to be photographed wearing glasses, watches (lower left) as the van is loaded aboard the ferry, August 1960.

"We must have been cooped up for around three hours," says Pete. "Then the lock turned in the door to admit the two gorillas who had originally broken our sleep. We were hustled into a police car and driven to the airport where we were marched to a plane.

"On arrival at Heathrow Airport we were given our passports and cleared customs with absolutely nothing to declare and no luggage to be searched."

A few days later John came home on a train. He carried his guitar and amp on his back.

Stu remained with Astrid in Hamburg.

What had promised to be the Beatles' first big professional tour had ended in disaster. Despite this setback, they did have something special—the Hamburg crowds had gone wild over their music.

For several days John stayed at home, completely disillusioned. He thought about how nice it would be to have the professional quality of Tony Sheridan and put some money into a savings account. Then he remembered his long trek home and it brought him back to the stark realities of life and the problems they had experienced with Koschmider.

Paul loafed around the house until his father persuaded him to get a job. He had not been pleased when Paul quit school to go to Hamburg. Paul signed up at the Labor Exchange and soon got a job as a truck driver's helper with an express company named Speedy Prompt Delivery. He carried packages for two weeks, then got laid off when the Christmas rush ended. He next found work winding electric coils at Massey and Coggins.

Pete Best made a few phone calls to Peter Eckhorn, who said he would send the Beatles' equipment to Liverpool.

"On the day the ship arrived," says Pete,

"Mother and I took a cab to the wharf and picked up the massive crate. Inside were my drums, a guitar, sound equipment, and personal gear. We piled the lot into the taxi and left the busted crate on the dock."

George Harrison did not know that the others had returned from Hamburg. He was still ashamed at being deported from Germany at the height of their success. He spent most of his time brooding at home in his room.

Toward the end of December, John, Paul, George, and Pete finally got together again and made plans to find work.

The Beatles played a gig at The Casbah and introduced a temporary guitarist, a chemistry student named Charlie Newby, who had been in Pete Best's earlier group, the Blackjacks.

Brian Kelly, a Liverpool promoter, was organizing a show for the Litherland Town Hall on December 27. On Christmas Day he phoned Bob Wooler, an associate of Allan Williams, and said he was one band short. Wooler suggested the Beatles, who were now at the Jacaranda Club, and would be happy to get the work. Kelly hired them.

They were billed as The Beatles—Direct from Hamburg. The show was held at a teen dance hall and is noteworthy for being the first time the boys caused a near riot. Afterward, the kids swarmed around them asking for autographs. When one of the Beatles spoke, a girl said: "You sure speak good English, being Germans."

"We had introduced a British audience for the first time to 'making show' at The Casbah," says Pete. "We had fun clowning and leaping and doing most of the things that Bruno Koschmider had demanded at the Indra Club. We also went through the paces of 'making show' at the Litherland. We were playing for a dance in a hall that could accommodate fifteen hundred, but they stopped dancing after we started playing. They surged forward to be near us and to scream. People didn't go to a dance to scream so this was news! The magic of the Beatles was busting out."

Hamburg had taught the Beatles how to respond to rough, wild crowds, and how to endure endless hours of singing to screaming, foot-stomping audiences. All of the sweat and toil and practicing seemed, finally, to have paid off.

Their performance at the Litherland Town Hall had given the Beatles a resurgence of confidence that was desperately needed. Just as they had considered giving up, they now sprang back with a lift.

PART TWO
1961

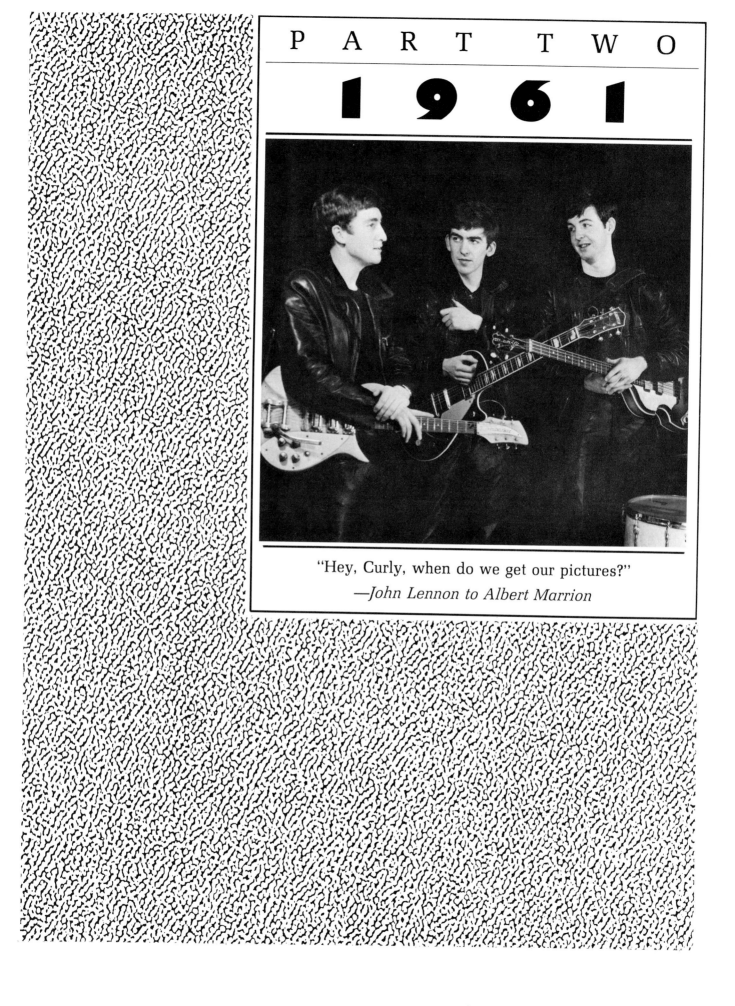

"Hey, Curly, when do we get our pictures?"
—*John Lennon to Albert Marrion*

During their tour in Germany the Beatles had, without musical intentions, created a new sound, a wild, almost frenzied sound. Their savage music and whimsical antics merely assured survival among the robust Hamburg audiences, but produced a near cataclysmic effect on the more docile folk in Liverpool.

"It was Hamburg," says John. "That's where we really developed. To get the Germans going and keep it up for twelve hours at a time, we really had to hammer. We'd try anything we could think of because there was nobody to copy. So we played what we liked and the Germans liked it, too, as long as it was loud."

The Beatles had become so popular among the Merseyside crowds that they deserved a club where their talents could be showcased as the resident band.

The showcase was the Cavern and the man responsible for getting them there was Bob Wooler.

The Cavern had been the brainchild of Alan Sytner, former owner of the successful West Coast Jazz Club in Liverpool during the late fifties.

In 1956, while vacationing in Paris, Sytner became interested in the numerous jazz clubs—known as Paris Caverns—built into the caves on the Left Bank. Since the Liverpool waterfront offered no caves, Sytner reasoned, a warehouse basement would be an adequate substitute. His diligent search for an appropriate cellar ended at 10 Mathew Street, an unswept, rancid section in the main business district.

Sytner began converting the former egg-packing station into his dream. The rough concrete floor was resurfaced, the brickworks were painted black, and a huge stage was placed at the end of the center section. The arches had already been strengthened during the war, when the basement provided shelter from Luftwaffe air raids.

A successful publicity campaign brought hundreds of people when the club opened on January 16, 1957. The Merseyside Jazz Band played to a packed house and became the resident weekend group. Although the club was named the Merseyside Jazz Union, its members began calling it the Cavern, an appropriate name that eventually became customary.

Everything went well until the end of 1958 when a rival, the Mardi Gras Jazz Club, opened in another part of Liverpool. The fickle fans were lured away. Another factor that contributed to the Cavern's decline was the exorbitant amounts of money Sytner had been spending to book guest attractions.

Alan Sytner decided to abandon his albatross. He got married, moved to London, and put his father in charge of the club. By mid-1959 the crowds were so sparse that the doors were about to close.

Raymond McFall was the man who brought the Cavern back to life. McFall, an accountant who had represented Alan Sytner, bought the ailing club and reopened it on October 3, 1959. Entertainment for this gala event came from Mr. Acker Bilk and his Paramount Jazz Band, plus two American guests, Sonny Terry and Brownie McGhee.

Under McFall's guidance the Cavern again became a popular jazz club, but McFall—like many area club owners—was facing a new kind of trouble. Several local skiffle groups—also known as "beat bands"—were used to fill the midevening gaps at the various clubs. In 1960, they began to create a stir among the audiences and were on the verge of becoming more popular than the big-name resident bands.

It was during this period that Bob Wooler was able to help the Beatles. Wooler was the Cavern's popular disc jockey, and although the club was devoted to jazz, he was devoted to the Beatles and did all he could to promote them. He convinced Ray McFall to give them a chance and that's how they came to play a lunchtime gig at the Cavern on February 21, 1961, when the resident group went on break. Most of the crowd were local Beatles fans whose enthusiasm was no surprise to anyone.

The Cavern could not be called a sophisticated nightclub, but it could easily be called a dungeon. It was a cramped, grimy, underground sauna where sweat rolled down the walls, onto the equipment, causing the amps to fail. There was no air, no carpets, and no tables, and the lighting was sparse. The hundreds of fans who came to see the Beatles would have found more room aboard a submarine.

"We probably loved the Cavern best of anything," says George. "We never lost our identification with the crowd and we never rehearsed anything. We were playing to our own fans who were like us."

And the fans would come for 274 shows from 1961 to 1963.

Fame brought a new problem for the Beatles following their scream-producing performance at the Litherland Town Hall right after Christmas 1960. As their popularity spread they began receiv-

Three photos of the Beatles—John, Paul, George, and Pete—outside the Cavern in 1961.

ing a few threats from angry Merseyside boys who believed that the Beatles were stealing their girl-friends.

"Stu Sutcliffe rejoined us halfway through January," says Pete, "and he was always a target because of his small stature. George also had to be rescued by bouncers. John, however, was always ready to have a go, and I usually had a go at his side as a sort of rescue squad for Stu."

The Beatles' crowds kept growing along with their popularity, and avid female fans began picking individual favorites. John and Paul had a rivalry going to see who could attract the most attention. Neither realized that several groupies were mesmerized by the silent, moody drummer, Pete Best.

As their popularity continued to grow, so also grew the squabbles among them. Paul wanted to play bass guitar and constantly tormented Stu, who could not play bass or any other instrument. Stu realized that he was no musician and was just taking up space onstage. He was with the group only because of his friendship with John and he knew it.

Throughout January and February 1961, Allan Williams booked local gigs at the Aintree Institute, Lathom Memorial Hall, Blair Hall, and Grosvenor Ballroom. Meanwhile, he had written to Peter Eckhorn, owner of the Top Ten Club, and was close to completing a deal for the Beatles' second tour in Hamburg. Williams first had to overcome a few official obstacles resulting from the group's unfavorable exit from Germany during their first trip, so he set about placating the German Consulate. He explained that the unfortunate arrangements with Bruno Koschmider at the Kaiserkeller had not been honored and created unfair hardships on the boys. He closed his letter by stating: "I can assure you all the musicians have very good character and come from first class families, and they have never been in trouble with the police in this country."

On March 2, after the work permits were granted, Williams prepared a contract for the Beatles to appear at the Top Ten Club for seven evening shows at 40 DM per performer per night, beginning March 27. However, Williams was completely unaware that this booking had already been arranged with Peter Eckhorn by Pete Best via telephone.

Pete Best says: "This time we went in style. We went by train and Astrid greeted us at the station.

She was wearing an all-leather trouser outfit."

The Beatles were also pleased with their improved living quarters, complete with bath. John, Paul, George, and Pete shared the dormitory with Tony Sheridan, while Stu returned to Astrid's house.

"We alternated each night at the Top Ten with Tony Sheridan," says Pete. "He was really popular in the Hamburg area, and one evening [record producer] Bert Kaempfert came into the club to see what all the commotion Tony had on the customers."

Astrid was still influencing the Beatles by introducing changes in Stu's appearance that were not initially accepted by the others.

"I remember one evening," says Best, "Stu came in with a special hairstyle that Astrid had given him. We all fell over laughing so much that Stu combed his hair back to the original James Dean look. But Astrid persuaded Stu to try it again. Then, one evening, George came in with the same hairstyle, and a few days later, Paul and John were wearing it, but not knowing if they should keep it. Eventually, they did and that's how the Beatles hairstyle came to be. I was never really fond of it myself, because I knew I would have looked awful that way."

Astrid also gets credit for those famous collarless suits. "She made one for Stu," says Pete, "and we also had one made for each of us. But the material was so sheer that it split at the seams when we sat down."

On March 22, ten months after the Silver Beatles auditioned in the basement of the defunct Wyvern Social Club at 108 Seel Street, the Blue Angel Club opened on the same site.

Allan Williams named the club after the 1930 German film starring Marlene Dietrich, and he hoped that the new club would provide a sophisticated contrast to the seedy clubs in this part of Liverpool. He designed an invitation imprinted with a drawing of Marlene Dietrich, a big favorite in England.

Alma Warren provided the entertainment on opening night, backed by the Terry Francis Quartet.

Williams stood in the doorway and considered the future of his new investment, but his thoughts were not so cheerful regarding the Beatles. They had betrayed him and he was now becoming aware of Pete Best's interference.

On April 20, Williams wrote a letter of resignation to the Beatles, ending his association as personal manager just one month short of a year, citing a contract violation by the group as his reason for resigning. He had discovered that Pete Best had telephoned Peter Eckhorn from Liverpool to arrange the Top Ten booking and Eckhorn had mailed the train tickets to Pete's home. It was Williams, however, who had prepared the written contract with Eckhorn and obtained the work permits. Williams's letter was typed, but the envelope he sent it in was handwritten and he misspelled the group's name in addressing the letter: The Beetles, c/o the Top Ten Club. The letter said it all:

> Dear All,
>
> I am very distressed to hear you are contemplating not paying my commission out of your pay as was agreed in our contract for your engagement at the Top Ten Club.
>
> May I remind you, seeing you are all appearing to get more than a little swollen-headed, that you would not even have smelled Hamburg if I had not made the contacts, and by Law it is illegal for any person under contract to make a contract through the first contract.
>
> I would also point out that the only reason you are there is through work that I did and if you had tried yourselves to play at the Top Ten without a bona fide contract and working through a British Government approved Agency you would not be in Germany now.

Allan Williams recalls: "I was very upset with the boys. I wrote all kinds of threats, like blackballing them from playing any Liverpool spots, getting the law on them for breach of contract, which meant reporting them to the Agency Members Association.

"Of course, I never did carry out any of my threats to get them blackballed. I arranged their German work permits and could easily have gotten them out of Germany. I may have a lot of bark but not much bite and am not the vindictive or petty-minded type. That letter ended our business relationship. I don't think I could have acted in any other way. Unknown to me, of course, I was saying good-bye to millions of pounds and worldwide success. But everybody can look back in wisdom."

During this stint at the Top Ten, Stu could no longer endure the ribbing about his love life and his pitiful attempts to play the bass guitar. Most of the wisecracks came from John and Paul. By mid-

May, Stu had left the Beatles and returned to art college, in Hamburg. At the end, there was no animosity, despite the constant bickering, and they all remained friends.

Meanwhile, Bert Kaempfert had signed Tony Sheridan to a Polydor contract and a recording session was to be scheduled as soon as a backup band could be found. Sheridan was interested in the four boys from Liverpool.

"I remember the Beatles were really getting to be popular at the Top Ten," recalls Sheridan. "They would sometimes sneak in and join me onstage, even though they were not supposed to. They even did that in 1960 on their first visit to Hamburg. The Beatles could be just the group to back me because they did just that onstage at the Top Ten."

And so it came to pass that the Beatles were chosen, and they were very excited about doing the session.

The boys got up bright and early and drove to the studio.

Pete says: "We wondered if we had come to the right place. We had been expecting a recording setup on the grand scale. After all, Bert was a big name and Polydor an important label. Instead, we found ourselves in an unexciting school gym with a massive stage and lots of drapes."

Blue Angel Club
108 Seel Street
Liverpool 1

Royal 7943

May we extend our reserved invitation to become a founder-member of the Blue Angel Club; tasteful in decor and luxuriously furnished, occupying three floors, comparable only with West End establishments and catering for ladies and gentlemen of taste.

We offer professional cabaret each evening and also dancing to the Terry Francis Quartet or a quiet evening in our cocktail lounge with incidental music played on the grand piano. For the gentlemen who wish to relax we have provided a gentlemen's lounge and for the ladies a luxurious powder room.

We open on Wednesday, March 22nd, starring Alma Warren for the opening week with dancing till 1 a.m. on weekdays and 2 a.m. weekends with light refreshments served. If you would like to become a foundation member we request that you fill in the necessary application form and return it with cheque or banker's order and we invite you to bring along a guest to our opening free champagne night.

We would respectfully mention that formal dress is required for the opening night from 8 p.m.

With the compliments of the Management,

A. R. Williams.

The songs to be recorded had already been selected by Sheridan and Kaempfert. "My Bonnie" had been a hit for Ray Charles in 1958, and in 1956 Bill Haley and His Comets had a hit with "When the Saints Go Marching In." Sheridan frequently sang both songs at the Top Ten and it seemed natural to record songs that he was used to doing and which were familiar to his fans.

Bert Kaempfert was so impressed with the Beatles that he signed them to a six-month contract as backup artists and set up a separate session without Sheridan. Lennon later referred to this event as the first true recording session for the four Beatles—John, Paul, George, and Pete.

After doing "Ain't She Sweet" with John on lead vocal, they recorded an original Lennon-Harrison instrumental, "Cry for a Shadow."

Sometime before they returned to Liverpool, Tony Sheridan recorded three more songs with the Beatles: "Why," "Sweet Georgia Brown," and "Take Out Some Insurance."

Back in Liverpool, Bill Harry had been toying with the idea of publishing a newspaper devoted to the Merseyside rock bands. A friend of Stu Sutcliffe, Harry was involved with the music scene in Liverpool. Harry recalls: "It was evident that the members of the groups had no conception of the scope of the scene they were involved in."

Harry borrowed £50 from his friend Jim Anderson and opened an office at 84 Renshaw Street. After enlisting the help of his fiancée, Virginia Sowry, and a photographer, Dick Matthews, he began compiling a file cabinet full of information on all the local bands. He persuaded Bob Wooler to become a columnist, and to this day credits Wooler as the individual who engendered more publicity for the local rock groups than any other person. Wooler also had a giant collection of American rock music, which he played at the Cavern.

Bill Harry says: "On July 6, 1961, Volume 1, Number 1, of the *Mersey Beat* hit the stands. That is to say, I personally distributed the copies, about 5,000. I took them to all the local stores, such as W. H. Smith, Conlan's, and Blackburns, which the kids would frequent. The local clubs and jive halls, anywhere the musicians would assemble were on my route. Naturally, all the record stores were on my list."

The Beatles returned from Hamburg about the time the first *Mersey Beat* was published, and Harry wanted to do a cover story about their Polydor contract for the next issue.

Volume 1, Number 2, the July 20–August 3 issue, headlined BEATLES SIGN RECORDING CONTRACT! A

Facing page: An announcement of the opening of the Blue Angel Club sent by Allan Williams to prospective members in March 1961. *Left:* Interior of the Blue Angel. It was at the piano that Williams told Brian Epstein all about the Beatles, late in the year.

Und das ist die Twist-Rangliste:

1. Peppermint-Twist	. . . .	Valente/Francesco
2. The Twist	. . . .	Chubby Checker
3. Let's Twist Again	. . . .	Chubby Checker
4. My Bonnie	. . . .	Tony Sheridan
5. Popocatepetl-Twist	. . . .	Valente/Francesco
6. Twist-Twist	. . . .	Chakachas
7. Liebestraum-Twist	. . . .	Charly Cotton
8. You Can't Sit Down	. . . .	Phil Upchurch
9. Let's Twist Again	. . . .	Johnny Halliday
10. Steiler Zahn	. . . .	Olivers Twist-Band

A 1961 Hamburg Top 10 listing of twist records.

photo taken by Astrid and provided by Lennon included Stu Sutcliffe, who was no longer with the group when the contract was signed. The article mentioned that Sutcliffe had remained in Germany to study at the Hamburg Art College, and that the Beatles "have no plans for taking on another guitarist, but have decided to remain a quartet."

In July, "My Bonnie"/"The Saints" (Polydor N24673) was released in Germany. Two versions had been produced—one featuring a slow introduction in German, and another in English. The German version would appeal to the fans of Tony Sheridan, and if sales indicated a potential hit the English version would be released to the Britons. Stu Sutcliffe sent the record to the Beatles, who intended to have Bob Wooler play it at the Cavern.

Although the Beatles had a contract as backup artists with Polydor, their name did not appear on the record label. They did not know that the Polydor executives had decided that all groups that backed Tony Sheridan would appear on the label as the Beat Brothers, regardless of the group's actual name.

When the Beatles returned to Liverpool in July they were without a manager, but this posed no problem for getting local bookings. Along with other promoters such as Sam Leach and Brian Kelly, Pete's mother, Mona Best, made sure that the boys did not stay idle.

Brian Kelly arranged for them to play regularly at the Aintree Institute starting August 12. Bob Wooler usually emceed the dances that Kelly set up, in addition to his deejay job at the Cavern. Wooler's first in-depth article on the Beatles appeared in the August 31–September 14 issue of *Mersey Beat*.

The Beatles continued their performances at the Cavern throughout September, along with other groups, including the Bluegenes, the Remo Four, Gerry and the Pacemakers, Ian and the Zodiacs, and Karl Terry and the Cruisers.

In his "The Hornet's Nest" column in the *Mersey Beat* for October 5–19, Bill Harry presented his personal list of the most popular rock bands on the Merseyside. The Beatles were number one, followed by Gerry and the Pacemakers, Rory Storm and the Hurricanes, the Remo Four, and the Strangers.

One of the most unusual music events at the Litherland Town Hall was reported by Bob Wooler in his column for the November 2–16 *Mersey Beat*.

THE ROVING I

It had to happen sometime. It was just a question of the right time and the right place—and the sharing of a carefree mutual mood of co-operativeness. Well it happened at Litherland Town Hall during the Thursday night jive session on 19th October. The curtains opened and the Beatmakers exploded on an astonished crowd with a sound that was bigger than the Guns of Navarone. You've never heard of the Beatmakers? Well, it may never happen again that The Beatles and The Pacemakers (The Beatmakers) are feeling in a sufficiently crazy mood to go on stage together in one terrific jam session. Gerry wore George's black leather outfit and capered about in a hilarious Faron-cum-Rory-cum-

Karl Terry type of act using the hand mike; Paul wore a castoff nightie that Freddie acquired from his mother to pack his drums with; John did a Marx Brothers style piano act; Freddie, in a railwayman's rig-out was on one drum kit. Pete was on the other; George wore a hood and played lead guitar, Les was on rhythm; the other Les was blowing wild on his sax. The whole thing was a gas, a riot! The octet zipped through four romping numbers: "Whole Lotta Shakin," "What'd I Say," "Red Sails," and "Hit the Road Jack." The crowd stopped jiving and went wild. Like I said it may never happen again. It was one of those things that now and then swings.

The Beatles were on a roll. *Mersey Beat* had named them the most popular local band, and they were playing regularly at the Cavern as well as at other bookings throughout Liverpool. But despite all the local pandemonium the Beatles were plagued by a new problem. Boredom. They were beginning to grow weary with the Cavern shows and felt that they would never find stardom beyond the Merseyside.

The boys were unaware that a stranger was about to appear who would influence their career more than anyone could imagine. The stranger's name was Brian Epstein.

Harry Epstein was the owner of two music stores called NEMS (North End Road Music Stores). The first had opened in Central Liverpool in 1957 and business was so good that another store was added two years later in Whitechapel Street.

Harry's oldest son, Brian, was a twenty-seven-year-old failure. He had failed as a student, a soldier, and as an actor before taking the job as manager of the record department at his father's store in Whitechapel. Here he had found his calling and became a successful salesman and executive.

On October 28, an eighteen-year-old boy named Raymond Jones came into the store and asked for a record called "My Bonnie."

Epstein asked for the artist's name.

"The Beatles," replied Jones, who then added that Bob Wooler had mentioned the record at one of the local dances and said it was a "good rocking dance song."

After checking his files, Epstein confessed that he had no such record nor any such listing by title or group. He could not know that this simple request by an ardent teenager was destined to change the rest of his life.

The next day, as Epstein began searching for the elusive record, two girls strolled into the store and asked for "My Bonnie." They told Epstein that the Beatles played at the Cavern, just a few blocks away on Mathew Street.

A thoroughly frustrated Epstein decided that

TONY SHERIDAN

My Bonnie
(Mein Herz ist bei dir nur)

The Saints
(When The Saints Go Marching In)

Sleeve and label for Tony Sheridan's "My Bonnie," the first commercial record on which the Beatles played. Released July 1961.

Jive Fans This Is It!

MEET THE BEATLES

every Saturday at

AINTREE INSTITUTE

(BUSES 20, 21, 22, 30, 61, 91, 92, 93, 95, 96 & 500 TO BLACK BULL, NEXT DOOR)

YES! PAUL, JOHN, GEORGE AND PETE

will be playing for you exclusively at Aintree Institute,
every Saturday, starting 12th August 1961.

You must be there, too!

Come early and bring your friends!

Jiving from 7-30 to 11 p.m.   Admission 4/-

Aintree Institute Your Saturday Dance Date

he'd better learn something about this local band that was causing so much interest and yet was unknown to him. Although he wrote for *Mersey Beat,* his column was devoted to the most popular songs by established artists, not the raucous sounds of hard-rock groups in Liverpool. Yet, the fact that a local band was creating so much excitement intrigued him.

Epstein called Bill Harry and explained his dilemma. Harry was amused and said he would arrange a visit with the band.

During his lunch hour on November 9, Epstein went over to Mathew Street and carefully waded through the rotting fruits and vegetables covering the pavement until he arrived at the Cavern. Inside, he knew he had made a big mistake. The place was a dark, wretched dump with dripping walls. There was no ventilation and his nostrils were begging for clean air. He could not understand why anyone would spend a minute in such squalor.

When Epstein was introduced to the Beatles he inquired about "My Bonnie." George told him it had been recorded in Hamburg on the Polydor label. Paul ran over to Bob Wooler and asked him to play it. Afterward, Epstein thought the song was good but nothing to get excited about. He forced himself to remain for the Beatles' second show and found himself liking them more and more. When it was over, he told the boys that he would like to invite them to the Whitechapel store for a meeting, to discuss the possibility of representing them.

Throughout November, Epstein continued his lunchtime visits to hear the Beatles at the Cavern. He was not impressed by their scruffy leather coats and jeans, but *was* impressed by their performances, music, and honesty. He had no idea about how he could help them but he had a strange

feeling that the Beatles were somehow special. They had a magnetic charm that affected fans like honey affects bees. Epstein felt that they were going to become very successful and he wanted to participate.

"Operation Big Beat" took place on November 10 at the Tower Ballroom in New Brighton, and featured five of the most popular jive bands in Liverpool.

This was promoter Sam Leach's first venture in producing a big show at the Tower. More than 3,500 fans were on hand to hear the Beatles, Gerry and the Pacemakers, the Remo Four, Rory Storm and the Hurricanes, King Size Taylor and the Dominoes.

A photograph of the Beatles performing during the show appeared in the November 30–December 14 issue of *Mersey Beat,* along with a coupon to be mailed to the paper's Popularity Poll to determine the top Merseyside bands. The first announcement

Classified section of the *Liverpool Echo,* August 25, 1961, with two listings advertising performances by the Beatles.

The Beatles back recording artist Danny White in the Cavern in 1961.

of the contest had appeared in the previous issue.

At 4:30 on the afternoon of December 3, Epstein met with John, Paul, George, and Pete at the Whitechapel store. Bob Wooler accompanied the boys as their adviser. Briefly, they talked about the possibility of a management contract, but the boys were uncertain and wanted more time to consider the idea. Epstein scheduled another meeting to be held three days later.

In the meantime, Epstein discussed the situation with E. Rex Makin, a friend and family lawyer. Makin had seen a lot of Epstein's grand ideas go up in smoke and offered no encouragement regarding a management agreement for a rock band.

Epstein also consulted Allan Williams, who advised him not to "touch them with a bargepole!" Obviously, Williams was still upset at losing his commission for the Beatles' Top Ten engagement.

On December 6, Epstein offered his services to the Beatles. "Quite simply," he said, "you need a manager. Would you like me to do it?"

Silence prevailed as the boys thought for a few moments. Paul wanted to know if the music they played would have to be changed and was assured that it would not.

Another uneasy silence followed, then Lennon spoke.

"Right, then, Brian," John blurted out. "Manage us. Where's the contract? I'll sign it."

At the time, Epstein would not have been able to distinguish a management contract from a Goon Show script. He stalled by telling the boys that he would have one at their next meeting.

A written agreement was executed by the Beatles and Brian Epstein on December 10. This historic occasion took place at The Casbah in the basement of Pete Best's home.

Alistair Taylor, a NEMS employee, appeared as a witness. Later, he said he felt like a complete fool because "I signed my name as a witness to Brian Epstein's signature, and Brian had forgotten to sign the contract!"

Albert Marrion, a distinguished photographer, has an impressive list of credits, which include serving as the official Liverpool photographer during the Blitz of World War II. He became more famous, however, as the man who took the first official pictures of the Beatles.

Marrion recalls: "Midway during the month of December 1961, Brian Epstein called me and asked if I could take some photos of four boys he had started to manage. At first, I was reluctant to accept the task. We were primarily a portrait and wedding studio. In fact, the reason Epstein called me was I had been the photographer for his brother Clive's wedding.

"Brian had told me they were a scruffy-looking

Left: Another *Echo* classified ad for the Beatles in the Friday, September 8, issue. *Above:* Sam Leach, Bob Wooler, and George Harrison, Liverpool, 1961.

group in all-leather outfits, but quite harmless. I agreed and told Brian to have them meet me at my Wallasey studio the following Sunday, December 17.

"At first, I asked my partner, Herbert Hughes, to take the photo session, but he flatly refused, wanting nothing to do with the beat group.

"Sunday morning arrived and the four Beatles arrived at my studio. I remember those leather pants and jackets, the polo sweaters, and suede shoes to this day. Brian had spoken to them prior to the meeting so they were half serious in attitude. Every once in a while, John Lennon would stick his tongue out and make a wisecrack. John and Paul joked and laughed throughout most of the session. George Harrison was quiet and Pete Best didn't speak almost at all.

"It was pouring down rain and Lennon was beginning to irritate me. I, being bald at the forehead, Lennon frequently referred to me as 'Curly.'

"This photo session was done for Epstein as a friendly gesture against the wishes of my partner, Hughes. I took about thirty photographs of the Beatles but discarded all but sixteen negatives because many showed Lennon and McCartney acting up and spoiling the pose. No doubt, those negatives should have been kept, looking back.

"Just before I processed the photographs that Bill Harry was to use in the 'Top 10 Poll' issue [of *Mersey Beat*], I was walking down North John Street and noticed the four Beatles on the opposite side of the street, just ready to turn off into Mathew Street. They were wearing the same leather outfits they had posed in for me, and again it was raining quite steady.

"Lennon spotted me. He cupped his hand over his mouth, and in his deep Liverpudlian accent, yelled, 'Hey, Curly, when do we get our pictures?' 'Soon boys,' I said and continued on my way. The Christmas holiday was starting and despite the

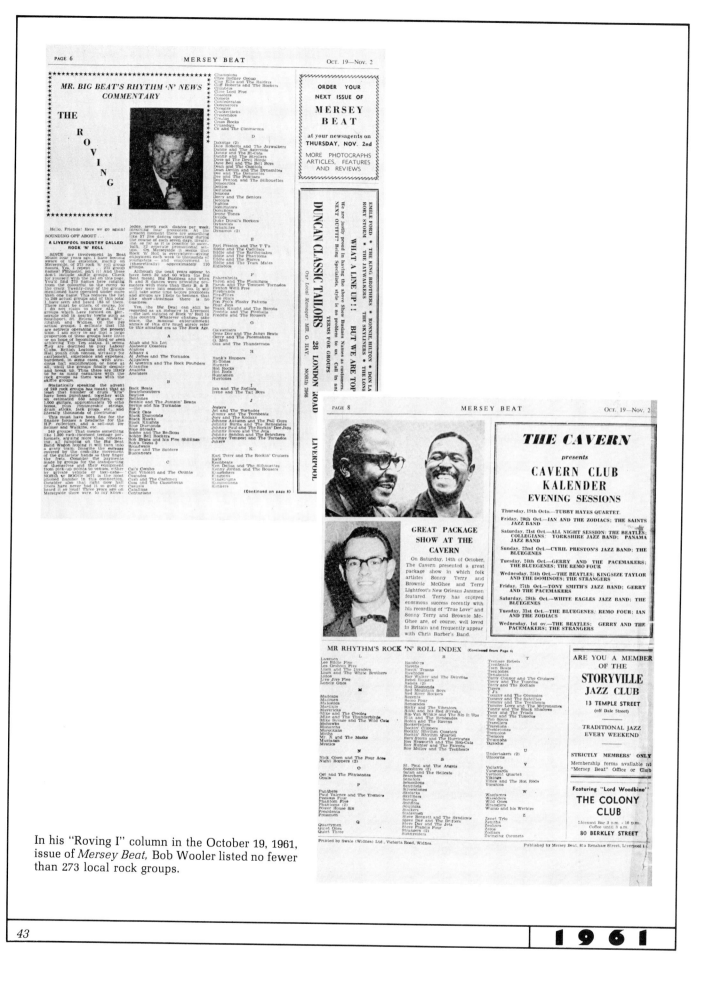

In his "Roving I" column in the October 19, 1961, issue of *Mersey Beat,* Bob Wooler listed no fewer than 273 local rock groups.

OPERATION BIG BEAT

THE HURRICANES RIP IT UP ! . . .

. . . Gold lame shirts included. Johnny Guitar, Rory, Ringo and Lu at New Brighton Tower.

LIFELESS OR DEAD

Listening to back alley talk does not really do good and I mean by this that small rumours have been spreading that the Liverpool rock scene seems to be lifeless or dead at the present time. How ridiculous can you get? Without myself referring to any files or notes I can now think of the wild fire business that has been going on and is going on right now. Gone are groups such as Robin and the Ravens, Faron and the Tempest Tornadoes, Cliff Roberts and the Rockers. But fresh on the scene are Faron and the Flamingoes, Earl Preston and the T.T.'s, the Detours, the Climbers, Steve Day and the Drifters and others. Frank Bowen joins the Cyclones, and there is a new drummer for both the Remo 4 and Frank Knight and the Barons.—Jeff Martin.

THE BEATLES IN ACTION . . .

Photo by Dick Matthews

George, Paul, Pete and John, appearing at the highly successful "Operation Big Beat" at the Tower Ballroom. Fans of this popular group will be pleased to hear that copies of their record will be available soon at Nems.

Left: "Operation Big Beat" was covered in the November 30 *Mersey Beat. Right:* The November 30 issue also contained the *Mersey Beat* Popularity Poll clip-out form that readers could mail in to vote for the top groups in Liverpool. *Below:* The first management contract between the Beatles and Brian Epstein, December 10, 1961. John, Paul, George, and Pete affixed their signatures, but Epstein forgot to sign (even though Alistair Taylor witnessed his signature!).

MERSEY BEAT POPULARITY POLL

Many, many forms have already been sent in. Here is your last chance to vote for your favourite groups. Fill in the form and post it to the "Mersey Beat" office on or before December 1st.

NAME

ADDRESS

1.
2.
3.
4.
5.
6.
7.
8.
9.
10.

If you have any difficulty obtaining "MERSEY BEAT" please fill in the form below:—

To the Newsagent:—

Please reserve me a copy of each issue of

"MERSEY BEAT"

NAME ....

ADDRESS ....

THE MERSEYSIPPI

ONE OF THE MOST vigorous changes in the pop field this year was the boom in traditional jazz. Kenny Ball, Terry Lightfoot, Acker Bilk and many British bands found their popularity at its peak; new bands formed, clubs thrived, and Clinton Ford at last received some acclaim. With all the activity of talent scouts searching for talent in the jazz field, I wondered why the Merseysippi didn't rocket to the top. The group was formed in 1948 and became Merseyside's top jazz group. They recorded for Esquire and Oriole and singles, e.p.'s and l.p's were issued. They appeared on television and radio. In fact they were doing well before the trad fad hit the pop field.

I went along to the Mardi Gras Club to see how they were getting on, and jovial trumpeter Pete Daniels was able to enlighten me on the situation. It was quite simple. The Merseysippi just have no intention of turning professional. As semi-pro's they find they can enjoy the music they love to the full; many professional players find their enjoyment curtailed by the fact that they have to earn their bread and butter in a highly competitive field. As the headquarters of the record companies and television studios are in London, the opportunities for a semi-pro band in the provinces are very limited.

There are still three of the founder members in the present line-up, which includes Trevor Carlisle on drums ("One has to practice all the time," he says, "it's the only way"); Dick Goodwin, who is the band manager, on bass; Ken Baldwin on banjo and guitar; Frank Robinson on piano; Don Lydiate on clarinet; Pete Daniels, trumpet; Johnny Laurence, trumpet; John Parkes, trombone; Jill Martin, vocals.

ON THE SCENE BY JAZZMEN

On the Scene is a new feature in which I hope to bring to your attention items of interest, comment and general chat, in, on and about jazz sights and sounds around town.

The big news for modernists is the happy association of the Cavern and London's Ronnie Scott Club, which promises to bring the best in British modern jazz to the Cavern every Thursday evening. On Thursday, Ronnie Scott, ex co-leader of the lamented Couriers blew a nice, warm-up set, and everyone yelled when guest tenor Zoot Sims came on-stage. A fine ovation for a fine musician, known over here for his work with Getz, Brookmeyer and Mulligan.

Zoot's Jazz, unlike the hard new school of Coltrane, Rollins and disciples, springs from the Lester Young idea. Blowing a varied set of standard's balladic and up, including "Soft Winds," "Broadway" and "Cubano Chant," Sims displayed his control to advantage, but as the man said: "If you can't hear nothin', you can't blow nothin'."

With squeals, grunts, howls, forceful hand-clapping, stamping of the feet and lusty revival shouts, Zoot tried hard to drive the rhythm men (Tracey, Napper, Dougan), but these three cool gents just refused to go. Tracy probed Monklike. Napper soloed well, but inaudibly and Dougan turned in rim-shots and triplets as per book. Something of the expected Sims fire and warmth got across in a swinging blues and the frantic "Broadway."

Fours all round by Zoot Scott, Dougan and a hesitant Jimmy Deuchar took the session to an entertaining, if disappointing end.

THE CAVERN

presents

CAVERN CLUB KALENDER

EVENING SESSIONS

November 28th—BLUEGENES, REMO FOUR, GERRY AND THE PACEMAKERS.

November 29th—THE BEATLES, IAN AND THE ZODIACS, JOHNNY SANDON AND THE SEARCHERS.

November 30th—DON RENDALL QUINTET.

December 1st—GERRY AND THE PACEMAKERS.

December 2nd—ZENITH SIX, THE BEATLES.

December 3rd—Empire: KENNY BALL. Club: ALAN ESDON'S JAZZBAND, THE BLUEGENES.

December 5th—JOHNNY SANDON AND THE SEARCHERS, GERRY AND THE PACEMAKERS, THE BLUEGENES.

December 6th—BEATLES, THE REMO FOUR, STRANGERS.

December 9th—THE SAINTS, GERRY AND THE PACEMAKERS.

December 10th—HUMPHREY LYTTLETON AND HIS BAND, THE BLUEGENES.

December 12th—BLUEGENES, THE REMO FOUR, GERRY AND THE PACEMAKERS.

December 13th—THE BEATLES, THE RAVENS, THE FOUR JAYS.

IN WITNESS whereof the parties hereto have hereunto set their hands the day and year first before written

SIGNED by the said
BRIAN EPSTEIN in the
presence of :—

J. A. Taylor.
FLAT C. "HEREMINDS"
THE SERPENTINE SOUTH
BLUNDELLSANDS
LIVERPOOL 23.

SIGNED by the said
JOHN WINSTON LENNON
in the presence of :—

J. A. Taylor.

SIGNED by the said
GEORGE HARRISON
in the presence of :—

J. A. Taylor.

SIGNED by the said
JAMES PAUL McCARTNEY
in the presence of :—

J. A. Taylor.

SIGNED by the said
PETER RANDOLPH BEST
in the presence of :—

J. A. Taylor.

Albert Marrion's 1961 business card with price quotes for his regular work—wedding photography.

cold and rain, my heart had a warm bit of sympathy for those four boys who would soon take the world by storm."

Mersey Beat, Volume 1, Number 12, was packed with information on the proposed activities of the Beatles for the new year. The cover had two photos—one of Emile Ford with the Beatles, and one of Billy Kramer.

In her "Mersey Roundabout" column, Virginia Harry wrote: "The Mersey Beat Christmas Party will take place at 11 P.M. on Friday, 22nd December. For Merseyside entertainment folk only, the party should prove a very entertaining affair. Tickets are obtainable only from *Mersey Beat* and cost 10/- [shillings] each. As there are only 150 tickets available we would suggest that entertainers contact us as soon as possible. . . . The results of the *Mersey Beat* Popularity Poll will be announced at the party and I would like to take the opportunity to say that, as yet, no one knows the results. The results of the poll will be fair and we invite anyone who doubts to come along to the office to examine them, upon application."

Virginia ended her column with a note: "Information from NEMS: Elvis' new disc 'Can't Help Falling in Love with You'/'Rock-a-Hula-Baby' is expected to be released by Decca in January."

On December 16, the day before the Beatles' historic photo session with Albert Marrion, *Cash Box* magazine announced: "Bert Kaempfert has opened up the first twist fight in Germany with two new records. The first is by a twister from England, Tony Sheridan, who sings in English and German.

The record 'My Bonnie' and 'The Saints,' both done in twist rhythm, is being released soon in the U.S. with six top record firms fighting over the master."

This was the first indirect mention in America of the Beatles, referring to the record on which they had backed Tony Sheridan.

After the photo session, the next objective in Epstein's plan was a recording contract. While working at NEMS he had made several important contacts with Decca Records in London. He called the record company and invited the top A&R (artists and repertoire) man, Mike Smith, to visit him in Liverpool.

On December 20, Epstein treated Smith to dinner and took him to see the Beatles perform at the Cavern. Smith seemed enthusiastic about the boys but said he would prefer to have them come to Decca for a proper audition. Epstein agreed and was told to be at the studio by 11:00 on New Year's Day.

Brian was ecstatic. At first, he kept the exciting news to himself. He knew that Smith wanted to hear how the boys would sound on a taped playback, and how they would handle themselves during the session.

When the boys heard the news, they suddenly felt as if the long road to success was beginning to shorten.

Epstein wasted no time in his relentless pursuit of ultimate success for his clients. Only two weeks after signing the management contract he had achieved three significant goals.

First, he was certain that the Beatles would be voted Number 1 in the *Mersey Beat* Popularity Poll. Since he knew that no professional photos of the boys were available, he had arranged for their first formal session with Albert Marrion.

Second, Epstein had arranged an audition with the top A&R manager at a major record company.

And, third, he had arranged for Polydor Records in London to release "My Bonnie"/"The Saints" in the United Kingdom. The record had been released in Germany only five months earlier.

On December 30, the Beatles played their last Cavern date of the year and shared the bill with the Yorkshire Jazz Band.

There was no doubt in Brian Epstein's mind that the year ahead would offer challenges and changes, but he was also certain that the future would be very prosperous for John, Paul, George, and Pete.

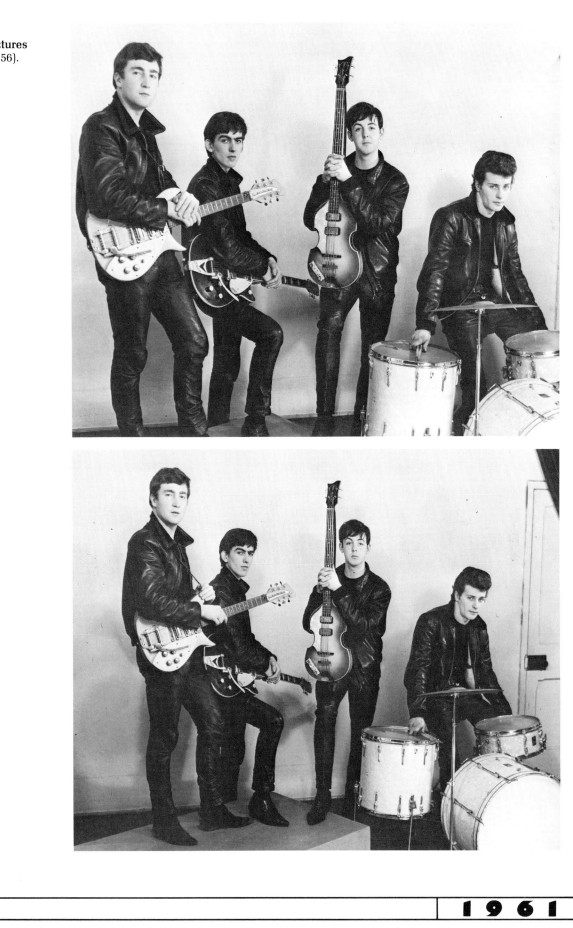

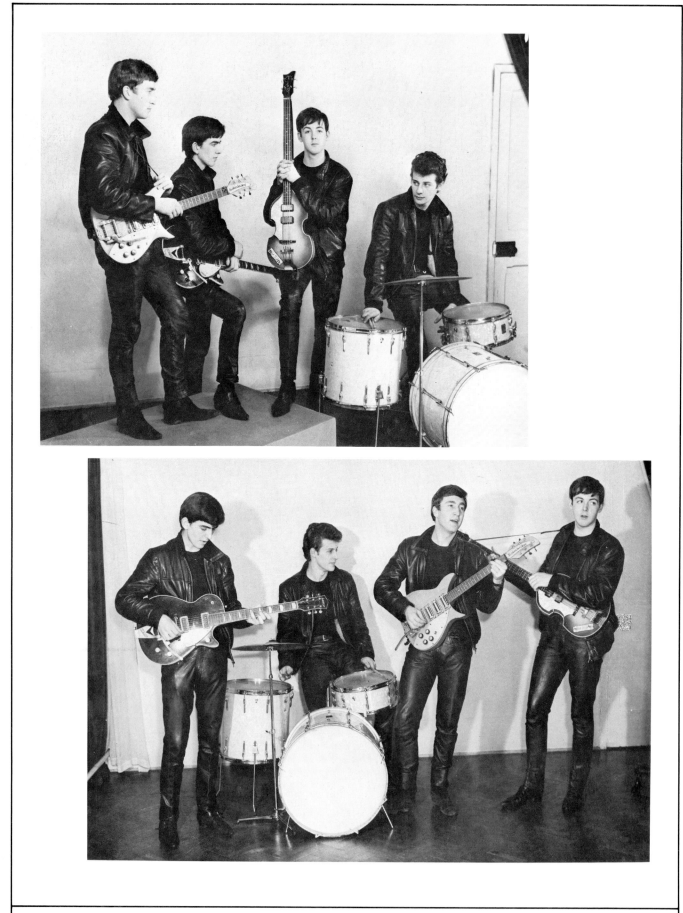

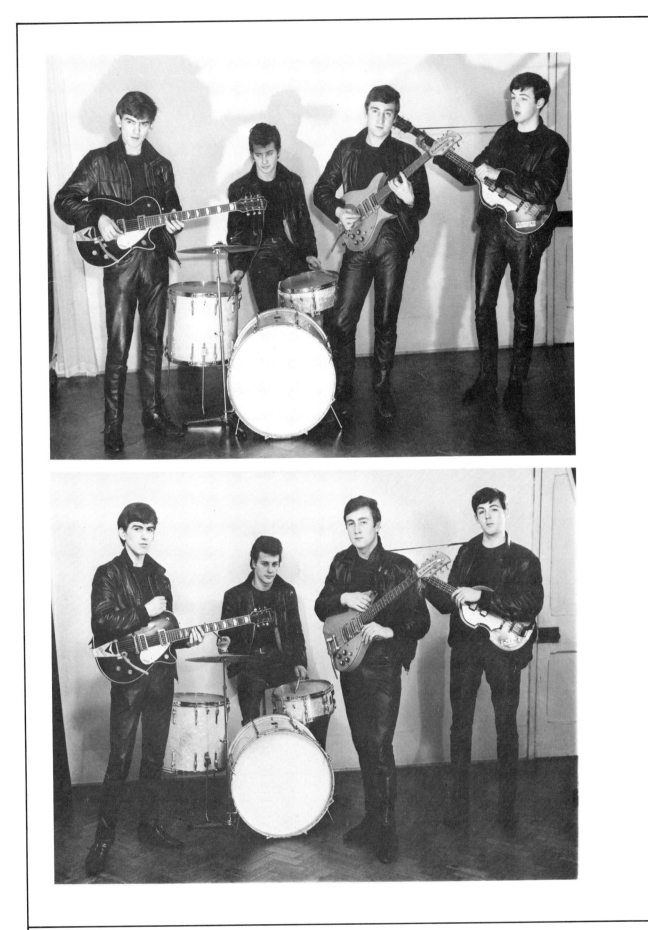

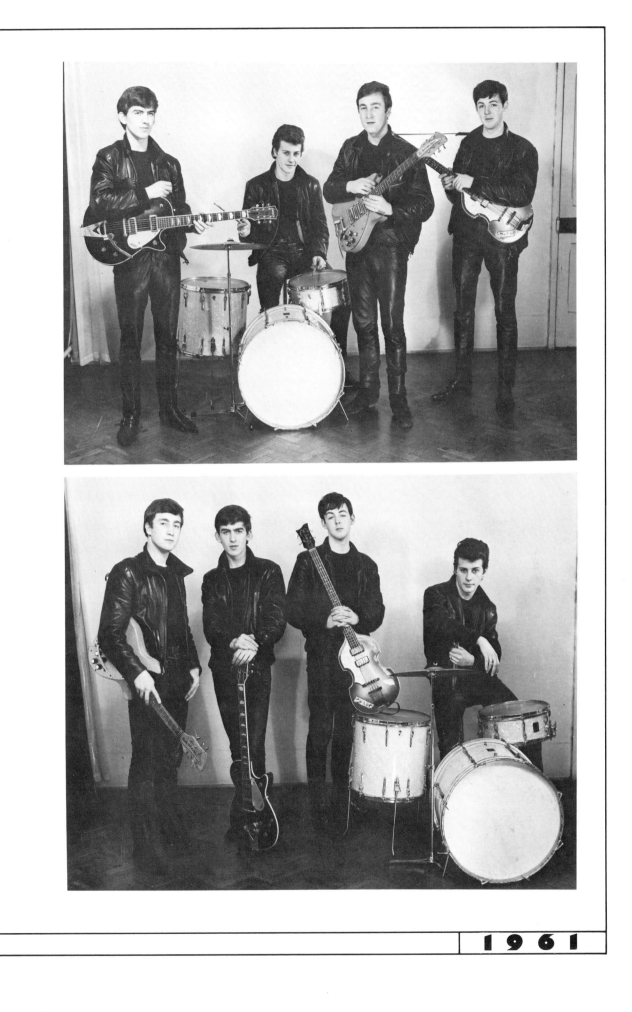

1961

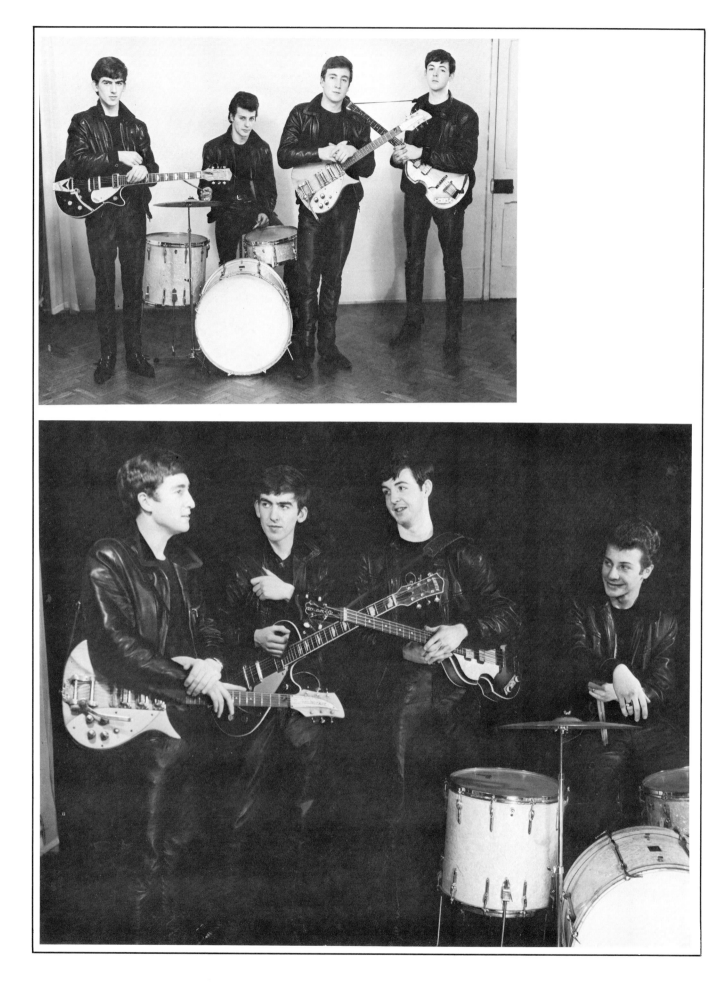

PART THREE
1962

"Sorry, Mr. Epstein, but groups with guitars are on their way out."

—*Dick Rowe*

Perhaps the best kept secret the Beatles concealed from *Mersey Beat* and their Liverpool fans was their audition for the Decca Record Company in London on New Year's Day 1962.

Nine days earlier in America, *Cash Box* had announced, "One of the most constructive moves to be made by Decca for many months is the formation of a new production team to handle the company's pop single output. Spearheaded by A&R manager, Dick Rowe, who will be directly responsible to the chairman, Sir Edward Lewis, the team is completed by Mike Smith, Rowe's assistant and co-producer, Peter Attwood, recording engineer of three years standing and Tony Meehan, former drummer for The Shadows. Rowe, who will act in an advisory capacity, feels that this youthful team with their fingers on the teenage pulse, will be more than capable of producing the kind of sound that makes for chart success."

Now the big day had arrived! Pete Best wondered if their reception at Decca would be warm and friendly or match the frigid weather that had greeted them when they awoke at the Royal Hotel in Russell Square. Also, the Beatles were not the only group who would be competing for a coveted recording contract today.

"The cold, stone appearance of the Decca West Hampstead studios looked more like an institution of learning than a recording studio," recalls Pete. "When we entered the building we met Eppie and he was in a fit because Mike Smith had not yet arrived." And the climate did not improve after the producer entered the room. "Mr. Smith told us that we could not use our own amplifiers, and told John, Paul, and George to plug their instruments into the studio speakers."

The situation worsened when the red recording light came on. Paul was too nervous to sing and his voice began to crack. George was having trouble playing his guitar. All of the boys were nervous and it showed, mostly during the solo vocals. But they played valiantly from midday until late afternoon.

During their "moment of truth" the Beatles sang fifteen songs. Three were Lennon-McCartney compositions: "Like Dreamers Do" and "Love of the Loved," featured Paul, then John sang lead on "Hello Little Girl."

George sang lead on "The Sheik of Araby," "Three Cool Cats," "Crying, Waiting, Hoping," and "Take Good Care of My Baby," which was currently the Number 2 song by Bobby Vee on the Merseyside Top 20.

Most of the songs performed at the audition were favorites at the Cavern. Paul sang lead on "September in the Rain," "To Know Her Is to Love Her," "Searching," "Till There Was You," and "Besame Mucho." Then John sang the lead on "Money" and "Memphis Tennessee," and sang a duet with Paul on "Sure to Fall."

An awkward incident further marred the day. Epstein began to criticize John's singing. Lennon burst into a violent rage. Everything stopped. The red light went out. Epstein, Mike Smith, the engineer, and the rest of the group stared uneasily at one another. Moments later, Epstein rushed out of the room and did not return for nearly thirty minutes.

When the session was finished, John and Epstein had recovered from their verbal explosion.

"We heard the playback," says Pete, "and we all were confident with the results. Looking back today, perhaps, we could have been a little more polished, like John or Paul on certain vocal tracks. But that New Year's Day we felt that a Decca recording contract was imminent. We all jumped back into [road manager] Neil Aspinall's van and headed home to Liverpool."

Three days later, *Mersey Beat* Number 13 hit the streets with the results of its popularity poll in bold headlines on the front page: BEATLES TOP POLL!

The news came as no surprise to the legion of Beatles fans. Others, however, questioned the poll's authenticity. Rumors suggested that many competitive groups—including the Beatles—had bought several copies of the previous two issues, put the name of their group on the voting coupons, and mailed them in.

Bill Harry, editor of *Mersey Beat,* was not concerned about this obvious ploy to stuff the ballot box. "There were enough legitimate votes from the girls to assure the Beatles first place," says Harry. "I could recognize the writing of most group members and really didn't count those sent in bundles with the same handwriting."

John, Paul, George, and Pete were elated. They knew that this public endorsement could not be ignored by Mike Smith at Decca and they would soon sign their names to a contract.

It was the quiet before the storm.

Tony Barrow, a free-lance writer who wrote cover notes for Decca record albums as well as a

BEATLES TOP POLL! *Mersey Beat,* January 4. Note the misspelling of Paul's last name! Inside, Brian Epstein's picks for the best records of 1961. And his predictions for 1962. . . .

MY TOP POPS—1961

Brian Epstein   Photo: Albert Marion

The chart that follows is a purely personal choice of discs selected from the records that have appeared in Britain's Top Twenty during 1961. Included here is what I consider to have been the most disappointing disc of the year from a commercial point of view. How Tony Newley's 'What Kind of Fool am I' did not make No. 1 spot I will never understand. In general it has been a poor year pop-wise. Most of the discs in the earlier part of the year were very run of the mill type. The second half of 1961 was certainly much more interesting. On the other hand the top five discs listed in my chart are probably among the best single records to have received commercial success in many years. 'Take Five' is certainly a phenomenon. It's appeal has staggered the musical world. It's my own belief that here was a brilliant example of a disc being presented to the public at the right moment. Anyway from the point of view of these first five discs things are certainly 'looking up boys'.

Looking at the future, January

1962 will see the issue of three very important records. Elvis Presley's 'Can't Help Falling in Love/Rock-a-hoola Baby' has climbed high quickly in the States. Already the soundtrack LP of Cliff Richard's 'The Young Ones' is selling fast. The title song from the film will be released on a single the first week in January. And thirdly of great interest to Mersey beaters the fabulous record on which The Beatles back Tony Sheridan will be issued on January 6th. This could be a big one for the Beatles whose records I look forward to seeing in the charts in 1962. These are the records I will remember of 1961:

TAKE FIVE
Dave Brubeck.

GEORGIA ON MY MIND
Ray Charles.

WHAT KIND OF FOOL AM I ONCE IN A LIFETIME
Anthony Newley.

THE TIME HAS COME
Adam Faith.

TAKE GOOD CARE OF MY BABY
Bobby Vee.

SEPTEMBER IN THE RAIN
Dinah Washington.

YOU'LL ANSWER TO ME
Cleo Laine.

REACH FOR THE STARS/ CLIMB EVERY MOUNTAIN
Shirley Bassey.

THAT'S MY HOME
Acker Bilk.

SAMANTHA
Kenny Ball.

And a Happy New Year to everyone.

Brian Epstein.

If you have any difficulty obtaining "MERSEY BEAT" please fill in the form below:—

To the Newsagent:—

Please reserve me a copy of each issue of

"MERSEY BEAT"

NAME ....

ADDRESS ....

....

PARISIAN ROCK

Unabridged, unexpurgated, uncensored, we now present a startling report on the rock and roll scene in Paris by The Beatles. This item has long lain in our files, collecting dust whilst we pondered over the thought 'dare we print it.' Due to Christmas feelings, we are a bit merry, so we brushed off the dust, and here it is:

It was 10 o'clock, o'clock it was, when we were entering the OLYMPIA in Paris to see the "Johnny Halliday Rock Show." The cheapest seats in "les theatre" (French) were seven and sixpence, so we followed the woman with the torch (English).

When Johnny Halliday came, everybody went wild — and loud was the cheering and many the dancing in the aisles, too. But the man said 'sit down,' so we had to.

The excitement rose, the audience rose to dance, like the many boys and girls dancing along the back rows. Also old men, which is stranger still, isn't it.

Meanwhile, later the same week, we go to "Les Rock Festival" held in a club in Montemartre, with Danny et les Pirates and many more groups for your evening's entertainment. Topping the bill was Vince (Ron, my boy, Ron) Taylor, star of English screen and "Two I's."

The atmosphere is like many a night club, but the teenagers stand round the dancing floor which you use as a stage. They jump on a woman with gold trousers and a hand microphone and then hit a man when he says "go away." A group follows, and so do others, playing "Apache" worse than many other bands. When the singer joins the band, the leather jacket fiends who are the audience, join in dancing and banging tables with chairs.

The singers have to go one better than the audience, so they lie on the floor, or jump on a passing drummer, or kiss a guitar, and then hit the man playing it. The crowd enjoy this and many stand on chairs to see the fun, and soon the audience are all singing and shouting like one man, but he didn't mind.

Vince (Ron, Ron) Taylor finally appeared and joined the fun, and in the end he had so much fun that he had to rest. But in spite of this is had been a wonderful show, lovely show . . . lovely.

music column, "Off the Record," for the *Liverpool Echo,* acknowledged the event in his column. "Latest episode in the success story of Liverpool's instrumental group The Beatles: Commenting upon the outfit's recent recording test, Decca disc producer Mike Smith tells me that he thinks The Beatles are great. He has a continuous tape of their audition performances that runs over 30 minutes and he is convinced that his label will be able to put The Beatles to good use. I'll be keeping you posted. . . ."

On January 5, one day after the Beatles had been named the number-one group in the Merseyside, Polydor Records released the United Kingdom recording of "My Bonnie"/"The Saints" (Polydor NH 66833) by Tony Sheridan and the Beatles.

The first record label on which the Beatles' name appeared. Released January 5, 1962.

When recorded and originally released in Germany the label credits read: "Tony Sheridan and the Beat Brothers," as all of Sheridan's backup musicians were identified. Before the record was released in London, however, Epstein had persuaded the Polydor executives to use the group's real name on the U.K. release. It was the first record with the name of the Beatles on the label.

On January 4, the *South Liverpool Weekly News* had a two-column story about the release of "My Bonnie"/"The Saints" in England. The headline read: THEY'RE HOPING FOR A HIT RECORD, and the last paragraph offered an accurate prediction: "The boys have always been full-time musicians, ever since they left school, and are making quite a name for themselves locally. Who knows it might

not be long before they achieve nation-wide acclaim."

Although the boys were the number-one group in the Merseyside, they were unknown in London and record stores there did not stock "My Bonnie"/"The Saints." While this considerably reduced their exposure to a new audience, it was no tragedy to their Liverpool fans. They had already been to Harry Epstein's NEMS in Whitechapel and bought the version that had been released in Germany.

In addition to serving as the Beatles' manager, Brian Epstein still wrote his regular column for the *Mersey Beat,* called "My Top Pops." Ironically, in the same issue that had announced "Beatles Top Poll," Epstein wrote, "The fabulous record on which The Beatles back Tony Sheridan will be issued on January 6th. This could be a big one for the Beatles." Unfortunately, Epstein's talents as a prophet deserted him this time. The record went unnoticed and was all but forgotten.

On January 6, the Beatles returned to the Cavern and continued their regular performances through the end of the month.

January was an exhilarating month of "firsts" for the Liverpool foursome. They had their first audition for a major record company; they topped the *Mersey Beat* Popularity Poll; the first record with their name on the label was released; and on January 13 they were mentioned in print for the first time in America when *Cash Box* said: "A new rock 'n' roll team, Tony Sheridan and The Beatles, make their debut on the [English] Polydor label with 'My Bonnie.' Sheridan was discovered by Polydor producer Bert Kaempfert while playing night spots in Hamburg's famous Reeperbahn."

On January 22, a contract was signed by Epstein and Manfred Weissleder, owner of the Star-Club in Hamburg. An engagement for the Beatles to play the Top Ten Club again never developed because

First mention of the Beatles by name in America was this January 13, 1962, issue of *Cash Box*.

Decca exploitation chief **Bob Crabb** has been appointed personal assistant to **W. Townsley** (assistant to chairman **Sir Edward Lewis**). Tony Hall moves over from Decca House to Hanover Square to take over the exploitation duties. Hall, who manages Brunswick and Coral labels, will also continue his d.j. activities. Both appointments are effective from January 1st.

Granada TV's Personal Appearance series recently starred **Paul Anka** in his own show. Tele-recorded last year, "This Is Anka" also featured **Linda Scott** and comedian **Johnny Carson**.

A new rock 'n roll team, **Tony Sheridan** and **The Beatles**, make their debut on the Polydor label with "My Bonnie." Sheridan was discovered by Polydor producer **Bert Kaempfert** while playing night spots in Hamburg's famous Reeperbahn.

Cash Box—January 13, 1962————International Section

Peter Eckhorn refused to pay Epstein's price. Eckhorn was dumbfounded when told that the fee was now 2,000 DM per week for the group.

Weissleder, however, wanted the most popular English rock band to open his new nightclub and did not flinch when Epstein quoted the financial terms.

An agreement was prepared for 500 DM per person per week ($125 U.S.) and the Beatles were booked to appear at the Star-Club from April 13 until May 31.

By February, they still had not heard from Decca and wondered why no contract had been offered.

The Beatles went to the BBC's Playhouse Theatre in Manchester on February 12 and auditioned for Peter Pilbeam, who was pleased with their performance.

They appeared at the Cavern, then received second billing as *Mersey Beat* poll winners at a very successful charity dance for the benefit of the Empire Cancer Campaign. More than 3,500 attended the Pre-Panto dance at the Tower Ballroom on February 15, which starred Terry Lightfoot's New Orleans Jazzmen.

On March 7, they returned to the BBC Playhouse Theatre and recorded three songs before a studio audience whose reaction was spontaneous and ecstatic. The boys opened with "Dream Baby," a recent hit for Roy Orbison. Then they sang "Memphis Tennessee," a Chuck Berry hit from 1959, and "Please Mr. Postman," a popular song by the Marvelettes in 1961.

Afterward many of the girls in the audience rushed outside and eagerly waited at the stage door for a glimpse of their idols. Most of them surrounded Pete Best, begging for his autograph and bombarding him with personal questions. As far as the girls were concerned, Pete was the most handsome Beatle.

At 5:30 P.M. the next day, the BBC Light Programme "Teenagers Turn" aired the show recorded the previous day at the Playhouse. Beatles fans sat at their radios, mesmerized as the boys sang "Dream Baby."

A few days later, Brian Epstein finally got a call from Dick Rowe with the disappointing news that Decca would not be offering a contract.

"Why?" inquired a dumbfounded Epstein.

"Sorry, Mr. Epstein, but groups with guitars are on their way out," replied Rowe, who then added that he was not satisfied with the group's sound.

The February 22 issue of *Mersey Beat* announced the Beatles' first BBC radio appearance. At the lower right is one of Brian Epstein's eye-catching adverts for his NEMS record stores.

"The Beatles are going to be bigger than Elvis Presley," Epstein blurted out confidently.

Rowe countered with a suggestion that if Epstein really believed that his band had potential he could hire an A&R man and produce a record for about £100.

Epstein was thoroughly disgusted with Rowe's attitude but considered the idea for a few days. He talked to Tony Meehan, a member of Rowe's staff, but was offended by Meehan's abrupt manner, and decided that a session would be a waste of money.

The real reason the Beatles were rejected had nothing to do with their sound. On that fateful January day several bands had auditioned for Mike Smith, including Brian Poole and the Tremelos.

Dick Rowe told Smith that he could select only one group. Smith chose Brian Poole because he lived near London and would be easier and more economical to use than a band that lived 200 miles away in Liverpool.

Epstein vented his frustration with relentless visits to record companies in a concentrated effort to get a recording contract. He exerted all of his influence, but his attempts fell on deaf ears.

During this time, the Beatles were preparing for a show at the Barnston Women's Institute, to be followed by their third trip to Hamburg.

Part of Epstein's master plan for success included many demands that were not readily acceptable to the Beatles. He insisted on a professional attitude and a respectable appearance onstage. He would not tolerate their childish antics and said they would have to play to the whole audience, not those in the first few rows. Punctuality for all meetings and performances would be mandatory. Also deleted was the random music selection. A precise list of songs must be prepared for each show.

Epstein had been planning to improve the boys' appearance with suits, because the leather outfits reminded people of Nazi uniforms. This was a guise they could do without. Arrangements were made for the Beatles to be fitted for new suits at Beno Dorn, a Birkenhead clothier.

John was not keen about wearing a tailored suit and refused to discuss the idea with Epstein. Paul, George, and Pete agreed to try a new look. They talked to John, who reluctantly accepted their decision.

On March 24, the Beatles performed at the Barnston Women's Institute. They wore their new suits and presented their new image for the first time.

Epstein took advantage of every achievement the boys had earned. On the poster he designed for their show at the Institute he billed them as "Mersey Beat Poll Winners! Polydor Recording Artists!" The only other group to appear in this "all-star" show was the Pasadena Jazzmen.

At this time, Pete learned that they would not be signed by Decca. "I was hurt," says Pete, "because I was the last to know about it. The others knew a couple of weeks earlier. They let it slip out in a casual conversation one day."

Pete asked why they had waited to tell him and they said "they didn't want to dishearten him." They tried to cheer him up by saying that something else would come along.

Pete felt that there was another reason but couldn't get any answers. "I had roared and rampaged through Hamburg with them, gone mugging with John, and waded into all sorts of things with him. What had changed to make any one of them

think I might be broken up by this particular kick in the pants? My reaction was as normal as their own."

When *Mersey Beat* Number 18 went on sale March 22, page 3 was devoted to the Beatles. The top half previewed a special Fan Club night to be held April 5 at the Cavern. A brief article by Bob Wooler praised the boys and mentioned that they would soon depart for a seven-week engagement in Hamburg.

"If it is possible for a Rock 'n' Roll group to become a status symbol," wrote Wooler, "then the Beatles have made it so. They are still a phenomenon; their appeal is legend!"

There were advertisements for the Beatles' regular shows at the Cavern, plus their first engagement at the Odd Spot Club for March 22, and a one-night-only appearance at the Pavilion Theatre for April 2.

Brian Epstein asked Alan Swerdlow, a friend, to take some photographs of the Beatles during their performance at the Odd Spot Club. The boys wore their new suits, allowing Swerdlow to preview the image that John, Paul, and George would present during their upcoming foreign engagement. The photos also capture Pete's taciturn, moody countenance that drove all the girls wild.

The night of April 5 was one that Beatles fans had been anticipating with eager enthusiasm. Yellow-and-black advertising posters proclaimed: "The Beatles Fan Club Presents an Evening with John, George, Paul, and Pete, at the Cavern, 7:30 P.M." Ticket holders would receive a free photograph and everyone would be able to apply for free membership in the fan club.

"This was a very exciting evening for us," says Pete. "The fans were wonderful and this was a very special evening for them. The photograph on the posters was misleading in that we had long abandoned our leathers in favor of suits Brian bought to present us with a more clean image.

"But we had a surprise in store for the fans that they were not prepared for. The old Cavern crowd had made us what we were, and they were not too keen on our new suit image. So on fan night we came out in our leathers to wild cheers from our fan club girls."

Bernadette Farrell, an early Beatles fan, remem-

The Alan Swerdlow pictures, taken in performance at the Odd Spot (through p. 78).

bers that special night. "The Cavern scene seemed to grow out of nothing," says Farrell. "We first saw the Beatles at a place called Hambleton Hall when we thought them very tough-looking. That was, of course, because of their leather gear. But after listening to their music we were hooked right away. They started to appear around Liverpool and we made the effort to see them anywhere within reach.

"In those days I used to be a hairdresser's apprentice and during my lunch hour I would dash to the Cavern for a cheese roll and a Coke (sometimes served by Cilla Black), then rush back to work, hot and smelling of disinfectant, which let everyone know where I'd been.

"We'd be on top of the world if one of the Beatles had spoken to us," adds Farrell. "By that time their popularity was growing and they were always surrounded by girls. As time went on, it became such a habit going to see them that our lives revolved around Beatles gigs. When we heard that they were going to Germany, there were cries of horror from the fans, saying they couldn't leave.

"Fan Club night was also a special farewell show at the Cavern. My friend and I were there early as usual to make sure we got our usual seats, which were in the left side alcove, right at the front of the stage. By now, people had started to queue all day to get near the front. I recall once feeling embarrassed, standing in the queue, when George came down early and made some jokes about us. Although we wanted to see them, we didn't like them to think we'd been there all day."

Bernadette still has fond memories of Fan Club night. "The atmosphere was electric, but the place was so overcrowded and badly ventilated that condensation was dripping off the walls and ceilings so badly it fused all the equipment. But we didn't care. As long as the Beatles stayed we were happy to listen to them chatting away, especially John, who was always quick-witted and cracking jokes."

George Harrison took one look at Bernadette's brother, Brian, and said, "He looks like Alfred E. Newman," the trademark character of *Mad* magazine. Regardless of Brian's looks, he captured highlights of the evening on film. He took five photographs and they are the only known photos

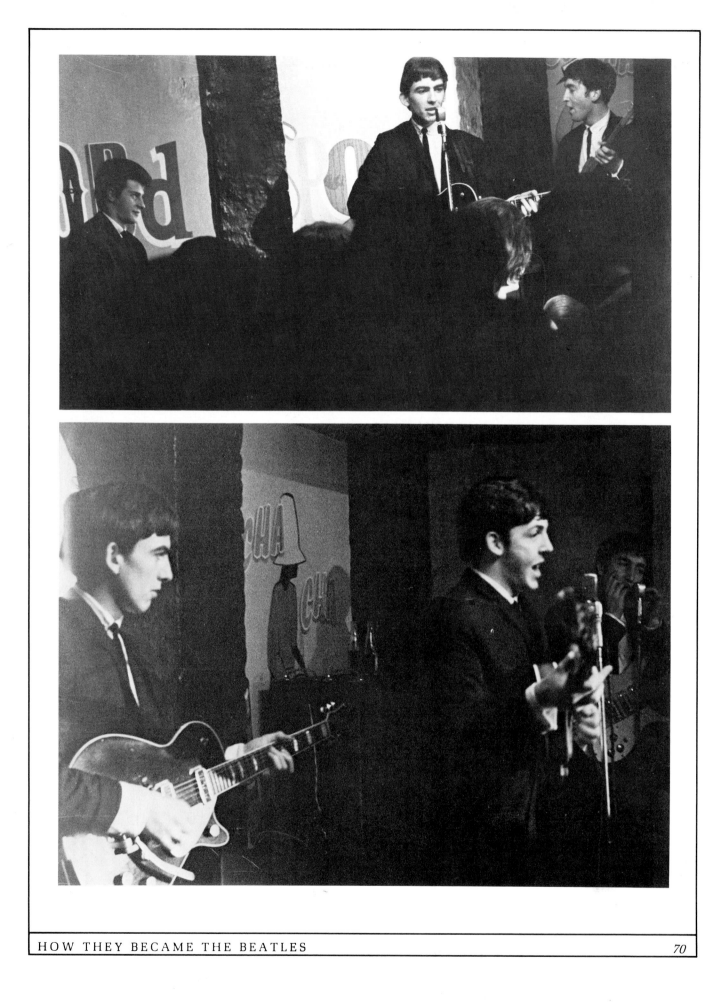

taken of the Beatles during their performance on Fan Club night.

During the first set, Paul sat on the edge of the stage. After a break the Beatles changed into their Beno Dorn suits.

Brian Farrell snapped a photo of Paul taking over Pete's duties on the drums, to show that he was more than just a bass player.

After the show most of the girls surrounded the Beatles and had them autograph the free photo all Cavern members had received at the door.

The free publicity photo was the same one used in the *Mersey Beat* "Beatles Top Poll" issue. Printed on the back for Fan Club members: "With Best Wishes from Paul-Pete-John-George. The Beatles. April 5, 1962."

Val Davies, another regular Cavern club member, remembers the solemn occasion following the show that night. She walked up to John at the piano and asked him to sign the back of her photo. Next she had George and Pete add their names. She did not ask Paul to sign because she was not pleased with his attitude.

"Paul was such a showoff," says Davies, "and that evening he was acting like he was a star. He would make like he noticed us and then say something smart. So, I passed him by.

"All in all," adds Davies, "we were sad to see them go off to Hamburg. The Cavern was not the same with the Beatles gone. Many good groups were still there, but none could be compared to the Beatles."

On April 10, John, Paul, and Pete flew into Hamburg from the Manchester Ringware airport. George was down with the flu and left the following day with Brian Epstein.

When John, Paul, and Pete stepped from the plane they were met by Astrid Kirchherr, who broke the sad and shocking news that Stu Sutcliffe had died that very day. Paul and Pete wept openly, but John was so shocked he couldn't speak or show any emotion.

After leaving the Beatles and returning to classes at Hamburg Art College, Stu had begun to suffer from severe headaches and blackouts. Astrid thought he was pushing himself too hard. "For days at a time he would not come down from his attic studio to eat or sleep," says Astrid. "And the headaches became violent, they seemed like fits."

In February Stu was examined by various physicians who could not diagnose the problem. During the next month his headaches were accompanied by temporary blindness.

On April 10 Astrid was working at the photo studio when her mother called to say that Stu's condition was worse. Astrid hurried home. At 4:30 P.M. Stu died in Astrid's arms during the ambulance ride to the hospital. Officially, the cause of death was labeled "cerebral paralysis due to bleeding into the right ventricle of the brain."

Although the hearts of the Beatles were filled with grief, there was a show to do and personal feelings had to be suppressed for the moment.

On Friday, April 13, the Star-Club, "the newest and largest club on the Reeperbahn," opened its doors. Manfred Weissleder, the owner, appointed Horst Fascher to handle crowd control. He had his hands full.

Astrid did not attend at first. She was mourning for Stu, but the boys gave her gifts and did everything they could to cheer her up.

The Star-Club was a welcome change from the small, seedy Liverpool hangouts. It was elegant and spacious, with a grand stage and curtains plus a winding staircase leading to a balcony. The Beatles were pleased with their large dressing rooms and actually felt as if they were being treated like stars. All of the bars were well stocked with pretty waitresses, as well as an army of bouncers to handle booze-filled barbarians.

"We returned to the endless round of booze and birds," says Pete. "The Star-Club was good 'turkin' ground,' a phrase derived from 'turkey' and 'stuffing,' meaning a place where girls were readily available. The barmaids especially saw to it that we never felt underprivileged in this respect. We used to finish our last set around 4:00 A.M., then our night's fun began."

Back in England, the April 14 issue of the *Liverpool Echo* carried an article about Stu Sutcliffe's death, along with his photograph. The story said there would be a probe into the mysterious death of the art student. Part of the article mentioned that "Stuart went to Germany 18 months ago with a Liverpool skiffle group . . . but he met 23-years-old Astrid Kirchherr and decided to stay and enter Hamburg College of Art." No reference that the skiffle group had been the Beatles was made. Obviously, the *Liverpool Echo* was not interested in stories about rock 'n' roll groups.

Michael McCartney, Paul's brother, told the *Echo* (in an April 16 follow-up story) of a premonition Stu had experienced. "When I met him in a jazz club when he was home on holiday a few weeks ago," said Michael, "he said he had a feeling that something was going to happen to him when he went back to Hamburg."

Bill Harry, editor of the *Mersey Beat,* offered his eulogy in an article entitled "Goodbye Stu!," which appeared in the April 19 issue.

On April 23, Decca released "My Bonnie"/"The Saints" (Decca 31382) in America through Deutsche Grammophon/Polydor. It was the first release in the United States of a record by the Beatles. Because the record was issued via Hamburg, the label credits read: "Tony Sheridan and the Beat Brothers," as stipulated by the terms of the contract. (A decade later, during an interview with the author, Tony Sheridan said he was not aware of the release in the U.S. by Decca.)

Bill Harry, always conscious of his readers' interests, was not about to let the Beatles' absence go unnoticed. The May 3 issue of *Mersey Beat* offered a review of the group's opening-night performance in Hamburg. "The Beatles," wrote Harry, "received a rapturous reception on their first night at the Star-Club in Hamburg. . . . In the first night audience was a television producer who was most impressed with the boys and arrangements are being made for them to appear on German television."

Meanwhile, Brian Epstein was walking the streets of London, trying to get a record company interested in the Beatles. Three companies—Columbia, Pye, and HMV—flatly refused him.

Epstein was getting desperate and felt that he was spinning his wheels. He decided it would be more practical to have a record disc of the boys' talents instead of hauling the Decca tapes all over town. On May 8 he went to the HMV record center and asked Ted Huntly, a recording technician, to put the tapes on a disc.

Huntly was impressed with the sound and offered to take the disc upstairs and let Sydney Coleman hear it. Coleman was the general manager of Ardmore and Beechwood, a respected music publishing firm and a subsidiary of EMI. Epstein agreed.

Syd Coleman was excited with the Beatles' music and said he would consider publishing some of their compositions. Also, he would play the disc for George Martin, a friend of his who was an A&R man at Parlophone Records.

Epstein suddenly felt that his unceasing efforts were about to bear fruit. After lugging the Decca audition tapes from record company to record company, after countless rejections and frustrations, he was now on the threshold of achieving a victory.

Epstein thought it ironic that this accomplishment had not developed through his usual tactics of trying to dazzle a producer, but from an accidental meeting with a recording technician who happened to know a publishing executive who had connections with a major recording studio.

Syd Coleman phoned George Martin, who was out of his office. Martin's assistant, Judy Lockhart-Smith, received the call and made an appointment to have Brian Epstein see Martin the next day.

Epstein made the arrangement and went to his hotel. Then an uneasy thought struck him. He remembered that Parlophone was a division of EMI, which had refused to see him on two previous occasions. Epstein went to sleep with little faith in what developments the morning might bring.

On May 9, Brian Epstein left the Green Park Hotel for his meeting with George Martin at EMI. Martin greeted him warmly and listened to the disc Epstein had brought. Martin really got excited and told Epstein that the group had an interesting sound—interesting enough to schedule an audition upon the band's return from Germany!

In Hamburg, the Beatles were still asleep when a telegram arrived from Epstein. A knock on the door stirred George, who staggered across the room, opened the door, and read the news:

CONGRATULATIONS BOYS. EMI REQUEST RECORDING SESSION. PLEASE REHEARSE NEW MATERIAL.

It should be noted that Ted Huntly and Syd Coleman deserve the credit for the Beatles' audition at EMI/Parlophone. If Epstein had not taken his tapes to Huntly to be put on a disc, Coleman would never have heard them and set up a meeting between Epstein and George Martin. In all probability, Epstein would have continued walking the streets, badgering record companies to give his band a chance. He would not have met George Martin because Parlophone was a division of EMI, and EMI controlled two other labels (Columbia and HMV) that had already rejected him.

Enthusiasm once again gripped the Beatles. After receiving the telegram, they ate breakfast and went to Polydor Records, boasting that they were going to audition at EMI. The boys emphasized that EMI was interested in them as a group, not as backup artists, which had been their role at Polydor for six months before they were dropped.

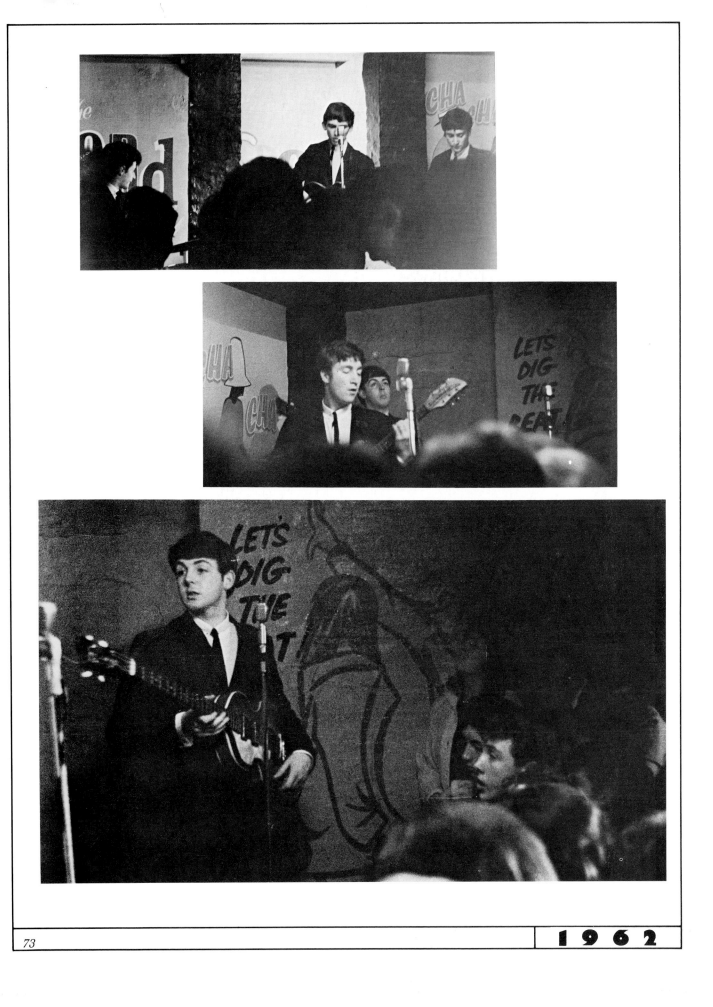

1962

John and Paul immediately began composing a song for the EMI audition and the final product was "P.S. I Love You."

GREAT NEWS OF THE BEATLES, was the *Mersey Beat* headline issued the day before the boys returned from Hamburg. "Impresario Brian Epstein," wrote Bill Harry, "informs *Mersey Beat* that he has secured a contract with the powerful EMI organization for the Beatles to record for the Parlophone label.

"This is terrific news! And the many people who voted the Beatles the No. 1 Rock 'n' Roll group on the Merseyside will now have the opportunity to vote again for their favorite beat music entertainers—this time by voting their first disc a hit and buying copies as soon as it is released in July."

The news was, to say the least, premature: the Beatles had been invited to audition and had certainly not been offered a recording contract.

On June 1, the boys returned to Liverpool and began rehearsing for their audition.

Five days later, they went to Studio No. 2 at St. John's Wood on Abbey Road in London and Epstein introduced them to George Martin. Martin told the boys about his background. John's eyes widened with interest when he learned that Martin had produced the Goon records. Throughout the fifties, "The Goon Show," starring Peter Sellers, Harry Secombe, and Spike Milligan, was one of the most popular comedy programs on British radio.

During the audition the boys performed a lot of standard selections such as "Besame Mucho," but included some original compositions such as "Love Me Do," "P.S. I Love You," and "Ask Me Why."

The Beatles left the studio after a round of handshakes from Martin, who thanked them and said it was nice to meet them after such a big buildup from Epstein.

While the Beatles were in Hamburg, Epstein had also secured enough bookings to keep them busy well into September. The first show was a "Welcome Home" night at the Cavern on June 9, where they set a new attendance record of 900 fans. Two days later they returned to the Playhouse Theatre in Manchester to record their second BBC Light Programme, "Here We Go." During this show they played "Ask Me Why," a Lennon-McCartney composition, followed by "Besame Mucho" and "A Picture of You," which had recently been released by Joe Brown and was on the pop charts in En-

gland. It was also Brian Epstein's favorite song.

After the recording session, Pete Best was mobbed by fans outside the studio. His popularity was rapidly increasing beyond the Liverpool area. However, Pete remained aloof, unapproachable, playing a steady beat on his drums but not calling attention to himself. His stoic appearance was such an enigma that the fans began calling the group, "Pete Best and the Beatles."

The second BBC Light Programme went on the air June 15 and was the last show Best did with the band.

When Brian Epstein gave Bill Harry the advertisements for the June 14 issue of *Mersey Beat,* he referred to the Beatles as "Parlophone recording artists," but it was only hype since no contract had yet been offered.

Meanwhile, the LP *My Bonnie* by Tony Sheridan and the Beat Brothers was released by German Polydor in Hamburg. The album contained only two songs on which the Beatles backed Sheridan ("My Bonnie" and "The Saints"). An asterisk appeared by the two song titles on the back cover, indicating in small print: "accompanied by The Beatles."

The credits on the album label, however, still appeared as Tony Sheridan and the Beat Brothers. Perhaps the information noted by the asterisk was included on the cover in deference to the success of the Beatles two months earlier at the Star-Club. Also, Polydor executives may have recalled the group's visit in May, when the boys had marched into their office and boasted about their invitation to audition for EMI as a group, not as mere backup musicians.

The album was well received in Hamburg. Unfortunately, English Polydor did not release the album and it was never exported to England by German Polydor.

On June 21, the Tower Ballroom in New Brighton was packed with more than 2,000 people to hear Bruce Channel sing his Number 1 hit "Hey! Baby." Channel was one of the hottest recording artists in America. *Mersey Beat* reported he was considered as "the only white artiste capable of singing true blues." Appearing with Channel were two groups familiar to English fans: "Parlophone recording artistes The Beatles and Fontana recording artistes Howie and the Seniors."

Eight days later the Beatles topped the bill at the Tower Ballroom, followed by ten top Merseyside groups. It was a special night for Paul McCartney.

He received a big cake from his fans and an electric shaver from Brian Epstein, to celebrate his twentieth birthday.

On July 1, the Beatles appeared at the Cavern with Gene Vincent, who spoke highly of them. He had heard them perform at the Star-Club in April. But Vincent was more interested in another Liverpool group, Gerry and the Pacemakers, and was trying to get them to accompany him on a tour of Israel.

The Beatles continued their shows at the Cavern throughout the remainder of July and performed with Joe Brown July 27 at the Tower Ballroom and at the Majestic Ballroom the next day.

During the last week in July, George Martin told Brian Epstein that he wanted to sign the Beatles with Parlophone Records.

The Beatles continued their shows at the Cavern. On August 3 they appeared with Gerry and the Pacemakers. On August 10 they performed in the "Riverboat Shuffle" aboard the M.V. *Royal Iris.* Also on the bill were Johnny Kidd and the Pirates plus the Dakotas with Pete MacLaine. Two days later the Beatles returned to the Cavern, along

Whether it was because of a magnetic stage presence or his popularity with the fans, Pete Best alone merited special attention from the photographer.

with the Red River Jazzmen, the Bluegenes, and the Big Three.

August 16, 1962, is a date forever etched in Pete Best's memory. It was the day he was fired.

"We played both the noontime and evening gigs at the Cavern on August 15," recalls Pete. "I remember after we finished the evening performance, I asked John if he would like a lift to the Riverpark Ballroom in Chester, where we were booked for the next day. John and I strolled out of the Cavern together and he said: 'No, I will go on my own.' Then we parted ways. There was nothing

unusual in this, as I presumed he had another ride. When I got home there was a note from Mom that Brian wanted to see me in his office the next morning.

"When I arrived the next morning, there was a look in his face I could not explain. Something was up but what he said to me was the last thing on my mind—or rather let me say, it really never entered my mind."

Epstein said: "I've got some news for you. The boys want you out and Ringo in," referring to Ringo Starr.

Pete was speechless but managed to ask why.

"They don't think you're a good enough drummer," answered Epstein.

"Why has it taken two years for them to decide that my drumming isn't good enough?" asked Pete. "I consider myself as good, if not better than, Ringo. Does Ringo know about this yet?"

"He's joining on Saturday," said Epstein.

"Well, if that's the way it is, then that's it," said Pete, and walked out of the room.

Epstein followed Pete into the hall and asked if he would stay with the group until Ringo ar-

rived. Pete didn't answer.

Neil Aspinall, the road manager, was waiting outside for Pete and one look told him that something was wrong.

"What's happened?" asked Aspinall. "You look as if you've seen a ghost."

"They've kicked me out," answered Pete.

Pete was still unaware that George Martin was going to sign the Beatles to a recording contract. On August 16, John, Paul, and George went to Chester for their performance at the Riverpark Ballroom. Pete did not appear, and Johnny Hutchinson, now with the Big Three, stood in.

Bill Harry broke the shocking news in the August 23 issue of *Mersey Beat*. MERSEY BEAT EXCLUSIVE STORY—BEATLES CHANGE DRUMMER! "Ringo Starr (former drummer with Rory Storm and the Hurricanes) has joined The Beatles, replacing Pete Best on drums. Ringo has admired The Beatles for years and is delighted with his new engagement. Naturally he is tremendously excited about the future.

"The Beatles comment, 'Pete left the group by

mutual agreement. There were no arguments or difficulties, and this has been an entirely amicable decision.'

"On Tuesday, September 4th, The Beatles will fly to London to make recordings at EMI Studios."

The article featured a photo of Pete.

During an interview Bill Harry gave a different account of what was going on.

"The article I wrote for *Mersey Beat*," said Harry, "was mild and not really a true story of what actually happened. One thing I never did print in the paper was the fact that I received many letters from irate fans demanding that Pete be returned to the group.

"Hundreds of girls came to my office and signed petitions. The popularity of Pete Best was strong and the fans who followed the Beatles' Cavern appearances through 1961 and 1962 were up in arms."

According to many who were present, the main reason for sacking Pete can be summed up in one word—jealousy. John, Paul, and George were extremely jealous of Pete's ability to attract girls. Too many female fans openly acknowledged Pete as the group's leader and the most handsome Beatle.

Another reason for Pete's dismissal concerned his stage presence. He was reserved and silent while the other three were wild and witty. Pete just didn't fit in.

Pete's numerous fans were not about to accept idly the reality of their idol being dumped—especially since the group was finally beginning to achieve success at local clubs, along with BBC radio shows, tours in Germany, and a recording contract with a major record company.

It was too much for Pete's fans to swallow. They marched along the streets, carrying protest signs, and shouting their scornful opinions at every Beatle concert.

Although John, Paul, and George received a lot of abuse, Pete's irate fans saved their greatest wrath for Brian Epstein, who suddenly found himself driven into a corner with a tiger on his heels. He couldn't walk the short distance from NEMS to the Cavern without protection, and refused to enter the club without bodyguards. The angry fans even damaged his new car.

On August 19, the Beatles arrived at the Cavern for their first performance with Ringo Starr. He had been officially welcomed into the group the preceding day.

On stage, George introduced Ringo to the crowd.

THE HESWALL JAZZ CLUB

Saturday, 24th March, 1962

The Fabulous
BEATLES
(Polydor Recording Artists)
(Mersey Beat Popularity Poll Winners)
(Prior to European Tour)

Plus

Wirral's Top Jazz Group
The Pasadena Jazzmen

Plus

The current TOP TWENTY records

★ ★

at Barnston Women's Institute
from 7-30 p.m. — 11-15 p.m.

Admission by Ticket only - 7/6

No Admission after 10-0 p.m.

After the show the Beatles walked outside, where angry Pete Best fans were waiting with signs and chanting, "Pete Best Forever—Ringo Never!" A scuffle began and during the battle, George Harrison received a black eye.

Alas, all of the fans' unhappiness could not alter the undeniable fact that the Beatles were now John-Paul-George-and-Ringo, and those were the names that would become known to the world eighteen months later.

Another big secret the Beatles kept to themselves occurred on August 23, when John Lennon married his longtime girlfriend, Cynthia Powell. The wedding was held at the Mount Pleasant Register Office and Brian Epstein was the best man. Paul and George also attended.

The reason for secrecy was John's belief that their popularity might suddenly decline if his marriage became public knowledge.

"I thought getting married would be good-bye to the group," said John. "We went mad keeping it

This card is to be shown at all meetings attended, to the Door Staff and also to the Desk Staff, and any other Club Official on demand.

A member who does not produce his or her Membership Card must "sign in" as a visitor.

Cards and passes are not transferable. Anyone found using another person's Card or Pass will be liable to be barred from the Club.

This card does not guarantee admission if the management deems the premises full, or for any other reason.

THE MERSEYSIDE PRINTING CO.
21 DALE STREET - - LIVERPOOL, 2
TELEPHONE : CENTRAL 4895

THE Cavern CLUB

MEMBERSHIP CARD
1962 SEASON

Ending 31st December, 1962

Show your friends how to get to the CAVERN!

N° 596

FULL NAME { BERNADETTE FARRELL
(in Block Capitals)

ADDRESS 79 CHILDWALL
(in Block Capitals)

LANE,

WOOLTON,

LIVERPOOL 25.

Member's signature

B. Farrell

Date 21 - 2 - 62

IMPORTANT

HANDBAGS
COATS
SHOES
UMBRELLAS
ETC.

Must NOT be Left Lying around the Club UNDER SEATS In the toilets . . . or anywhere where you cannot look after them.

The Cavern membership card of Bernadette Farrell, then Harrison's girlfriend and a Cavern regular. The well-worn card was carried to the club more than one hundred times.

John

The Beatles at the Star-Club, December 1962. These are the first color photographs to surface from that period. *(Courtesy Thomas J. Meenach III)*

Paul

Pete

Top: John. *Above:* The end of a long night. At left is Gene Vincent.

secret. But I did feel embarrassed being married. Walking about, married. It was like walking around with odd socks on, your fly open."

"The Beatles, by this time, were surrounded by girls," recalls Bernadette Farrell. Except for John, Farrell says, "they dropped their steady girls and started dating their fans, although I must say it was kept reasonably discreet. There were many rumors about who was going with who."

The boys' social life continued after performances at the Cavern with visits to a local bowling alley or the Blue Angel Club, owned by their first manager, Allan Williams.

"One place they used to go," says Farrell, "was Vi Caldwell's house (Rory Storm's mother) but I know they liked going there because she treated them as one big happy family.

"As the Beatles started going to the Blue Angel, so did their fans, and a whole social circle developed which was good to be a part of. My friendship with the Beatles developed after receiving lifts home from them after leaving the Cavern. They never made very obvious advances in front of other fans because even as early as this they were recognized and pestered, which sometimes spoiled the night out."

On August 22, the day before John's wedding, a Granada TV crew had come to the Cavern to film the noontime show. The Beatles sang but the place was packed with a boisterous crowd anxious to be on television. The room was sweltering so the Beatles removed their coats and were filmed wearing their black vests. Granada TV did not broadcast the show until November, after the Beatles' first record had been released.

On August 24, the Beatles performed at the Cavern for the first time with a secretly married Beatle.

With so much going on, Epstein was again thinking of ways to publicize his group, and called Peter Kaye.

"Brian Epstein phoned me," says Kaye, "and asked if I could take some photographs of the Beatles. I was aware that Albert Marrion had already taken some very excellent photographs of the group, and I didn't have the foggiest idea how I could do better."

When the Beatles arrived at the studio they met Les Chadwick, a staff photographer. Chadwick decided to take some group shots in the studio while Kaye was out scouting locations for background shots.

"How'd it go?" Kaye asked upon returning to the studio.

"It's hopeless," replied Chadwick.

The Beatles had been very inattentive and had never undergone a session that lasted three hours. Besides, Albert Marrion had been a more experienced, authoritative person than Chadwick.

Kaye had been looking for a new concept, different from the Beatles pictures that had been published. He found what he was seeking in the rubble of Liverpool. "Nobody ever did this before. We wanted to do something different. They were a Liverpool group so we decided to use Liverpool landmarks.

"Next thing," Kaye says cynically, "even dogs were being photographed in the rubble!"

The first exterior session was scheduled on a rainy Wednesday afternoon. "It drizzled the whole time," says Kaye. "We went to all the prearranged locations we'd worked out earlier. Then we returned to the studio to develop the film."

Epstein met Peter Kaye at the studio the next morning.

"What have you got?" asked Epstein.

Kaye showed him the results and described what had been done. "We worked on a principle, contrasting their appearance in suits against

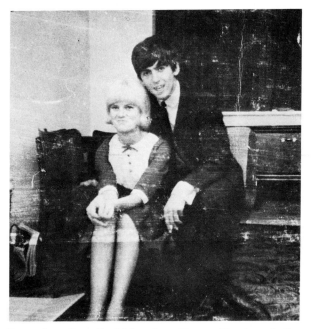

Bernadette Farrell with her date, George Harrison, in the living room of her parents' house. The snapshot was taken by her brother.

First photo poster of the Beatles. For Fan Club night at the Cavern, April 5. (Note the credits: Albert Marrion took the pictures, Alan Swerdlow did the layout.)

drains and rubble,'' explained Kaye. ''The group would look neater than they really were. Toward the end of the session we finished up on the Pier Head, against the Liver Building with the Liver Bird atop.''

This photo was widely used by the press to establish the Beatles' Liverpool roots.

''Then we used the fire salvage vessel, the *Salvo*,'' continued Kaye.

Epstein took one look at the picture and told Kaye that he wanted the negative, but Kaye informed him that the studio did not give up their negatives.

Epstein soon received a small photo of the Beatles to be sent to the news media.

''These weren't for sale, mind you,'' says Kaye, ''or for free. They were press handouts for agencies. Brian sent them everywhere, not the national papers, but the local rags. He did a tremendous public relations campaign on the group. This was in September, before their first vocal came out, so I believe all of those press photos were tossed in the trash.''

On September 4 at 8:15 A.M., the Beatles assembled on the tarmac at the Speke Liverpool airport. Amid the pouring rain and wild winds, a photograph was taken that would later be published in the *Mersey Beat*. The photo clearly shows George Harrison still with the shiner he received on August 19 at Ringo's debut with the group.

Moments after the picture was taken, the Beatles boarded a plane and flew to London for their first recording session at EMI. After checking into the Chelsea Hotel, they went to the studios in St. John's Wood.

George Martin was aware that Ringo Starr had replaced Pete Best. When Pete was fired, Mona Best called Martin to see if he had influenced the Beatles' decision. Martin assured her that such was not the case.

''I never suggested that Pete Best must go,'' said Martin. ''All I said was that for the purposes of the Beatles' first record I would rather use a session man. I never thought that Brian Epstein would let him go. He seemed to be the most salable commodity as far as looks went.

''It was a surprise when I learned that they had dropped Pete,'' adds Martin. ''The drums were important to me for a record, but they didn't matter much otherwise. Fans don't pay particular attention to the quality of drumming.''

But Martin wasn't going to take chances on a drummer he had never heard. He decided to audition Ringo while John, Paul, and George rehearsed two songs tentatively selected for their first record on the Parlophone label.

As the boys practiced, George Martin eyed each Beatle and wondered if it was possible for one of them to be the new Cliff Richard. There wasn't a producer alive in England who didn't dream of discovering someone to top Cliff Richard, who had reigned as the number-one British male vocalist for the past four years.

The first song recorded that day was ''How Do You Do It,'' composed by Mitch Murray and pub-

Brian Farrell's five snapshots are the only known photographs of Fan Club night. *Above:* The sign on the wall was designed for Fan Club night and was never used again. *Right:* Although the boys were regularly performing in suits and ties, they put on the leathers for their fans one last time that night. (They continued to wear the black outfits to please the rougher Hamburg crowd.)

lished by Dick James. James had asked Martin to consider putting the song on the B side of the Beatles' first release. Martin liked the song and thought it could be a big hit for his new group.

The Beatles, however, had other ideas. Martin was suddenly feeling opposition from John, Paul, and George, who wanted to record their own compositions.

"In due time," Martin told them, "when you can write a song as good as this."

The Beatles had just started a revolution in the recording industry. They couldn't read a note of music, but were trying to tell a seasoned producer what songs were best for them to record!

Martin threw a signal to the engineer, Norman Smith, to stop. Smith shut down the tape recorders and the red light went out.

George Martin began to explain the intricacies of producing records to the four lads. He informed them that recording sessions were very expensive and that planning for each session was essential. A record could be produced in stages by recording a music track first and later dubbing in a voice track. Studio engineers were very good at editing and mixing various tracks to produce a flawless

master. So, Martin said, instead of taking chances and wasting time and money, he would make all of the decisions, then added: "Right. Is there anything you don't like?"

Silently, the boys looked at one another; then George said, "Yeah, I don't like your tie."

A trace of a smile crossed Martin's lips, then he told the boys to sing "Love Me Do." Next, he had them do "How Do You Do It" one more time, then another run through "Love Me Do."

Finally, Martin realized that they were not making any progress. He told them to go practice during the week and return for another session on September 11.

The Beatles flew back to Liverpool that evening. Their first recording session had been a flop, but John, Paul, and George had managed to overcome their studio nervousness.

George Martin called Dick James and came straight to the point. "About your song—the boys will do 'Love Me Do' as the A side. I suppose they could do yours as the B side, but I think it's a waste of a good song."

James listened to "Love Me Do" and thought it was rather effective.

Left: During a break, the Beatles changed back into their new suits. *Below:* A very rare moment with Paul on drums. He also occasionally played the piano at Cavern gigs.

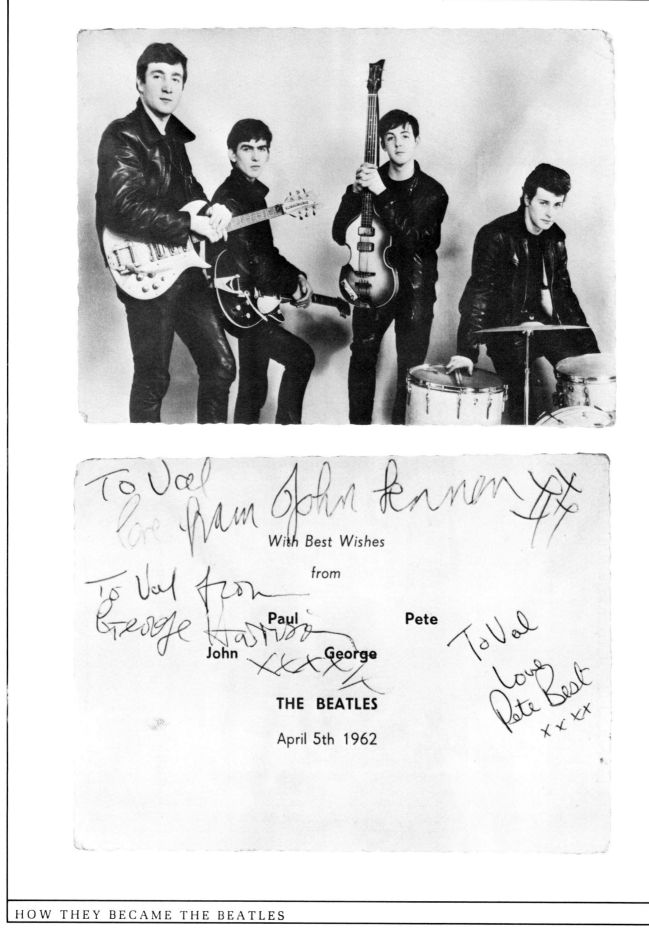

To Val
Love from John Lennon XX

With Best Wishes

from

To Val from
George Harrison

Paul   **Pete**

John   **George**
XXXXX

THE BEATLES

April 5th 1962

To Val
love
Pete Best
x x xx

In Liverpool, the Beatles continued to rehearse their own material. They appeared at the Majestic Ballroom on September 8, and the Cavern the next two days. During the week nothing was said regarding their disastrous session at EMI.

Mersey Beat Number 30 hit the stands on September 6. There was an article about the group's days with Stu Sutcliffe—written by Paul McCartney (his name was misspelled)—and a story by Bill Harry about their new drummer, Ringo Starr.

On September 11 the boys summoned their courage and returned to London for their second EMI session (usually referred to as the first).

George Martin greeted the boys and told them he had canceled "How Do You Do It." The two songs to be recorded were "P.S. I Love You" and "Love Me Do."

Unknown to Ringo, a studio drummer named Andy White was standing in the wings. Since producing a session was very costly—a fact constantly belabored by studio brass—Martin wanted an experienced drummer available in case Ringo's performance was inadequate. On many occasions a studio musician will be called to stand by and never be used. Unfortunately for Ringo, this was not to be one of those occasions.

After rehearsing both songs, Norman Smith turned on the tape machines and the Beatles went into "P.S. I Love You."

Instantly, Ringo felt that they were doing a "Pete Best" on him. It was obvious that Ringo was nervous and frightened while in the studio, but he had become a Beatle to play drums—for concerts and records. Now he felt that although he was fine for clubs and concerts, they didn't want to use him on recordings. Martin really wasn't satisfied with Ringo's ability. "He hit good and hard and used the tom-tom well, but he couldn't do a roll to save his life."

It was a shattering blow to Ringo's ego but he went along and played the maracas during the first take of "P.S. I Love You." On the second take he exchanged the maracas for a tambourine and banged it on every third beat.

After the second take was done, Martin was confident that a salable record could be achieved

From Fan Club night, the first-ever handout photo—front and back. Val Davies had John, George, and Pete sign hers that very night.

by the delicate mixing of a sound engineer.

For the most part, Ringo had remained silent during the session and made no objection to relinquishing his job to Andy White. The Beatles knew when to keep quiet. Martin had authority and their immediate recording future could dissolve without the support of the influential producer.

As the Beatles began the retake of "Love Me Do," Andy White still occupied the drummer's seat, and a total of eighteen takes were recorded before George Martin considered they had a successful one. Ringo banged the tambourine as instructed all the while. It was getting late, and a vain attempt to record "Please Please Me," was abandoned after a few takes.

"Right, lads," Martin said with a weary smile, and the session was done.

The Beatles had recorded their first commercial record and left the studio shortly after one o'clock in the morning of September 12.

During September and October the Beatles had a busy schedule. Upon returning to Liverpool they played their Cavern dates plus an engagement at Queens Hall, Widnes, with Billy Kramer and the Coasters.

The September 20 issue of *Mersey Beat* carried the photo showing George's black eye. An advertisement for NEMS appeared in the lower left corner: "We are now accepting orders for the Beatles first record on Parlophone—"Love Me Do" c/w "P.S. I Love You"—Released Friday October 5th."

Eight days later the boys performed aboard the *Royal Iris* during a river cruise.

Brian Epstein officially signed a management contract with the Beatles on October 2, with the fathers of Paul and George as witnesses. It was a five-year agreement with Epstein getting 25 percent of the group's earnings.

Three days later, EMI released Parlophone R4949. On the original single, Ringo plays drums on "Love Me Do," but Andy White is the drummer on "P.S. I Love You."

On October 6 the Beatles made an appearance at the Dawson Music Shop in Widnes and autographed copies of their first record.

Two days earlier, the *Mersey Beat* had carried a short article in which a former Beatle was mentioned. "Lee Curtis and the All-Stars," wrote Bill Harry, "are now the resident Friday night group at the Majestic Ballroom, Birkenhead. . . . Drummer Pete Best has now settled comfortably in the group and he says 'I've never enjoyed playing so much.' "

Probe Into Mystery Death Of City Student

Mother In Germany: Father Cannot Be Told

An investigation into the mystery death of a 21-years-old Liverpool art student, Stuart Sutcliffe, who died in a German ambulance with his fiancee by his side, was being held to-day.

Mrs. Millie Sutcliffe, aged 54, of 37 Aigburth Drive, Aigburth, flew to Hamburg after a telegram told her of her son's death. His father, Mr. Charles Sutcliffe, a second engineer, sailed for South America on Sunday and cannot be told of the death for at least three weeks.

"He has a weak heart and we cannot radio his ship to tell him. He will be told when he reaches port," said his daughter, Joyce, aged 20.

Stuart went to Germany 18 months ago with a Liverpool skiffle group for three months, but he met 23-years-old Astrid Kirchherr and decided to stay and enter Hamburg College of Art.

The couple planned to marry when he finished his course in June. A former pupil of Prescot Grammar School and Liverpool College of Art, Stuart was described by a close friend as "one of the most promising young artists I've ever known."

LETTER

He had a painting bought by Mr. John Moores after a city exhibition.

In a room decorated with half-a-dozen of her brother's

STUART

paintings, Joyce last night said: "We had a letter from Stuart on Monday which said he had been taken ill and the doctors could not find out what was the matter. He died in an ambulance on Tuesday while he was being taken to hospital with Astrid by his side. Stuart came home for a holiday a few weeks ago, quite unexpectedly, and he didn't seem his usual self at all. He was very quiet."

She added: "Stuart lived for painting. It was his whole life and his biggest wish was to have his own exhibition in Liverpool."

Stuart's body is to be flown home on Monday after a postmortem.

Premonition Of Death

City Art Student Died In Germany

A 21-years-old Liverpool art student, who died with his fiancee by his side in a Hamburg ambulance, had a premonition that he would die young, a friend told the Echo.

Stuart Sutcliffe, whose home was at 37 Aigburth Drive, Aigburth, died of a blood clot on the brain, a post mortem examination revealed over the week-end. His body will be flown home to-morrow or on Wednesday.

A friend, Michael McCartney, aged 18, of 20 Forthlin Road, Allerton, said:

HAD FEELING

"When I met him in a jazz club when he was home on holiday a few weeks ago he said he had a feeling that something was going to happen to him when he went back to Hamburg. He was obviously w o r r i e d and nervous."

Stuart's mother, Mrs. Millie Sutcliffe, who flew to Germany when she heard of her son's death, returned home last night accompanied by her son's fiancee, Astrid Kirchherr. They were to have married at the end of his art course in June.

His father, Mr. Charles Sutcliffe, has not been told of the tragedy. A second engineer, he is at present sailing to South America, and as he has a weak heart, the family thinks it is unwise to radio his ship.

Liverpool Echo, Saturday, April 14, and Monday, April 16. Stu's friends and former band are referred to only as "a Liverpool skiffle group."

Brian Epstein bought a full page in the October 4 issue of *Mersey Beat* to announce his boldest coup to date. He was going to present Merseyside's Greatest-Ever Rock Spectacular, "starring America's fabulous Little Richard!"

The concert was held October 12 at the Tower Ballroom in New Brighton. Also appearing were the Beatles, the Big Three, the Mersey Beats, the Four Jays, Billy Kramer and the Coasters, the Undertakers, Rory Storm and the Hurricanes, Lee Curtis and the All-Stars, Pete MacLaine with the Dakotas, and Gus Travis and the Midnighters.

Alan Swerdlow, who had taken photographs of the Beatles at the Odd Spot Club, designed the colorful program that had a double-page layout with individual photos of the four boys.

The October 18 issue of *Mersey Beat* revealed yet another big "first" for the Beatles. Their recording of "Love Me Do" was the Number 1 hit on the Merseyside Top 20!

BEATLES HEAD MERSEYSIDE TOPS was the headline. The following article included praise from Decca recording artist Buddy Brittain, who said he considered the Beatles "to be the best group in the country, and this opinion is shared by many people in the show business world."

On October 25, the boys returned to the Playhouse Theatre in Manchester to record their third BBC program, "Here We Go." This was the first radio show for Ringo. The group did "Love Me

Do," "A Taste of Honey," "P.S. I Love You," and "Sheila." The set, except for "Sheila," was aired the following day.

The Beatles also filmed an appearance for Granada TV's show "People & Places."

By popular demand, the Beatles appeared in a second show starring Little Richard on October 28 at the Liverpool Empire Theatre. Dave Reid, the Breakaways, Craig Douglas, Sounds Incorporated, Kenny Lynch, and Jet Harris and the Jetblacks also performed.

On November 1 the Beatles went back to Hamburg for their second engagement that year at the Star-Club. Although their salary was increased to 600 DM each per week, they weren't thrilled about leaving Liverpool, because they wanted to promote "Love Me Do" as much as possible. However, the Star-Club agreement had been made long before they had auditioned for EMI, and a contract had to be honored.

The cover of *Mersey Beat* issued November 1 had a large photograph of Lee Curtis and the All-Stars. The picture reveals Pete Best's expression of being "settled comfortably in the group."

Well, almost.

During an interview with the author sixteen years after the photo appeared, Pete offered his real thoughts about the Beatles' success in 1962.

"I really could not get them off my mind," confesses Pete. "Everywhere we went before August was John, Paul, George, and Pete. Now, whenever I saw the Beatles mentioned, it was John, Paul, George, and Ringo. I'd be playing the Cavern or the Majestic, and the Beatles would be playing the same clubs the very next night. I never was there to see them, but I knew they were performing and would just stay home and try to think things clear."

Pete's frustration increased significantly when "Love Me Do" was released.

"The song was on the radio all the time," says Pete. "They were going up and I was continuing in a group not as popular, doing the same old gigs I'd done up to August with the Beatles. I still had a large following of girls, but it wasn't the same without the Beatles. It was eating at me something terrible but I couldn't show it openly."

The Beatles returned from Hamburg on November 15 and went to the West End Hotel in London. The next day they were interviewed by reporters and publicity men. During the afternoon they appeared on "The Friday Spectacular," a Radio Luxembourg show sponsored by EMI.

Top: Promo label of the Beatles' first American record, released April 23. Side A. *Above:* Commercial label.

On November 26 the boys went back into the studio for another session with George Martin. Again, he wanted them to do "How Do You Do It," but John became evasive. He would keep changing the subject and hastily improvise one of their own compositions.

Finally, they recorded "Please Please Me" and

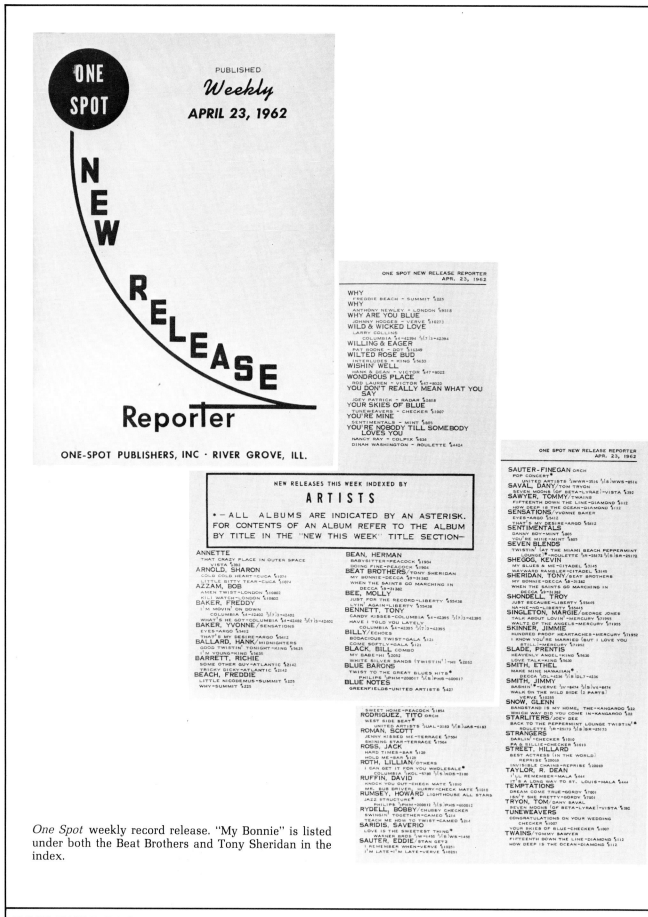

One Spot weekly record release. "My Bonnie" is listed under both the Beat Brothers and Tony Sheridan in the index.

"Ask Me Why," which became the songs for their second Parlophone single.

On November 27 they went to the BBC Paris studio to record their first radio show in London. They sang "Love Me Do," "P.S. I Love You," and "Twist and Shout." The program, called "The Talent Spot," aired on December 4.

On December 2, through an arrangement with veteran London promoter Arthur Howes, the Beatles appeared onstage with Frank Ifield at the Embassy Cinema in Peterborough. The Beatles received second billing. At the time, Frank Ifield had the Number 1 song, "Lovesick Blues," as well as the Number 14 song, "I Remember You."

The audience had come to see Frank Ifield, not an unknown rock group called the Beatles. This became evident by the crowd's weary expression and complete silence as the boys sang "Love Me Do" and "P.S. I Love You." The audience preferred the sentimental ballads of Mr. Ifield and did not appreciate having their senses bombarded by the Beatles' wild rock music, played loudly with enthusiasm. It was a disastrous rejection for the boys.

The Beatles returned to Liverpool for shows at the Cavern on December 5 and 9.

The story "Beatles Record" actually announced their upcoming recording *audition* for George Martin. Pete's popularity is amply demonstrated by *Mersey Beat*'s choice of his photo to illustrate the cover story.

Five days later the Cavern presented a special "Stars of TV, Records and Radio" show. Robin Hall and Jimmy McGregor topped the bill, along with the Beatles, the Four Masts, and the Mersey Beats.

On December 13, *Mersey Beat* revealed BEATLES TOP POLL FOR SECOND TIME, along with a huge photo on the cover. Brian Epstein had bought another full page that listed all of their accomplishments.

The same day, "Love Me Do" became Number 17 on the British pop charts—the highest position it would attain.

Three days after appearing at the Majestic Ballroom on December 15, the Beatles grudgingly left Liverpool to fulfill the last two weeks of their contract at the Star-Club in Hamburg (December 18–31). They were now earning 750 DM each per week but displayed none of the excitement they had once shown the frenzied fans at the Indra, Kaiserkeller, and Top Ten—or, indeed, when they opened the very club where they were now appearing for the last time.

Ted Taylor, leader of King Size Taylor and the Dominoes, set up his tape recorder at the Star-Club on Christmas. His recordings captured the sounds of the Beatles for future generations who never had the opportunity to hear their Hamburg shows.

Lady Luck had merely smiled on the Beatles in 1962, but the year ahead would bring enormous success and set the stage for worldwide acclaim.

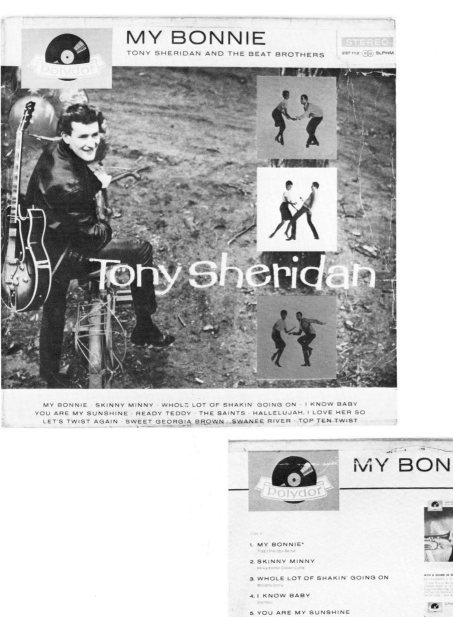

MY BONNIE · SKINNY MINNY · WHOLE LOT OF SHAKIN' GOING ON · I KNOW BABY
YOU ARE MY SUNSHINE · READY TEDDY · THE SAINTS · HALLELUJAH, I LOVE HER SO
LET'S TWIST AGAIN · SWEET GEORGIA BROWN · SWANEE RIVER · TOP TEN TWIST

Clockwise from lower left: The hand-written Abbey Road sessions log covering the June 6, 1962, audition (with Pete Best) through three songs recorded at the album session, February 11, 1963. A 1962 German newspaper ad for the Star-Club. The German Polydor LP (label, front, and back) *My Bonnie,* released June 1962; on the back, the Beatles are credited by name on two of the songs.

CHANNEL

Appearing at the Tower Ballroom on Thursday, June 21st, is **Bruce Channel**, currently one of the hottest recording artistes in the United States. Rated as the only white artiste capable of singing true blues, Bruce will be accompanied by his star harmonica player, **Delbert McClinton**.

★

"The Prince of Blues," as he has been dubbed, is touring Britain on the strength of one smash hit record—"Hey! Baby"—which has been high in the hit parade since March. Bruce cut this number when he was a small-time local boy in his home town of Dallas, Texas. The small private company who made the record issued only 200 copies for local distribution.

★

A friend of Bruce's (Marvin Montgomery, who is now his manager) took it along to a local radio station and managed to get it played. From that one airing the record caught on like wildfire throughout Dallas and then Nashville and, finally, throughout the United States and Britain until it became a world wide hit. Bruce now has a gold record to mark the 1½ million copies sold so far. His latest release is "Number One Man."

★

Two other recording groups are also on the bill, groups familiar to all our readers—Parlophone recording artistes **The Beatles** and Fontana recording artistes **Howie and the Seniors**.

Both of these groups owe their success to the people of Merseyside, who have been aware of their talent for quite some time.

★

Our cover stars, **The Big Three** will also be appearing, together with that uproariously funny quartet of goonery, the **Four Jays**.

★

Bruce and Delbert McClinton will be backed by an English group—**The Barons** (not to be confused with our own **Lee Castle and the Barons**.)

The June 14 *Mersey Beat* advertised Bruce Channel's Tower Ballroom show, which featured the Beatles, "of Stage, Radio and Record Fame."

MERSEY BEAT

MERSEYSIDE TOPS

Week ending 9/6/62

1. I'M LOOKING OUT THE WINDOW
CLIFF RICHARD
2. GOOD LUCK CHARM
ELVIS PRESLEY
3. PICTURE OF YOU
JOE BROWN
4. COME OUTSIDE
MIKE SARNE
5. GINNY COME LATELY
BRIAN HYLAND
6. LAST NIGHT WAS MADE FOR LOVE
BILLY FURY
7. A LITTLE LOVE, A LITTLE KISS
KARL DENVER
8. I DON'T KNOW WHY
EDEN KANE
9. NUT ROCKER
B. BUMBLE & THE STINGERS
10. THE GREEN LEAVES OF SUMMER
KENNY BALL
11. HOW CAN I MEET HER
EVERLY BROTHERS
12. STRANGER ON THE SHORE
ACKER BILK
13. SHARING YOU
BOBBY VEE
14. AS YOU LIKE IT
ADAM FAITH
15. LOVE LETTERS
KETTY LESTER
16. UNSQUARE DANCE
DAVE BRUBECK
17. THREE STARS
RICHARD CHAMBERLAIN
18. WONDERFUL LAND
THE SHADOWS
19. WHEN MY LITTLE GIRL IS SMILING
JIMMY JUSTICE
20. ORANGE BLOSSOM SPECIAL
THE SPOTNIKS

Spotlight LP—'Sinatra and Strings' Frank Sinatra
Best Selling EP—'Follow that Dream' Elvis Presley.

CLIFF RICHARD is looking very happy. "Looking Out The Window" is the best-selling record on Merseyside, and heads "Mersey Beat's" charts this issue—the only full Merseyside top twenty listing.

Printed by Swale (Widnes) Ltd., Victoria Road, Widnes.

Published by Mersey Beat, 81a Renshaw Street, Liverpool 1.

The June 14 issue also showed Cliff Richard and Billy Fury in the Top 10.

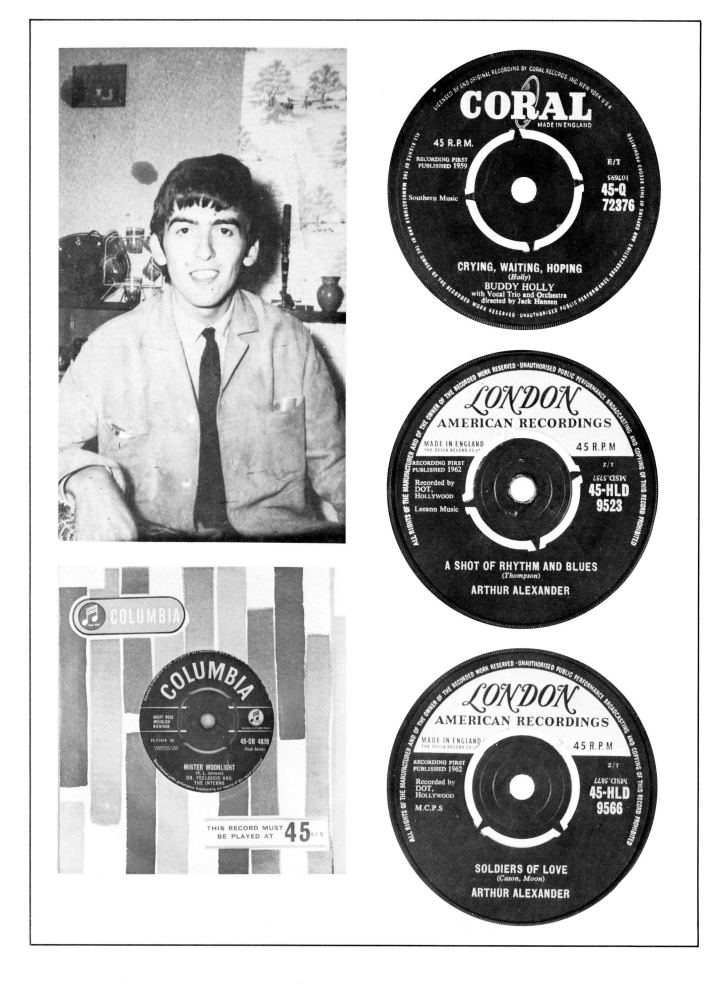

Facing page, top left: George Harrison.

British-release records by American recording artists of songs performed by the Beatles at the Cavern. The Cavern Girls bought other recordings of favorite "Beatles" songs, since no Beatles records were available. This set was purchased during 1962 by Val Davies in the NEMS Whitechapel store, at Cranes, and at Rushworths.

Below: The August 23 *Mersey Beat,* announcing the Beatles' "change" of drummer. *Right:* The letterhead of Peter Kaye's studio, where the first professional photos of the newly constituted Beatles were taken.

Peter Kaye STUDIO '9' PHOTOGRAPHY

Studio. 24. Newington Liverpool 1. Head Office 174. Park Road Liverpool 8. Tel. ROY 1316

LOOKING AT WIDNES AND RUNCORN
by CLIFF HAYES

First-class groups, first-class hall, and first-class production. At last, this is what Widnes has been waiting for! On Monday, September 3rd, Nems Enterprises will commence, for a trial period of three weeks, dances at the Queens Hall, Victoria Road, in which Bob Wooler will be presenting The Beatles and other leading groups.

The first show will include Billy Kramer and the Coasters and Runcorn's No. 1 group, Sonny Kaye and the Reds. Admission is by ticket only, so I suggest that Widnes readers ensure they do not miss these fine productions by obtaining tickets as soon as possible, from The Music Shop (Widnes), Dawsons (Runcorn and Widnes), El Cappuccino Coffee Bar (Runcorn), The Brazilian Coffee Bar (Widnes), Nems (Liverpool) or myself.

Poll Results

All votes have been counted and the groups performance at Deacon Road Labour Club has been taken into account. And the final result of the Mersey Beat Widnes and Runcorn Popularity Poll is as follows:—
1. Sonny Kaye and the Reds;
2. The Cheetahs/The Wanderers.
3. The Mustangs;
4. The Vikings;
5. The Senators.

NEMS ENTERPRISES PRESENT
THE NORTH'S No. 1 ROCK COMBO
THE BEATLES
AT THE
QUEENS HALL
W I D N E S
FOR A SEASON OF
THREE MONDAYS
Sept. 3rd, 10th & 17th
Supported by Top Merseyside Groups including
BILLY KRAMER
with THE COASTERS
RORY STORM
AND THE HURRICANES
SONNY KAYE
AND THE REDS
A BOB WOOLER PRODUCTION
—of course !
Tickets MUST be purchased in advance at 3/6 from
THE MUSIC SHOP (Widnes)
DAWSONS (Runcorn and Widnes)
THE BRAZILIAN COFFEE BAR
EL CAPPUCCINO (Runcorn)
and NEMS (Liverpool)

MERSEY BEAT EXCLUSIVE STORY

BEATLES CHANGE DRUMMER !

Ringo Starr (former drummer with Rory Storm and the Hurricanes) has joined **The Beatles**, replacing Pete Best on drums. Ringo has admired The Beatles for years and is delighted with his new engagement. Naturally he is tremendously excited about the future.

The Beatles will fly to London to make recordings at E.M.I. Studios. They will be recording numbers that have been specially written for the group, which they have received from their recording manager George Martin (Parlophone).

THE BEATLES TO PLAY CHESTER

As a result of the phenomenal Box Office success of The Beatles during their 4-week season of Monday nights at the Plaza Ballroom, St. Helens, the directors of Whetstone Entertainments, controllers of the ballroom, have engaged The Beatles for a series of four Thursday night sessions at the Riverpark Ballroom, Chester, which commenced on 16th August.

PETE BEST
Photo by Arthur Miller

The Beatles comment "Pete left the group by mutual agreement. There were no arguments or difficulties, and this has been an entirely amicable decision." On Tuesday, September 4th,

WE'RE STILL
The Four Jays
(Watch for a new name in the near future)
BACK FROM A SUCCESSFUL SEASON at the ISLE OF MAN
BROmborough 3454

ERIC'S
9 Commutation   8 & 10 Manchester
Row   Nor 1121   Street
Liverpool's leading group makers
STAGE JACKETS made from £5-15-0

When visiting Liverpool stay at the
GRENVILLE HOTEL
Recommended by top recording Artistes
61 Mount Pleasant (opp. Y.M.C.A.)
LIVERPOOL
Prop.: Bill Powell. Phone ROYal 7300

SEE THE STAR SHOW
with recording artistes
Brian Poole and the Tremilos
* * *
Ian and the Zodiacs
* * *
The Spidermen
on THURSDAY
SEPTEMBER 6th

TOWN HALL   LITHERLAND

RORY STORM
AND THE HURRICANES
Available for bookings from September 7th onwards
Phone STOnescroft 9517
NOW !

Have a "Merry" Evening at the
BLACK CAT CLUB
Above Sampson & Barlows, Lond'n Rd
FRIDAY: JAMBOREE CLUB
SATURDAY and SUNDAY
Rock with . . . Sonny Webb & Cascades . . . The Kentuckians . . . The Kansas City Five . . . The Thunderbirds . . . & others
MEMBERS ONLY   LICENSED

NEMS ENTERPRISES PRESENT
MIKE'S NIGHT
AT THE
CAMBRIDGE HALL
LORD STREET
SOUTHPORT
on FRIDAY, AUGUST 31st
STARRING

MIKE BERRY
with THE PHANTOMS
AND
★ THE DAKOTAS
WITH PETE MACLAINE
★ THE BIG THREE
★ BILLY KRAMER
WITH THE COASTERS
★ THE MERSEY BEATS
★ AND IT'S A BOB WOOLER PRODUCTION—OF COURSE !

TICKETS 6/- (in advance)
FROM ALDRIDGES
MORRISON'S TRAVEL AGENCY
and NEMS (in Liverpool)
7/-ON NIGHT AT DOOR
★ ★ ★ ★ ★
AND ALSO SEE
MIKE BERRY
AT
Sunday, Aug. 26th.
CAVERN CLUB
Monday, Aug. 27th.
CAVERN CLUB
(mid-day)
Monday, Aug. 27th.
PLAZA BALLROOM
ST. HELENS
Wednesday, Aug. 29th.
MAJESTIC BALLROOM
CREWE
Thursday, Aug. 30th.
MAJESTIC BALLROOM
BIRKENHEAD
Friday, Aug. 31st.
CAMBRIDGE HALL,
SOUTHPORT
Saturday, Sept. 1st.
CLEETHORPES
Sunday, Sept. 2nd.
OASIS CLUB, Manchester

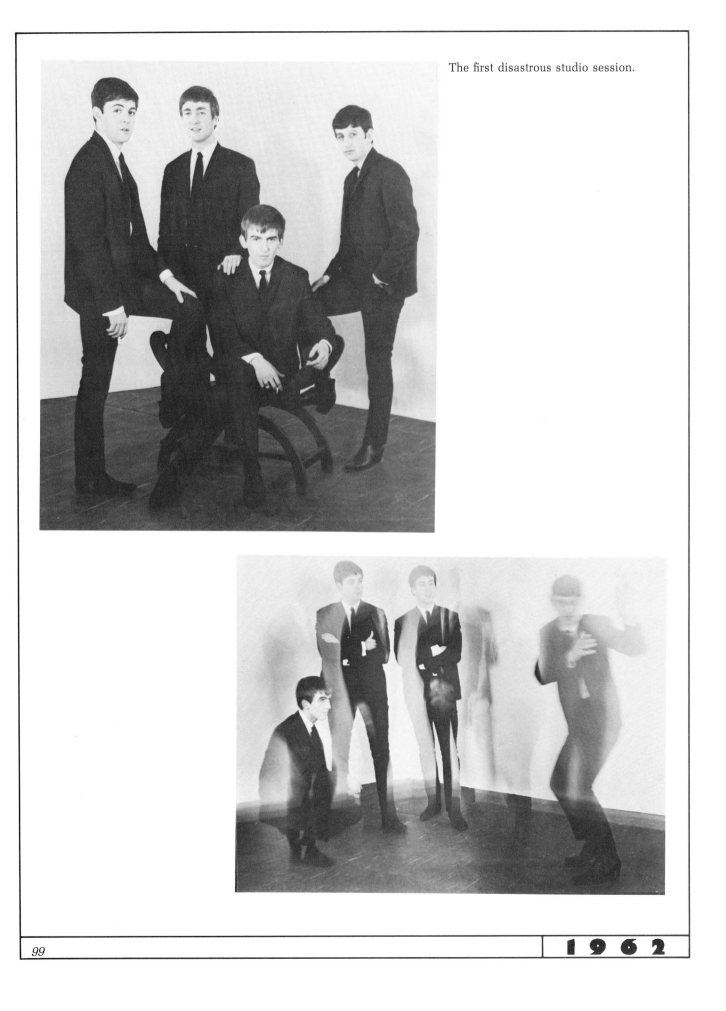

The first disastrous studio session.

Chadwick's brainstorm—the rubble.

Above: The fireboat *Salvor* session, which was the source of the first Ringo handout photo. An informal shot taken just before going aboard. *Right:* The first Ringo handout photo. Epstein sent the cards to radio stations and newspapers, but given that the boys were hardly known outside the Cavern, it's likely that all of them were filed in media trash cans. This copy was supplied by Chadwick himself.

DIRECTION.

NEMS ENTERPRISES LTD.
12-14 WHITECHAPEL
LIVERPOOL 1   ROYal 7895

THE
BEATLES

THE NORTH'S OWN ENTERTAINMENTS PAPER

MERSEY BEAT

FRANK HESSY
Limited
62 STANLEY STREET
(Corner of Whitechapel)
LIVERPOOL 1
FOR ALL MUSICAL INSTRUMENTS
OUR EASY TERMS ARE "EASIER"

Vol. 2 No. 31   SEPTEMBER 20—OCTOBER 4, 1962   Price THREEPENCE

BEATLES RECORD FOR EMI
story inside

WE ARE NOW ACCEPTING ORDERS FOR
THE BEATLES
FIRST RECORD ON PARLOPHONE
LOVE ME DO
c/w
P.S. I LOVE YOU
RELEASED **FRIDAY OCTOBER 5th**

NEMS   12-14, WHITECHAPEL. Tel. ROYal. 7895
50, GREAT CHARLOTTE ST.   70-72, WALTON RD.

HAVE A BALL!
AT
LITHERLAND TOWN HALL
YOUR THURSDAY JIVE DATE
DON'T BE LATE, MATE—FOR
SHANE FENTON
AND THE FENTONES
27th SEPTEMBER
TICKETS - 4/6 (at Door 5/6)

TIP TOP VARIETY
JIM GRETTY
V.A.F. M.A.A.   Tel. SEF 3482
also THE JIM GRETTY VARIETY
AGENCY
Artistes and Bands for all occasions

Visit the
ODD SPOT CLUB
89 BOLD STREET
LIVERPOOL

ONE OF THE
CITY'S LEADING
NIGHT SPOTS

PAGE 3

...OW ...T ...M

...is Presley
...t Dream'
...e novel
...nel" Elvis
...wonderful
...rt The
... Sound
...r That
...ngel."
...e role of
... member
...h no set
...g around
...amily car
...etrog in
...y set up
...the road,
... stretch
...roadside
...r family
...stead the

...ney sell-
...bait to
...spurred
...initial
...go into
...their own
...t of row-
...long bo-
...d home-
...into the
...m.

...nds that
...s outside
...county
...d makes
...an offer
...d, which
...at follows
makes for an exciting
film.

**ELVIS AND ANNE HELM IN
FOLLOW THAT DREAM**

REVIEWS

Norman Wisdom takes a step
back into the Roaring Twenties
in his latest film "The Girl on
the Boat," currently showing at

THE YOUNG SAVAGES (Cert. X)

doctor, Robert Bloch, author of
"Psycho" is responsible for the
screenplay—and has introduced
a surprise climax. On the same
bill, Richard Widmark stars in
"Pick-up on South Street," a
story of a bunch of underworld
characters who become unwit-
tingly involved with Communist
agents.

THE STRANGERS
THE UNDERTAKERS

TWO TOP TEN GROUPS

ALL ENQUIRIES TO: RALPH WEBSTER

MAG HULL **3763**   **AIN** TREE **4230**

BEATCOMBER

ON SAFAIRY WITH WHIDE HUNTER
In the Jumble . . . the mighty
jumble . . . . Whide Hunter sleeps
tonight. At the foot of the bed,
Otumba kept wogs for poisonous
snacks such as the deadly Cobbler
and Apple Python.
Little did he nose that the next
day, in the early owls of the Mor-
cambe, a true story would actually
happen.
Otumba awoke him with a cup of
teeth, and they lit up towards the
jumble.
"Ain't dat Elepoon Pill?" said Wipe
Hudnose, "wearing his new Beuul?"
"Could be the Flying Docker on a
case."
"No he's walking," said Otumba
in swahily which is not arf from here
as the crowbars. All too soon they
reached a cleaner in the jumble and
set up cramp.

Jumble Jim, whom shall remain
nameless, was slowly, but slowly asking his way through the underpants
(underware he was being washed by
Whide Hunter).
"Beat the bus Otumbath!" com-
manded Wheat Hoover.
"No, but maybe next week it will
be my turn to beat the bus now
standing at platforbe nine."
Jumping Gym, who shall remain
Norman, spotted Whit Monday and
the Barking Doctrine shooting some
rhinostrils and hippoposthumous
and Otumbark.
"Stop shooting those animoles!"
But it hab no influence upod them.
They carried on shooting, alligarters,
wild boats, garriffes, lepers and
Uncle Tom Cobra and all . . . Old
Buncle Ron Gabble and all . . . Bold
Rumple Bom Dobby and all . . . Bad
Runcorn Sad Toddy and all.

Above: This photo was taken
at Speke airport on September
4 as the Beatles departed for
their first Parlophone recording session. George's black eye
is clearly visible. *Right: Mersey Beat,* September 6. The un-
credited "Beatcomber" column
is by John Lennon.

Chadwick's photos of a Cavern performance. Ringo still has his name pasted on the drum.

Top: Chadwick's photo of a rehearsal at the Cavern.
Left: The cover of the October 4 *Mersey Beat* announced that the Beatles' first record was now available at Epstein's NEMS record stores. *Above:* Card-stock handout for the *Royal Iris* Grand River Cruise. The Beatles top the bill.

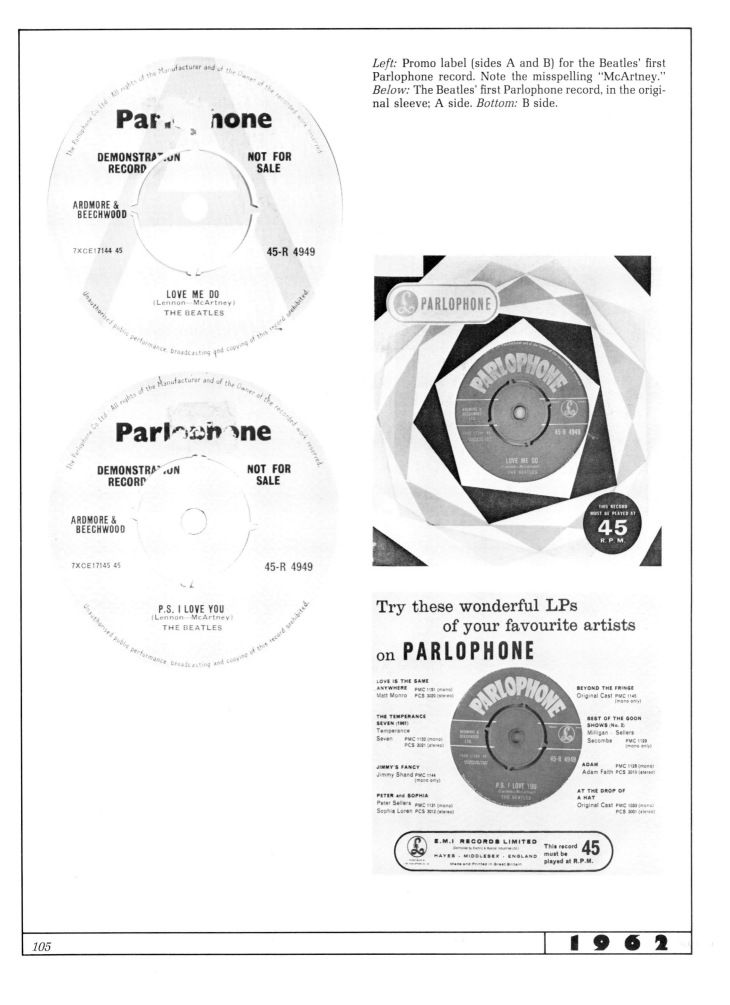

Left: Promo label (sides A and B) for the Beatles' first Parlophone record. Note the misspelling "McArtney." *Below:* The Beatles' first Parlophone record, in the original sleeve; A side. *Bottom:* B side.

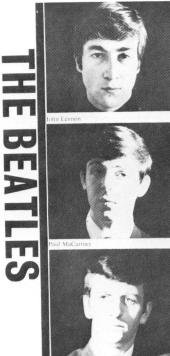

John Lennon

George Harrison

Paul MaCartney

Ringo Starr

John, Paul and George met when at school in 1956 and have remained together ever since. They have played as a group with numerous names, various drummers and other augmentations. Their present drummer, Ringo Starr, has only recently joined the group but they have admired and known him since their schooldays.

1962 has been an exciting and important year for The Beatles. They have spread their wings and their appearances in many different parts of the country have always effected the same result . . . an invitation to return. They have made three broadcasts on the Light Programme in Peter Pilbeam's 'Teenagers Turn', Granada T.V. filmed the group at the Cavern Club, Liverpool. They play at the Cavern (in the heart of the city) sometimes as many as three times a week, often a mid-day session . . . always it's a full house.

In May they were the principal attraction to open the fantastically successful Star-Club in Hamburg. Whilst they were away their manager took tapes to A. & R. Manager George Martin who subsequently signed them for Parlophone records. Both sides of their first single have been written by Paul and John. 'Love Me Do' was written in 1958 in the skiffle days and 'P.S. I Love You' was written whilst the group was playing in Germany at the Star-Club.

The Cavern Club

offers congratulations and
best wishes to

The Beatles

on the release of their first recording
for Parlophone

Love me do/P.S. I love you

It is with pleasure that the Club
announces that **The Beatles** will
continue to be featured regularly

at **The Cavern**

10 Matthew Street
off North John Street
Liverpool 1

Telephone Central 1591

Program for Little Richard at the Tower, Friday, October 12, 1962. Inside, Beatles photos and bios. Also, the announcement of their first record.

Right: This October 1962 German Polydor EP was the only release of the original 1961 version of "Sweet Georgia Brown" with the Beatles backing.

Little Richard at the Empire, October 28.

Above: Pete Best and his new band were the *Mersey Beat* cover story, November 1. *Right:* The November 15 *Mersey Beat* issue carried a story about "the extent to which the magnetic personality of Pete Best appeals to girls."

1962

Above: German newspaper ads for the Star-Club: November (left) and December (right). *Right and facing page:* The Beatles onstage at the Star-Club, December.

Three more photos of the same Star-Club appearance. This was to be their final (and Ringo's only) engagement in Hamburg. *Right:* In January, it had been John, Paul, George, and Pete, but by December, it was Pete, Wayne, Tony, Frank, and Lee Curtis wishing a Merry Christmas to fans and thanking them for making the All-Stars a success.

Brian Epstein placed this full-page ad.

P A R T   F O U R
1 9 6 3

"If the Beatles made a disc of themselves snoring for two minutes, it'd go to Number 1!"

—*Brian Matthew*

Although 1963 was the year that Beatlemania conquered England, the slow march to victory began with an inauspicious campaign in Scotland. The tour had been arranged in November 1962 between Jack Fallon at the Cana Variety Agency and Albert Bonici, a Scottish promoter. Although Bonici got the Beatles at a bargain rate of £42 per night, he actually lost money because bad weather canceled the first of five shows.

In fact, harsh weather created overwhelming hardships before the tour began. Scotland was embraced by a merciless storm that made air and road travel impossible.

On January 2 the Beatles' flight from London to Edinburgh was diverted to Aberdeen owing to bad weather. It was too late to call Neil Aspinall, who was anxiously pacing the floor in Edinburgh with all the equipment. So the first engagement, scheduled that night at Longmore Hall, was canceled.

The Beatles must have remembered their disastrous first Scotland tour with Johnny Gentle in 1960. They had no desire to experience that embarrassing ordeal again.

Alas, the campaign began on January 3 at the Two Red Shoes Ballroom in Elgin, and the next night at the Town Hall in Ross and Cromarty. On the fifth they were at the Museum Hall in Bridge of Allan, Stirlingshire, and the five-date tour ended the following evening in Aberdeen.

The Beatles remained in Scotland for two more days. On the eighth they went to Glasgow and sang their soon-to-be-released single, "Please Please Me," during an appearance on "Round Up," a children's show on Scottish television.

"Touring was a relief," said John. "We were beginning to feel stale and cramped. We'd get tired of one stage and be deciding to pack up when another stage would come up. We'd outlived the Hamburg stage and hated going back to Hamburg those last two times. There was a bit of screaming in Glasgow. We always got screams there when we played rock 'n' roll. I suppose they haven't got much else to do up there."

The January 3 issue of *Mersey Beat* featured a full-page story of the magazine's December 1962 awards night. Editor Bill Harry presented a special shield to the Beatles for winning the paper's popularity poll for the second straight year.

Brian Epstein presented a NEMS award to Billy Kramer and the Coasters as the "top nonprofessional group." Epstein, who had become Kramer's manager, was about to drop the Coasters and have his new protégé perform with a popular Manchester band called the Dakotas.

The Beatles returned to Liverpool and performed to a record-breaking crowd at Grafton Rooms on the tenth. Afterward, they were interviewed by Maureen Cleave of the London *Evening Standard.* She had been impressed by the large crowd of fans queueing outside the ballroom two hours before showtime.

"The Beatles made me laugh immediately," Cleave told her readers. "Their wit was just so keen and sharp—John Lennon, especially. They all had this wonderful quality. It wasn't innocent, but everything was new to them. . . . John Lennon has an upper lip which is brutal in a devastating way. George Harrison is handsome, whimsical, and untidy. Paul McCartney has a round baby face while Ringo Starr is ugly but cute. Their physical appearance inspires frenzy. They look beat-up and depraved in the nicest way."

On January 11 the Beatles' second single, "Please Please Me"/"Ask Me Why" (Parlophone

The cover of *Mersey Beat* for January 17 advertised the Beatles' second single.

1.(a) Do you prefer blondes or brunettes (b) Why?

2.(a) Where do you like to be kissed? (b) Why there?

3.(a) Do you prefer dizzy blondes or intelligent brunettes, or vice-versa? (b) If the answer is just vice, please disregard the question.

4.(a) How do you spend your free time (b) If this is a leading question or if the answer will in any way incriminate you please leave a blank.

5. To quote a friend of yours 'How Do You Do It?'

6. You may refuse to answer the above on the grounds that it may incriminate you. However, should you condescend to answer it, you may be liable to legal entanglements.

7. Why did you choose the name 'Beatles' apart from the obvious facial characteristics?

8. What is your favourite dish - food that is?

9. What is your favourite indoor sport?

10.(a) Have you, or are you ever likely to, publish a book on Faith & Morals? (b) If so what will be the underlying theme of the book (c) Do you think it will be banned?

11.(a) Would you do anything once (b) More than once? (c) Why?

12.(a) Would you make a girl happy? (b) In what way?

N.B. WHEN ANSWERING THESE QUESTIONS PLEASE AVOID THE USE OF ABSURDITY & TERMINOLOGICAL INEXACTITUDES.

1. (a) Either, as long as they're female. (b) because they're female.

2. (a) The answer seems too obvious (b) Why not?

3.(a) Intelligence is an advantage; colour of hair - immaterial
(b) Question too interesting to disregard.

4. (a) Biological research (b) What's incriminating about biological research?

5. ——

6. ——

7. —— HA! (said with disgust.)

8. ——   P.T.O.

9. Flying.

10(a) Haven't you bought it? (b) Chastity in an Atomic Age.
(c) Henry Miller wasn't.

11. (a) Anything (b) If I enjoyed it, yes. (c) Because of my insane interest in research ... biological, or otherwise

12. (a) One can but speculate. (b) For an answer to this question, interested parties should realise that research plays a large part, and for this, such particulars as bodily statistics, facial features (photographs accepted) and proof of genuine interest (photographs accepted) are, of course, ... vital. Without them there is nothing more to be said than ......

Yours Sincerely
—— A Friend.

This "application" was typed up by Valerie Keene, one of the Cavern girls, and filled out by hand by Paul McCartney.

R4983), was released and reviewed by *Disc:* " 'Please Please Me' will undoubtedly please the growing band of fans who are following the Beatles. The boys chant this one briskly to a dark twangy background. 'Ask Me Why' moves with a Latin groove. . . ."

Keith Fordyce of the *New Musical Express* said, " 'Please Please Me' . . . has been publicized as The Beatles' Record of the Year. 'Ask Me Why' has really good flipside value. This vocal and instrumental quartet has turned out a really enjoyable platter, full of beat, vigor, and vitality, and what's more, it's different. I can't think of any other group currently recording in this style."

The Beatles played to the noonday crowd at the Cavern on the eleventh, and the following night at the Invicta Ballroom in Chatham, Kent.

On January 13 the boys went to Aston, Birmingham, to record their first appearance for the BBC-TV show "Thank Your Lucky Stars." They sang "Please Please Me" and the show was aired six days later.

On the fourteenth they played to a huge audience at the Wolverham Welfare Association Dance in Wirral. Two days later, at the Playhouse Theatre in Manchester, they recorded a show for the BBC Light Programme "Here We Go." They sang "Chains," "Please Please Me," "Ask Me Why," and "Three Cool Cats." All but the last song were aired on January 25.

The Beatles thrilled the Cavern lunch crowd on the seventeenth and that night they were at the Majestic Ballroom in Birkenhead. Every ticket had been sold in advance and the police had to be called to restore order when 500 fans were turned away at the door.

On January 19, "Please Please Me" debuted in *Melody Maker* at Number 47 and stayed on the chart for eighteen weeks. For two weeks, beginning March 2, it reigned as the Number 1 song. It made its last showing on May 18 at Number 49.

The number of British artists being aired in the United States was sparse. At that time, Frank Ifield's "I Remember You" and an instrumental by the Tornadoes called "Telstar" were big hits. The Beatles dreamed of getting on the American charts and the possibility of that dream coming true was improving greatly. The *New Musical Express* announced: "The Beatles, yet to have a major British hit, have been snapped up for America by Vee Jay, the label responsible for the U.S. success of Frank Ifield's 'I Remember You' and 'Lovesick Blues.'"

Very rare Japanese Polydor release of "My Bonnie" in January 1963. The bio on the sleeve describes Sheridan as "Mr. Twist."

"The deal was completed on Monday [January 21] by Barbara Gardner, Vee Jay's international chief, who was visiting London."

On January 22, the boys spent a hectic day recording a trio of BBC shows ("Pop Inn," "Saturday Club," and the "Talent Spot") at different locations and returned to Liverpool the next day.

That evening they played to an enthusiastic crowd at the Baptist Youth Club Dance in Lancashire.

"Fabulous!" said the *Port Sunlight News.* "That was the comment everyone made who heard The Beatles at the Co-operative Hall on Friday night. . . . The Beatles were the main attraction at the dance held by the Baptist Youth Club. . . . Every one who attended—and many more—are asking the question, 'When are they coming again?' "

The "Friday Spectacular" show that aired January 25 over Radio Luxembourg was different from all others. On previous shows the boys always mimed the lyrics in front of an invited audience. The radio listeners heard the original record plus the audience reaction. This time, however, the Beatles actually performed "Please Please Me," the Chuck Berry hit "Carol," and a Carl Perkins song, "Lend Me Your Comb."

On the last day of January "Please Please Me" became the Number 1 song on the Merseyside Top 20, and the boys performed a double-header at the Majestic Ballroom. The manager, recalling the melee by irate fans who had been turned away on January 17, wisely scheduled shows for 8:00 P.M. *and* 11:00 P.M.

There was no doubt that the Beatles were now the most popular group on the Merseyside. Their fans were delighted but also worried about losing their two-year bond with their idols.

During the month, the boys had appeared on six radio or TV shows, completed a successful Scotland tour, and signed an American recording contract. As their popularity increased beyond Liverpool, the number of local bookings decreased. It was just a matter of time before the Merseyside crowd would have to share these four young lads with the world.

Brian Epstein was anxious to get a Beatles album on the market as soon as possible. He knew from experience at NEMS that April and May were not profitable months for record sales and reasoned that retailers would welcome an album by the Beatles during the slump period. Also, a successful album would give Epstein more bargaining power regarding schedules and fees for summer concerts and tours. He wanted fees to rise with the release of every new Beatle record.

On February 2 the Beatles began their first nationwide tour, appearing at the bottom of a six-act bill starring Helen Shapiro. The sixteen-year-old star had already achieved fame as the Best British

Female Singer in 1961 and 1962. The tour would be presented in two parts by promoter Arthur Howes, who would later produce all but one of the Beatles' British tours.

This engagement was important because the boys could plug their current single by singing it throughout England. On opening night at the Gaumont Cinema in Bradford they did "Chains," "Keep Your Hands Off My Baby," "A Taste of Honey," and "Please Please Me."

February 3 was an open day in the tour and the Beatles returned to Liverpool for an eight-hour rhythm & blues marathon at the Cavern. The next afternoon—after 152 shows—they did their final lunchtime performance at the Cavern.

The Helen Shapiro tour continued through the next five days. One unpleasant incident occurred after an appearance at the ABC Cinema in Carlisle on the eighth.

As Miss Shapiro was heading for her room at the Crown and Mitre Hotel, a young man asked her to join him in the ballroom for a dance. It was a very conservative affair for members of the Carlisle Golf Club.

Miss Shapiro politely declined the invitation but was persuaded to change her mind by the Beatles.

"I nipped upstairs and freshened up my face,"

Although Capitol Records at first chose not to issue Beatles recordings, Capitol in Canada did, beginning with "Love Me Do," released February 1963.

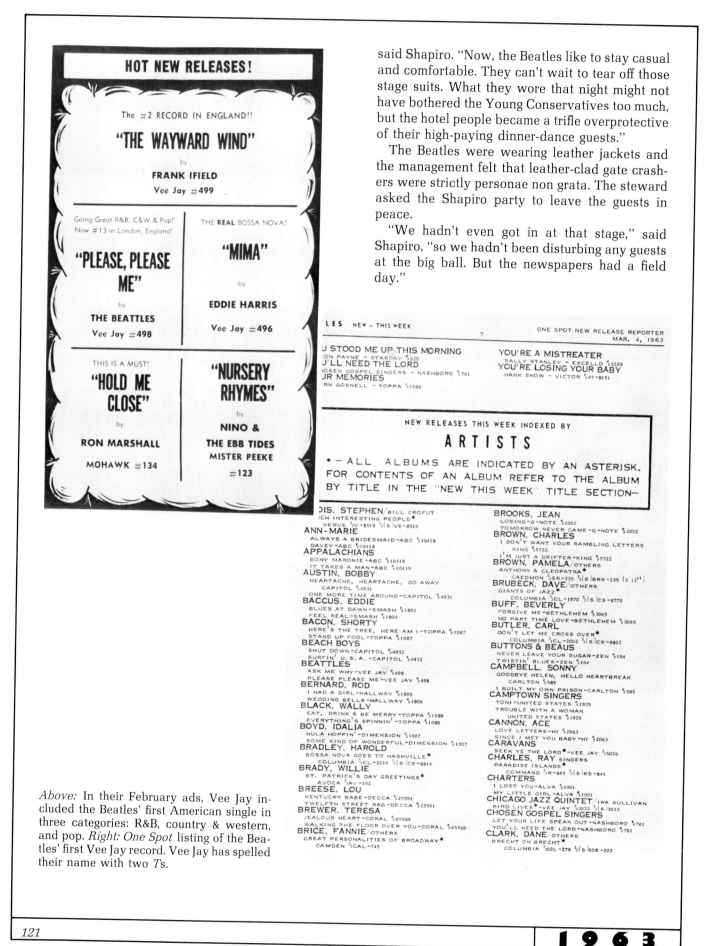

said Shapiro. "Now, the Beatles like to stay casual and comfortable. They can't wait to tear off those stage suits. What they wore that night might not have bothered the Young Conservatives too much, but the hotel people became a trifle overprotective of their high-paying dinner-dance guests."

The Beatles were wearing leather jackets and the management felt that leather-clad gate crashers were strictly personae non grata. The steward asked the Shapiro party to leave the guests in peace.

"We hadn't even got in at that stage," said Shapiro, "so we hadn't been disturbing any guests at the big ball. But the newspapers had a field day."

LES NEW – THIS WEEK

7

ONE SPOT NEW RELEASE REPORTER
MAR. 4, 1963

...U STOOD ME UP THIS MORNING
...ON PAYNE – STARDAY #620
...U'LL NEED THE LORD
...OSEN GOSPEL SINGERS – NASHBORO #761
...UR MEMORIES
...RN GOSNELL – TOPPA #1086

YOU'RE A MISTREATER
SALLY STANLEY – EXCELLO #2229
YOU'RE LOSING YOUR BABY
HANK SNOW – VICTOR #47-8151

NEW RELEASES THIS WEEK INDEXED BY

ARTISTS

* – ALL ALBUMS ARE INDICATED BY AN ASTERISK. FOR CONTENTS OF AN ALBUM REFER TO THE ALBUM BY TITLE IN THE "NEW THIS WEEK" TITLE SECTION—

...DIS, STEPHEN/BILL CROFUT
...ICH INTERESTING PEOPLE*
...VERVE ³V-8519 ³(S)V6-8519
ANN-MARIE
ALWAYS A BRIDESMAID-ABC #10418
DAVEY-ABC #10418
APPALACHIANS
BONY MARONIE-ABC #10419
IT TAKES A MAN-ABC #10419
AUSTIN, BOBBY
HEARTACHE, HEARTACHE, GO AWAY
CAPITOL #4931
ONE MORE TIME AROUND-CAPITOL #4931
BACCUS, EDDIE
BLUES AT DAWN-SMASH #1804
FEEL REAL-SMASH #1804
BACON, SHORTY
HERE'S THE TREE, HERE AM I-TOPPA #1087
STAND UP FOOL-TOPPA #1087
BEACH BOYS
SHUT DOWN-CAPITOL #4932
SURFIN' U.S.A.-CAPITOL #4932
BEATTLES
ASK ME WHY-VEE JAY #498
PLEASE PLEASE ME-VEE JAY #498
BERNARD, ROD
I HAD A GIRL-HALLWAY #1806
WEDDING BELLS-HALLWAY #1806
BLACK, WALLY
EAT, DRINK & BE MERRY-TOPPA #1089
EVERYTHING'S SPINNIN'-TOPPA #1089
BOYD, IDALIA
HULA HOPPIN'-DIMENSION #1007
SOME KIND OF WONDERFUL-DIMENSION #1007
BRADLEY, HAROLD
BOSSA NOVA GOES TO NASHVILLE*
COLUMBIA ³CL-2014 ³(S)CS-8814
BRADY, WILLIE
ST. PATRICK'S DAY GREETINGS*
AVOCA ³AV-142
BREESE, LOU
KENTUCKY BABE-DECCA #25591
TWELFTH STREET RAG-DECCA #25591
BREWER, TERESA
JEALOUS HEART-CORAL #65569
WALKING THE FLOOR OVER YOU-CORAL #65569
BRICE, FANNIE/OTHERS
GREAT PERSONALITIES OF BROADWAY*
CAMDEN ³CAL-745

BROOKS, JEAN
LOSING-G-NOTE #2002
TOMORROW NEVER CAME-G-NOTE #2002
BROWN, CHARLES
I DON'T WANT YOUR RAMBLING LETTERS
KING #5722
I'M JUST A DRIFTER-KING #5722
BROWN, PAMELA/OTHERS
ANTHONY & CLEOPATRA*
CAEDMON ³SR-235 ³(S)SRS-235 (3 12")
BRUBECK, DAVE/OTHERS
GIANTS OF JAZZ*
COLUMBIA ³CL-1970 ³(S)CS-8770
BUFF, BEVERLY
FORGIVE ME-BETHLEHEM #3065
NO PART TIME LOVE-BETHLEHEM #3065
BUTLER, CARL
DON'T LET ME CROSS OVER*
COLUMBIA ³CL-2002 ³(S)CS-8802
BUTTONS & BEAUS
NEVER LEAVE YOUR SUGAR-ZEN #104
TWISTIN' BLUES-ZEN #104
CAMPBELL, SONNY
GOODBYE HELEN, HELLO HEARTBREAK
CARLTON #585
I BUILT MY OWN PRISON-CARLTON #585
CAMPTOWN SINGERS
TONI-UNITED STATES #1929
TROUBLE WITH A WOMAN
UNITED STATES #1929
CANNON, ACE
LOVE LETTERS-HI #2063
SINCE I MET YOU BABY-HI #2063
CARAVANS
SEEK YE THE LORD*-VEE JAY #5026
CHARLES, RAY SINGERS
PARADISE ISLANDS*
COMMAND ³R-845 ³(S)RS-845
CHARTERS
I LOST YOU-ALVA #1001
MY LITTLE GIRL-ALVA #1001
CHICAGO JAZZ QUINTET/IRA SULLIVAN
BIRD LIVES*-VEE JAY #3033 ³(S)3033
CHOSEN GOSPEL SINGERS
LET YOUR LIFE SPEAK OUT-NASHBORO #761
YOU'LL NEED THE LORD-NASHBORO #761
CLARK, DANE/OTHERS
BRECHT ON BRECHT*
COLUMBIA ³O2L-278 ³(S)O2S-203

Above: In their February ads, Vee Jay included the Beatles' first American single in three categories: R&B, country & western, and pop. *Right: One Spot* listing of the Beatles' first Vee Jay record. Vee Jay has spelled their name with two *T*s.

The tour continued on the ninth in Sunderland, and the first part of the engagement ended in Peterborough. Peter Jay and the Jaywalkers took the Beatles' place on stage that night as the boys hurried back to London for a very special engagement on Abbey Road.

On February 11 the Beatles went to EMI's Number 2 studio and recorded their first album. Producing an album was a whole new experience. It gave them and their producer, George Martin, a chance to share ideas and techniques. Martin had exercised absolute control over the choice of songs produced as singles, but now inspired a keen sense of motivation by allowing the Beatles to select all of the material for this project.

George Martin had originally intended for the boys' first album to be recorded during a live performance at the Cavern, but realized that it would be impossible to position microphones and equipment among the boisterous audience. Also, the low ceiling and sweaty stone walls threatened to cause engineer Norman Smith to yank out all his hair while trying to capture an acceptable sound on his tape machines.

Although the session could not be recorded at the Cavern, Smith was able to create an illusion of a live performance.

During an interview many years later for a monthly magazine, *The Beatles Book Monthly*, Smith said, "It wasn't too difficult. Instead of sticking the mikes only a few inches away from the speakers I put them several feet away, so that the sound bounced off the walls of the studio.

"The whole idea was just to let them record numbers exactly as they've been doing onstage. I added to the performance feel in the studio by positioning them much as they are onstage, with Ringo and his drums at the back, then George in front of him, and Paul and John in the center doing their vocals.

"The main things I remember were a large tin of Hack cough sweets which were stuck into a handy position on the piano, so that Paul and John could dig into it whenever they wanted to, and a couple of cartons of Peter Stuyvesant cigarettes that they steadily worked through during the day.

"The boys were very, very happy when they heard the playback at the end of the day," added Smith. "I hadn't done the final master tape, of course. I have to do two of those—a mono one for this country and a stereo one for America. I do a stereo version in the studio by putting all the in-

struments on one track and the voices on another."

Fourteen songs were recorded during the thirteen-hour session. Ten were selected for the album.

Despite their exhaustion following the EMI session, their relentless schedule continued. They performed a double-header the very next night at the Azena Ballroom in Sheffield, and the Astoria Ballroom in Oldham.

After appearing at the Majestic Ballroom in Hull on the thirteenth, they did a special show on Valentine's Day for hometown lovers at the Locarno Ballroom in Liverpool.

On February 16 the boys were at the Carfax Assembly Rooms in Oxford. The next day they sang "Please Please Me" during a second appearance on "Thank Your Lucky Stars," to be aired on February 23.

The Beatles gave two sellout performances on the eighteenth at Queen's Hall in Widnes. The next night they played the Cavern after a fourteen-day absence. The long line for admission had started forming two days before showtime. Lee Curtis and the All-Stars were also on the bill. This was the last time the Beatles saw Pete Best.

Afterward, the boys went to London for their first live appearance on BBC's "Parade of the Pops" on February 20. They sang "Love Me Do" and "Please Please Me."

Following a show that night at the Swimming Baths in Doncaster, they did another double-header on February 21 at the Majestic Ballroom, and performed the next night in Manchester.

A seemingly impossible goal was achieved when the Beatles reached Number 1 on the *New Musical Express* chart for the week ending February 22. "Please Please Me" was tied for the prized spot with "The Wayward Wind" by Frank Ifield, but massive sales indicated that in another week the Beatles would exclusively occupy the coveted Number 1 position.

Naturally, the boys were ecstatic as they began the second phase of the Helen Shapiro tour, performing in Mansfield on the twenty-third and in Coventry the next evening.

During a break in the tour the Beatles played at

Top row: Promo label of the first Vee Jay record (note two *T*s), side A (left) and side B. *Middle row:* Commercial label of the Beatles' first Vee Jay record, with error remaining side A (left) and side B. *Bottom row:* Corrected commercial label, side A (left) and side B.

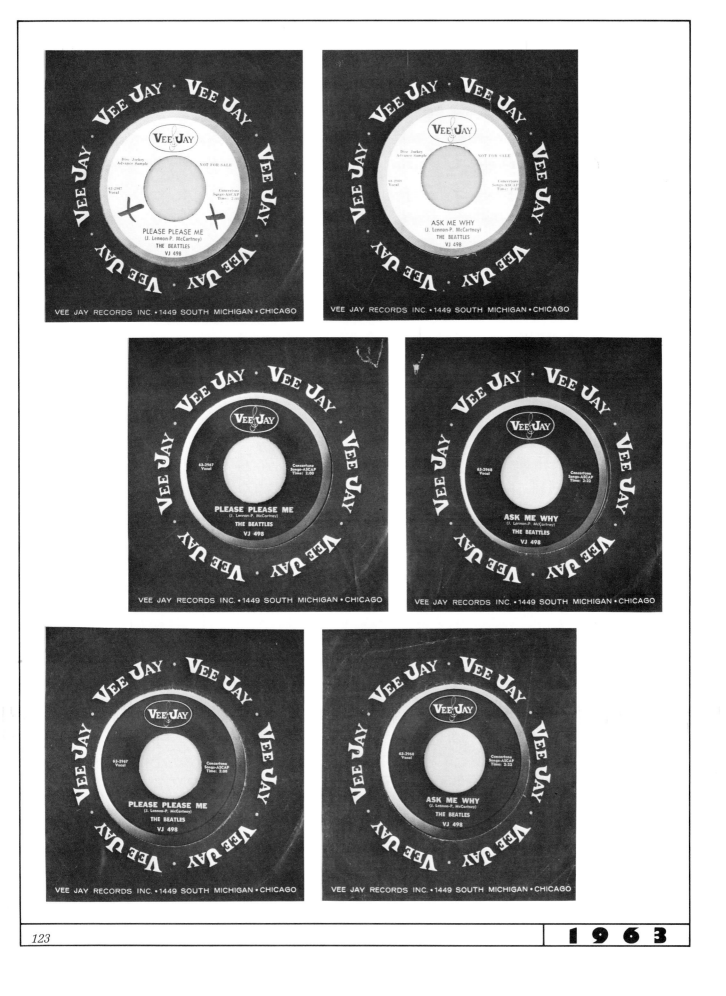

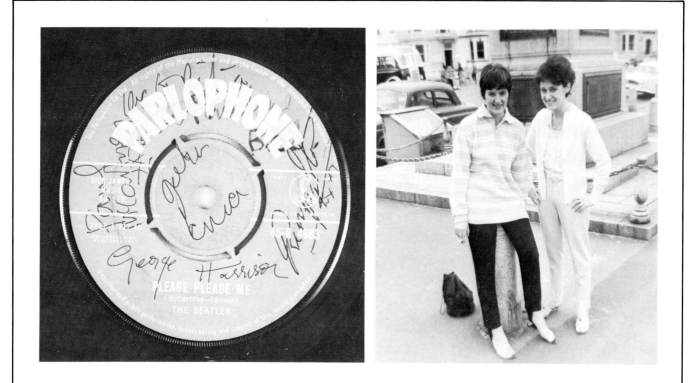

the Casino Ballroom in Leigh on February 25.

On that day in America, Vee Jay released "Please Please Me"/"Ask Me Why" (Vee Jay 498). The deejay copies as well as the first commercial pressings had the group's name spelled *the Beattles*. The spelling error also appeared on all promotional and advertising material, but was later corrected when the publicity department at Vee Jay became aware of the mistake.

On February 26 Brian Epstein created another source of future income for the Beatles by forming Northern Songs Limited in partnership with London publisher Dick James. Northern Songs would publish all material written by John Lennon and Paul McCartney. This would include Lennon-McCartney songs recorded by other artists as well.

"I've explained to the boys," said Epstein, "how important it is that we attract other recording artists. I wanted to make demo recordings so that all of us can let the maximum number of outsiders hear what the boys have to offer."

Helen Shapiro caught the flu during the final week of the tour and was unable to appear at Taunton or York. Although the Beatles had the Number 1 hit, they did not top the bill in her absence. Instead, Danny Williams became the headliner for two days until Shapiro rejoined the tour in Shrewsbury on February 28.

During the coach ride to Shrewsbury from York on the twenty-seventh, John and Paul composed a new song called "From Me to You."

On March 1 the Helen Shapiro tour appeared at the Odeon Cinema in Southport.

The next day, as the tour arrived in Sheffield, "Please Please Me" became the Number 1 song on the *New Musical Express* and *Melody Maker* charts.

The tour's final engagement was on March 3 at the Gaumont Cinema in Hanley. The Beatles were just another band when the tour began. By now, they had become the star attraction to the ardent crowds whose adulation had grown with every show.

Gordon Sampson, a reporter who covered the tour, told his readers: "Helen Shapiro did her best to keep her fans happy by turning in a first-class performance every night. A great reception went to the colourfully-dressed Beatles, who almost stole the show, for the audience repeatedly called for them while other artists were performing!"

The Beatles returned to the Abbey Road studios in London on March 5 to record their next single, "From Me to You," and the B-side, "Thank You Girl." They also did a demo of an original composition, "Tip of My Tongue," for singer Tommy Quickly.

Facing page, left: The Beatles' second Parlophone single, signed by them to loyal fans Rita and Bel on March 7. *Facing page, right:* Rita and Bel before the show, that night. *This page:* The Beatles' van, same evening. Before the Beatles had chauffeured limousines, they had this van, which carried them everywhere. On this night, as on others, excited fans scrawled messages on the body and windows: "EDDY LOVES RINGO Please Please *Me,*" "ANN LOVES JOHN," "I Love George."

On the sixth the boys went to Manchester for their fifth and final "Here We Go" show. They sang "Please Please Me," "Do You Want to Know a Secret," and "I Saw Her Standing There." All but the last song were aired six days later.

Brian Epstein's fertile imagination spawned another money-making idea when he created the "Mersey Beat Showcase." It was a series of one-night stands featuring all the groups he managed. The first showcase—emceed by Bob Wooler—debuted March 7 at the Elizabethan Ballroom in Nottingham and starred the Beatles, Gerry and the Pacemakers, the Big Three, and Billy J. Kramer and the Dakotas.

Another big tour began March 9 starring two Americans—Tommy Roe and Chris Montez. At least they were the stars on opening night at London's Granada Cinema. Afterward, it was obvious to everyone in the entourage that the Beatles had stolen the show.

SCREAMS ACCLAIM BEATLES was the headline of the *New Musical Express* in a story by Andy Gray. "This all-action quartet from Liverpool has everything, exciting new sound, terrific instrumental attack, exhilarating solo and group vocal effects, and a fresh energy that leaves them limp at the end of each act.

"Admittedly they still need better production

and a good choreographer, tailor, and barber, but this apart they are the most exciting newcomers in Britain today."

During this tour the Beatles' repertoire consisted of "Love Me Do," "Misery," "A Taste of Honey," "Do You Want to Know a Secret," "Please Please Me," and "I Saw Her Standing There."

Other performers in the package were the Terry Young Six, the Viscounts, Tony Marsh, and Debbie Lee.

At every show the Beatles were greeted by screaming fans whose enthusiasm was so overwhelming that it suddenly became the Beatles' tour. Another "first" was added to their list of accomplishments. Although Tommy Roe and Chris Montez were the headliners, they were also from America, and no British act had *ever* topped an American act. The Beatles were clearly elated but also embarrassed when the crowds screamed for them instead of the American stars.

On March 11 the boys recorded their third and last "Friday Spectacular" show on Radio Luxembourg.

The tour continued the next day in Bedford minus John, who was in bed with the flu. Songs performed by the Beatles were rearranged so that John's lines could be done by Paul and George.

At the Rialto Theatre in York two days later, the

Program from the Chris Montez/Tommy Roe show, which included the Beatles. An ad in the program for the Beatles' soon to be released LP used a paste-up of the album design.

CHRIS MONTEZ AND TOMMY ROE

ARTHUR HOWES

in association with Evelyn Taylor presents

CHRIS MONTEZ
and
TOMMY ROE

with

THE VISCOUNTS
DEBBIE LEE
TONY MARSH
THE TERRY YOUNG SIX
and
THE BEATLES

flu bug struck again. The Beatles and the Terry Young Six both performed with one man missing. Lennon rejoined the tour at the Colston Hall in Bristol on the fifteenth.

On March 16 the Beatles appeared live on BBC's "Saturday Club" in London before performing that night in two shows in Sheffield.

During March 17–20 their performances thrilled the crowds in Peterborough, Gloucester, Cambridge, and Romford.

The boys made a quick trip to London on the twenty-first to record an appearance for the radio program "On the Scene," then rushed to meet the tour in West Croydon.

On March 22 the Beatles' first album, *Please Please Me* (Parlophone PMC 1202), was released in mono sound as the tour reached Doncaster. On the same day, "Misery" (HMV POP 1136) by Kenny Lynch was released. This Lennon-McCartney song had been turned down by Helen Shapiro in February, but Kenny thought it could be a hit for him.

On March 24 the tour reached the Beatles' hometown for their first show there in over a month. The boys always felt a little self-conscious whenever they performed in Liverpool.

"Being local heroes made us nervous," said John. "When we did shows there they were always full of people we knew. We felt embarrassed in our

suits and being very clean. We were worried that friends might think we'd sold out. Which we had, in a way."

During March 26–30 the tour performed in Mansfield, Northampton, Exeter, Lewisham, and Portsmouth.

On the twenty-ninth the Beatles' album debuted on the *New Musical Express* chart at Number 9.

The last day of March was also the last day of the Roe-Montez tour at DeMontfort Hall in Leicester, but there was no reprieve in the Beatles' incessant one-night stands throughout England.

On April Fool's Day they recorded two inserts for "Side By Side" in London. The resident band for this BBC show was the Karl Denver Trio, which opened every show with a guest band, after which each band would alternate solo performances during the half-hour program.

Two days later the boys recorded another appearance for "Easy Beat" at the BBC Playhouse Theatre.

One of the Beatles' most unusual bookings resulted from a letter to Brian Epstein from a Liverpool lad who wanted the popular quartet to perform for his class at Stowe School. Epstein arranged a date for April 4 at a fee of £100. This was the only show where the audience was exclusively made up of boys, who sat in dignified silence during a Beatles' performance.

1963

PLEASE PLEASE ME ★ THE BEATLES

mono

PARLOPHONE

THE BEATLES

PLEASE PLEASE ME

with Love Me Do and 12 other songs

Photo: Angus McBean

On the fifth, prior to a show at the Swimming Baths in Leyton, the group gave a "behind-closed-doors" performance to EMI executives after being awarded their first Silver Disc for the single "Please Please Me."

A significant event occurred soon after for one Beatle. In fact, it was a blessed event for John and Cynthia. Cynthia had been living with John's Aunt Mimi, pretending she was Cynthia Powell, a girl with no connection to the Beatles. On April 6, while shopping in Penny Lane, she began having labor pains and was taken to Sefton General Hospital. Two days later, at 7:45 A.M., she and John became the proud parents of John Charles Julian Lennon.

John was in London and phoned her that night.

He was delighted and promised to hurry home soon. Upon his arrival at the hospital he wore a disguise as he rushed through the public ward to Cynthia's private room. He didn't want to be identified as a Beatle, especially one with a wife and new baby. But the ruse failed. The Beatles were household names in Liverpool and some of the patients recognized him.

John was like any other father, deliriously happy and bursting with pride, exclaiming "bloody marvelous" to everyone. Naturally, Cynthia wanted John to spend some time with her and their new son, but Brian Epstein's relentless schedule precluded any family activities.

On April 12 the Beatles headlined another eight-hour rhythm & blues marathon at the Cavern; this was the day after their latest single, "From Me to You"/"Thank You Girl" (Parlophone R5015), was released. It entered the *Melody Maker* chart on April 20 at Number 19. Beginning May 4 it became the Number 1 song for six weeks and remained on the charts a total of twenty weeks before its final listing on August 31 at Number 43.

On the thirteenth the boys went to the Lime Grove studios in London for their first BBC-TV appearance on "The 625 Show." The program catered to promising new artists and the Beatles performed with all the other acts.

The next day, at the BBC-TV studio in Teddington, they recorded another insert for "Thank Your Lucky Stars." Afterward, they went to the Crawdaddy Club in Richmond to see a new group from London, the Rolling Stones.

Keith Fordyce reviewed "From Me to You" in the *New Musical Express:* "The singing and harmonizing are good and there's plenty of sparkle. The lyric is commercial, but I don't rate the tune as being anything as good as on the last two discs by this group." His opinion had no effect on the mass of fans racing to the record stores.

On April 15 the Beatles performed at the Riverside Dancing Club in Tenbury Wells, then hurried back to London the next day for a live TV appearance on "Scene at 6:30."

After a show at the Majestic Ballroom in Luton

Facing page: Cover of the Beatles' first LP—mono. *Top:* Rare first-pressing label of the Beatles' *Please Please Me,* released March 22. *Middle:* Cover of the extremely rare stereo issue of the Beatles' first LP. *Bottom:* Label of the stereo issue of the first album, released May 3.

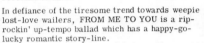

THE BEATLES

■ **GEORGE HARRISON** (lead guitar) ■ **JOHN LENNON** (rhythm guitar)
■ **PAUL McCARTNEY** (bass guitar) ■ **RINGO STARR** (drums)

HERE'S NEWS OF THAT EAGERLY-AWAITED NEW PARLOPHONE SINGLE WHICH
IS SURE TO GIVE THE BEATLES THEIR SECOND CONSECUTIVE CHART-TOPPER!

"FROM ME TO YOU"

coupled with

"THANK YOU GIRL"

Parlophone: R-5015   Released:Thursday 11 April 1963.

"FROM   ME   TO   YOU"

Words and Music: John Lennon and
Paul McCartney

Published by Northern Songs Limited

Vocally and instrumentally this new deck matches
the high spirits of PLEASE PLEASE ME with
John, Paul and George chanting and harmonising
expertly. BUT don't get the idea that this is a
carbon copy of their last single - in fact it is
the most unusual number THE BEATLES have
recorded to date.

In defiance of the tiresome trend towards weepie
lost-love wailers, FROM ME TO YOU is a rip-
rockin' up-tempo ballad which has a happy-go-
lucky romantic story-line.

EAR-CATCHING HIGH-SPOT: Those unexpected
falsetto-voice high-kicks on the line "If there's
anything I can do".

OFF-BEAT FINALE: Sudden switch of speed and
rhythm for that end-of-the-track instrumental
climax.

UNANIMOUS VERDICT: The sturdy beat plus the
unique Beatle-blending of harmonica, guitars and
voices plus the thoroughly infectious tune must
make FROM ME TO YOU another dead-cert
Number One chart-smasher!

SCHEDULE OF SUCCESS :: DATE-CRAMMED DIARY FOR THE BEATLES!

The Beatles have already completed major 1963 concert tours with Helen
Shapiro and with the Tommy Roe/Chris Montez package. They've a strenuous
but exciting schedule of top bookings ahead of them including................

......THESE APRIL RADIO AND TELEVISION DATES - THANK YOUR
LUCKY STARS (ABC Television) EASY BEAT (BBC Light) TUESDAY
RENDEZVOUS (A-R TV) THE 6.25 SHOW (BBC TV) SIDE BY SIDE (BBC
Light) and SWINGIN' SOUND '63 which is the second of three BBC Light
Programme pop shows to be broadcast from the Royal Albert Hall,
London, on Thursday 18 April.

......AN APPEARANCE BEFORE MORE THAN 10,000 FANS AT THE EMPIRE
POOL, WEMBLEY in the NEW MUSICAL EXPRESS POLLWINNERS' CONCERT
OF 1963 on Sunday 21 April.   The same evening The Beatles have a special
guest appearance at the West End's smart nighterie THE PIGALLE, Piccadilly.

......A NATIONWIDE CONCERT TOUR OF BRITAIN WITH COUNTRY &
WESTERN VOCALIST ROY ORBISON plus GERRY AND THE PACEMAKERS.
The tour begins at Slough on Saturday 18 May and will visit 20 venues through-
out the country.

......TOP-OF-THE-BILL APPEARANCES IN A SERIES OF STAR-
STACKED STAGE SPECTACULARS ENTITLED "MERSEY BEAT
SHOWCASE". Organised by Nems Enterprises of Liverpool "MERSEY
BEAT SHOWCASE" will visit Britain's key towns and cities in April,
May and June. These spectaculars feature the cream of Merseyside's
recording groups including GERRY AND THE PACEMAKERS, THE BIG
THREE and BILLY J. KRAMER AND THE DAKOTAS. Dates range
from KINGS HALL, STOKE (Friday 19 April) and MAJESTIC, FINSBURY
PARK (Wednesday 24 April) to FAIRFIELD HALL, CROYDON (Thursday
25 April) and IMPERIAL, NELSON (Saturday 11 May).

......SUMMER SEASON SUNDAY CONCERTS AT LEADING SEASIDE RESORTS
including GREAT YARMOUTH, BLACKPOOL and TORQUAY.

EMI press release for the Beatles' third single,
released April 11, 1963.

on the seventeenth they shuffled back to London for another BBC special. The Beatles appeared with fifteen other acts on "Swingin' Sound '63," which was broadcast live from Royal Albert Hall on April 18. Afterward, Paul was introduced to Jane Asher, a devout Beatle fan.

On April 19 the boys appeared in the second "Mersey Beat Showcase" at King's Hall in Stoke. The next night they were in Frobsham for their first and only booking at the Mersey View Pleasure Grounds Ballroom. Other Liverpool groups had performed there for two years.

The Beatles' biggest date came on April 21, when they played at the *New Musical Express* Poll Winners' Concert in Wembley. Cliff Richard headed the fourteen-act all-star show, and although the Beatles had not won a poll, they appeared as the penultimate act on the strength of their two recent chart-topping singles. During a performance before 8,000 eager fans they sang "Please Please Me," "From Me to You," "Twist and Shout," and "Long Tall Sally."

That evening they were back in London for a one-time only show at the Pigalle Club, a chic restaurant that would soon become the "in" place for the Mod crowd.

Gerry and the Pacemakers joined the Beatles on April 24 for the fourth "Mersey Beat Showcase" before an audience of 2,000 at Finsbury Park. The fifth "Showcase" took place the next night in Croydon.

Finally, it was playtime! On April 28 Paul, George, and Ringo were off for a well-deserved holiday in Santa Cruz de Tenerife, while John, without his wife and baby, and Brian Epstein hopped aboard a jet to Spain.

On May 1 the Beatles were on the cover of *Hit Parade,* and their smiling faces had graced the covers of nearly every pop magazine throughout April. Two days later their chart-topping Number 1 album, *Please Please Me,* was released in stereo.

The boys returned to Liverpool from their vacation on the ninth and plunged into a series of shows in Nelson, Sunderland, Chester, and Northwich, plus a live performance for a BBC-TV children's show, "Pops and Lenny," on May 16.

The Roy Orbison–Beatles Tour began two days later at the Aldelphi Cinema in Slough. It was the boys' third United Kingdom tour in as many months.

Although Rob Orbison was the headliner, the Beatles quickly captured that position when it be-

Top: Promo label of the Beatles' third record. *Above:* Only the first-pressing labels of "From Me to You" had this smaller type-style.

came obvious that the four lads were the crowds' favorites. It became the Beatles' tour after the first week and souvenir program covers were reprinted, placing the Beatles' name above Roy Orbison's. Their repertoire consisted of "Some Other Guy," "Do You Want to Know a Secret," "Love Me Do," "From Me to You," "I Saw Her Standing There," and "Twist and Shout."

Even though the Beatles were being mobbed at theaters and hotels, Roy Orbison was getting his fair share of adulation from audiences. "We would be backstage," said Ringo, "listening to the tremendous applause he was getting. He was just doing it by his voice. Just standing there singing, not moving or anything."

Although Brian Epstein had miraculously changed the boys' wardrobe and presentation to reflect a more polished act, the group had not completely succumbed to his influence. They were still goofing off onstage, ad-libbing when equipment failed, and having lots of fun with the audiences. Maureen Cleave of the London *Evening Standard* said, "It was like living it up with the four Marx Brothers."

The Beatles were unable to rest during a tour break on May 22 and spent six hours in London, recording a pair of BBC music inserts for "Saturday Club" and "Steppin' Out."

Their popularity on various radio and television shows prompted BBC executives to give the boys their own radio show, to be aired on Tuesday evenings. The half-hour program of music, which was called "Pop Go the Beatles," became so successful that a total of fifteen were produced, beginning May 24.

Also on that day Polydor Records in London reissued a former single that was announced in the *New Musical Express:* "You may have noticed a new Beatles' single in the shops this week. It isn't a new recording, but was actually taped in 1961, while the boys were in Hamburg. And the lead singer on the record isn't one of the Beatles but rock 'n' roller Tony Sheridan! The single 'My Bonnie'/'The Saints' (Polydor NH 66833) . . . was actually released in Britain last year on January 5th, 1962, credited to Tony Sheridan and the Beatles. It wasn't a hit then (except in Germany, where it made the local Top Ten) but Polydor obviously feels it stands a much better chance second time around—especially with the Beatles at No. 1!"

On May 26 the Beatles made their first hometown appearance in more than six weeks when the tour played the Empire Theatre. After that show, a fan who worked at NEMS said what all local fans felt about the group's success. "In the expert opinion of our little lot . . . we were seeing our Beatles in a completely different light. They were still *our* Beatles so far as the music was concerned, but we were in a vast theatre, a far more formal atmosphere than the Cavern, and we were a long

way away from John, Paul, George, and Ringo. We could feel the change in them as they returned to Liverpool. They were touring celebrities now. We didn't feel they were letting us down by leaving Liverpool but things would never be the same."

The next day, Vee Jay Records in America released its second Beatles single, "From Me to You"/"Thank You Girl" (Vee Jay 522). It instantly became the "Pick of the Week" in *Cash Box.*

A wave of excitement hit Liverpool on the heels of a rumor that a live version of "Some Other Guy" had been released as the new Beatles single. Anxious fans, however, soon discovered that the record was not for sale. Granada TV had recorded the boys during a show at the Cavern last year and had produced a few copies of the song as demo discs. A few of these demos had inadvertently turned up in local record stores.

Meanwhile, Chris Hutchins reviewed the tour for the *New Musical Express:* "As was expected, the Beatles virtually raised the roof, although little could be heard of them above the screams. . . . The Beatles prove again on this tour that they are currently the most exciting entertainers in the country."

On June 1 the boys spent eight hours recording two radio shows for "Pop Go the Beatles" and appeared that evening at the Tooting Granada in London.

Songs by Lennon-McCartney were so popular that they quickly attracted other artists. The Kestrels followed up their version of "There's a Place" by including "Please Please Me" on their new album. Bobby Sansom recorded "There's a Place," while "Misery" was the latest single by Dick Rivers, and French singer Johnny Halliday had released "I Saw Her Standing There."

"From Me to You," recorded in America on Bigtop Records by Del Shannon, was released on June 3. Vee Jay executives were worried. They had released the Beatles version of the same song only eight days earlier and feared that Shannon's cover would become the bigger hit, since he was more well known in America than the four boys from Liverpool. Their fears came true.

The Beatles-Orbison tour continued with shows in Brixton, Woolwich, Birmingham, Leeds, Glasgow, Newcastle, and came to an end on the ninth at King's Hall in Blackburn.

However, there was no break for the Beatles, because they played the Pavilion in Bath the next night, then rushed to Liverpool for a special chil-

The cover of the March 28 *Mersey Beat* mentioned the Beatles' first LP.

dren's charity show at Grafton Rooms on June 12.

One Liverpool fan thought it was like old times. "The Grafton was a relatively intimate place, big but much more friendly than the Empire and no orchestra pit keeping people away from the stage. When the doors opened we all made a dive for the front. A good 'spec' was vital so that we wouldn't miss a thing. We managed to get ourselves into a wonderful spot right in the center immediately in front of the stage. The tension was incredible.

"Bob Wooler [the emcee] spoke but his voice floated over our minds. Nothing mattered until *they* came on the stage. All of a sudden the four were ambling towards us. They fooled around a bit as usual and we knew at once that it was going to be much better than the Empire. George said 'hello' and the others nodded in our direction. I wondered if they were really glad to see old friends after so long away from the Cavern crowd.

"All too soon they were on their last number. They just did their forty-minute set and left. Instantly, the withdrawal symptoms set in. There was no way we could have a 'natter' with them after the Grafton show as we always did at the Cavern."

A double show occurred on the thirteenth. First, at the Palace Theatre Club in Offerton, and then ten miles away at the Southern Sporting Club in Manchester.

An enthusiastic audience was on hand at New Brighton's Tower Ballroom on June 14 as the Beatles joined Gerry and the Pacemakers for another "Mersey Beat Showcase."

A crowd of 1,500 welcomed the Beatles for their first appearance at City Hall in Salisbury the next day. It was the largest audience ever to attend a local show for any group.

Another "Mersey Beat Showcase" was presented on June 16 in Romford. It was the only time in which the show's three top stars occupied Numbers 1, 2, and 3 on that week's *New Musical Express* music chart.

It was also a magnificent achievement for their producer, George Martin. He became the first A&R man ever to have the top three songs on the weekly singles chart. The hits that brought the honor were "From Me to You," by the Beatles, "Do You Want to Know a Secret" by Billy J. Kramer, and "I Like It" by Gerry and the Pacemakers.

The Beatles were back in the BBC studios on the

Program for the Beatles/Roy Orbison show.

seventeenth to record their fourth "Pop Go the Beatles" show.

June 18 was Paul McCartney's twenty-first birthday. He was unable to have his party at home because all of the Beatles' groupies knew where he lived. So the festivities were held at his Aunt Jin's house in Birkenhead. The affair turned into a drunken orgy that resulted in some adverse publicity for the boys—not because everyone was drunk as a lord, but owing to a fight between John Lennon and Bob Wooler.

Heavy drinking and noisy quarrels were common at parties for musicians and a bit of revelry was always part of the fun. This time was different. John was livid about a comment made by Bob Wooler and began using the popular disc jockey's face as a punching bag. Wooler was injured more than anyone suspected.

As John marched out of the house he saw Billy J. Kramer and Billy Hatton of the Fourmost talking with a girl.

"John had really had a skinful," said Kramer, "and he grabbed the girl. She shoved him away and he swore at her so I persuaded him to calm down. Cynthia came out and she was in tears and she asked us if we could put John in a taxi. So we did."

John's aggressive nature was well known and he loved to argue with anyone. Wooler, however, presented a gentlemanly image and a reputation for good humor.

John refused to apologize or feel any remorse.

"You know as well as I do what happened," John told Tony Barrow, their press agent. "The bastard called me a bloody queer so I punched him one. It wasn't the drink that made him say it and I wasn't pissed when I smacked him for it. He just went too far. I'm not having that sort of thing, Tony, and I don't care what the papers make of it!"

Tony Barrow discussed the incident with Brian Epstein, who was very upset and thought that John should have exercised more control. Barrow sent a harmless press release that revealed nothing to the media.

"I guess Lennon has lost a few friends," Barrow told Epstein, "but no professional disaster is involved here. I do believe that both the Beatles and John will survive this little summer crisis." And they did.

On June 19, still suffering from hangovers, the Beatles were in London to do another "Easy Beat" show.

Top: Promo label of the Beatles' second Vee Jay record, side A. *Above:* Commercial label, side B.

Three days later, road manager Neil Aspinall took Paul, George, and Ringo to Wales in the van. John stayed in London to record an appearance for "Juke Box Jury" on BBC-TV. After reviewing songs by various artists he flew to Abergavenny in a chartered helicopter, arriving just in time to join the others for a show at Town Hall.

On June 23 the Beatles filmed a segment for a special All-Liverpool edition of "Thank Your Lucky Stars." On the twenty-fourth they did six songs for "Saturday Club" and played the next night in Middlesbrough.

The June 25 issue of *Cash Box* featured an article about Vee Jay Records, announcing their fall LP releases, which included *Introducing the Beatles.*

The boys gave their final Majestic Ballroom performance in Newcastle on June 26. After the show John and Paul wrote the group's next single, "She Loves You."

"John and I wrote it together," said Paul. "I thought of it first and thought of doing it as one of those answering songs. You know, the sort of thing the American singing groups keep doing. A couple of us would sing 'she loves you' and the others would do the 'yeah yeah yeah' lines. The one would be answering everything the other two sang. Then John and I agreed it was a pretty crummy idea as it stood and since we were borrowing an American thing, I suppose it was crummy. But at least we had the basic idea of writing the song. That night in Newcastle we just sat in the hotel bedroom for a few hours and wrote it."

Two days later, more than 3,000 excited fans jammed the Queen's Hall in Leeds to hear the Beatles, plus Acker Bilk and his Paramount Jazz Band.

On June 29, John's appearance on "Juke Box Jury" was aired and created a storm of controversy. Apparently, John's candid remarks angered a lot of viewers, and his opinions about Elvis's new song stunned Presley fans. John was not impressed with "Devil in Disguise." He said that Elvis was "today's Bing Crosby" and that "he ought to return to the rock 'n' roll material that made him famous."

Angry fans claimed that John was in no position to criticize anyone as successful as Elvis and should have shown more respect for such an important figure. Lennon's supporters replied that it was pointless for John to appear on the show if he could not honestly say what he thought. Elvis, however, had the last laugh because "Devil in Disguise" was then Number 2 on most music charts.

The Beatles were on a roll. Besides their weekly radio show, the music newspapers—*Melody Maker, New Musical Express, New Record Mirror,* and *Disc*—were smothering fans with stories about the boys' frantic recording and performance activities. Magazines for teenage girls offered weekly features, interviews, and color posters of the popular quartet. And the Beatles reigned supreme on the music charts.

Throughout June and July they were doing shows for contracts written back in March, long before the emergence of the screaming crowds that now idolized them. Brian Epstein, a fair and honest entrepreneur, honored each agreement at the originally established fee. He never canceled a show by using the "illness" ploy, and he never reneged on a booking. Epstein was known everywhere for his integrity and exemplary business dealings.

On July 1 the Beatles went to the studio on Abbey Road and recorded "She Loves You" and "I'll Get You."

The next day they did their fifth "Pop Go the Beatles" show and sang "That's All Right," which was Elvis Presley's first single for Sun Records, "There's a Place," "Soldier of Love," "Carol," "Lend Me Your Comb," "Clarabella," "Three Cool Cats," "Sweet Little Sixteen," and "Ask Me Why." These songs allowed the boys to demonstrate their versatility as singers, yet seven of these numbers never were commercially released as Beatles records.

On July 3 they did another "Beat Show" at the Playhouse Theatre and made their second appearance at the Plaza Ballroom in Oldhill on the fifth. Also on the bill was Denny and the Diplomats, led by Denny Laine, who would later sing with the Moody Blues before joining Paul McCartney's post-Beatle band, Wings.

Prior to their performance at Memorial Hall in Northwich on the sixth, the Beatles created a near riot when they attended the annual Northwich Carnival at Verdin Park, where Paul crowned the new carnival queen.

The next day was Ringo's twenty-third birthday, but there was no celebration because the Beatles had to play in Blackpool.

During July 8 through 13 the Beatles appeared twice nightly at the Winter Gardens in Margate. They taped two "Pop Go the Beatles" shows on the tenth in London, then rushed back to Margate.

The *New Musical Express* reported that the "Liverpudlian invasion of the Kent Coast was a tremendous success." Packed audiences of screaming teens applauded each performance by the Beatles and Billy J. Kramer and the Dakotas. An unbelievable reaction occurred whenever the Beatles were introduced to the explosive crowds. An estimated 20,000 people were exposed to the

Beatles' special style and music during the Margate shows.

On July 12 two EPs by the Beatles went on sale. One was authorized by their company, and one was released by another firm in hopes of attracting sales based on the boys' current success.

The first EP, *Twist and Shout* (Parlophone GEP 8882), was released three weeks ahead of schedule. It contained "Twist and Shout," "A Taste of Honey," "Do You Want to Know a Secret," and "There's a Place." The decision for the early release came from EMI executives after the EP's title song was covered as a single by Brian Poole and the Tremelos. EMI did not wish it to eclipse the Beatles' version, which had become a show-stopping highlight of their stage act.

The second EP was . . . *My Bonnie* (Polydor EPH 21-610). It included the title song plus "Why," "Cry for a Shadow," and "The Saints." All of the songs were recorded in Germany by John, Paul, George, and Pete Best when they served as backup artists for Tony Sheridan, who did the lead vocals.

An ad for Lybro jeans in *Mersey Beat*. Could anyone resist "The BEATLES view of the MERSEYSIDE Jean-scene"?

Twist and Shout debuted on the EP chart on July 27 in the Number 14 position and peaked at Number 2 on August 17. The EP was on the charts for thirty-one weeks and last appeared on February 29, 1964, at Number 48.

The busy Beatles recorded three editions of their radio show on July 16, followed by another "Easy Beat" appearance the next day.

On the eighteenth they were back on Abbey Road to record four songs for their second album.

Earlier, Paul and George had visited the office of Beatles press agent Tony Barrow. They brought him a copy of "She Loves You," because Barrow didn't like to sit in during recording sessions. "I found long sessions very, very boring, and much worse, they give an outsider, a nonmusician, a falsely optimistic impression of new songs," said Barrow. "You hear a fresh title a dozen or more times in the studio and even if it's rubbish you tend to come away from the session humming the theme and quite convinced you've just heard a number-one hit in the making. I prefer to wait until Brian Epstein or somebody in the group brings an acetate into the office for me to hear. Often it's not the finished product but it gives you a fair idea. I like to hear it once or twice and no more. That's the only chance record reviewers and radio producers give each new release."

During an interview with Tony Barrow, Paul discussed writing songs for the Beatles. "What John and I normally do is start off songs on our own," said Paul. "I go away and write something or he does. It would be daft to sit around waiting for a partner to finish your song off with you. If you

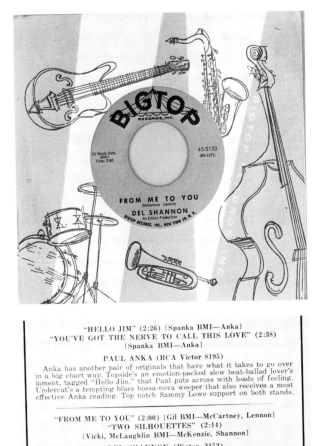

"HELLO JIM" (2:26) [Spanka BMI—Anka]
"YOU'VE GOT THE NERVE TO CALL THIS LOVE" (2:38)
[Spanka BMI—Anka]

PAUL ANKA (RCA Victor 8195)

Anka has another pair of originals that have what it takes to go over in a big chart way. Topside's an emotion-packed slow beat-ballad lover's lament, tagged "Hello Jim," that Paul puts across with loads of feeling. Undercut's a tempting blues bossa-nova weeper that also receives a most effective Anka reading. Top notch Sammy Lowe support on both stands.

"FROM ME TO YOU" (2:00) [Gil BMI—McCartney, Lennon]
"TWO SILHOUETTES" (2:14)
[Vicki, McLaughlin BMI—McKenzie, Shannon]

DEL SHANNON (Bigtop 3152)

Shannon, who recently did chart business with "Two Kinds Of Teardrops," can have another big one in "From Me To You." It's an infectious, thump-a-twist version of the tune that's currently riding in the number one slot in England—via the Beatles stand (available here on VJ). More of the top teen sounds on the cha cha twist "Two Silhouettes" coupler.

"I ALMOST LOST MY MIND" (2:12) [St. Louis, BMI—Hunter]
"STRAWBERRIES" (3:07) [Progressive BMI—Calabria]

JERRY BUTLER (Vee Jay 526)

The years-back Ivory Joe Hunter favorite, "I Almost Lost My Mind," can be in for another solid chart go-round. The reason is this striking new beat-ballad approach by Jerry Butler. Infectious instrumental

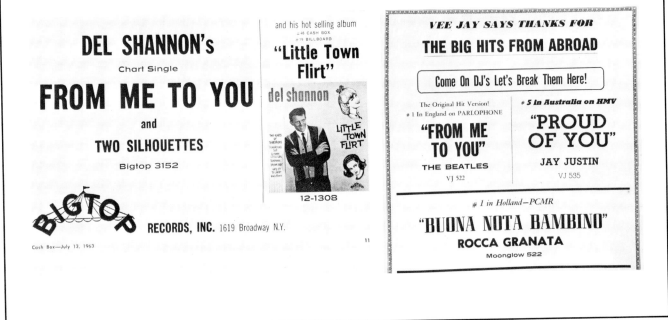

Facing page, top: Del Shannon was the first American recording artist to cover a Lennon-McCartney composition. *Facing page, middle:* The June *Cash Box* review of Del Shannon's "From Me to You." *Right:* On July 6, "From Me to You" entered the *Cash Box* Top 100 at Number 86. Number 1 that week was Kyu Sakamoto's "Sukiyaki." *Facing page, lower right:* Once the single entered the charts, Vee Jay advertised "The Original Hit Version!" in their publicity.

happen to be on your own, you might as well get it finished yourself. If I get stuck on the middle eight, if I can't get a middle bit for a new number, I give up, knowing that when I see John he will finish it for me. He'll bring a new approach to it and that particular song will finish up half and half, Lennon and McCartney. It really will be a fifty-fifty job."

A pair of sellout shows took place on July 19–20 at the Ritz Ballroom in Rhyl, Wales, then on to the Queen's Theatre in Blackpool on the twenty-first.

The Merseyside sound was quickly spreading. Recording executives were signing up Liverpool groups at an incredible pace, thus proving the extent to which the Liverpool beat had influenced other bands. The Beatles' special style was starting to appear in songs by other artists, who openly admitted a debt to the Fab Four.

From July 22 to 27 the Beatles, Gerry and the Pacemakers, and Tommy Quickly appeared at the Weston-Super-Mare Odeon with the same astonishing success they had previously enjoyed in Margate.

The boys were in Great Yarmouth on July 28, then spent the next day recording more songs for their second album.

They did another "Saturday Club" on July 30 and sang "She Loves You" and "I'll Get You," which would become their fourth Parlophone single three weeks later. They closed out the month with a riotous performance at the Imperial Ballroom on the thirty-first.

Sales of the *Twist and Shout* EP began to astonish everyone. It was selling faster than any extended-play release in history, as 150,000 copies passed over the counter in the first four days after its release.

Alan Smith of *New Musical Express* suggested it would make a "knock-out single."

"No," replied Paul quickly. "It's not really single material. It's a bit too off-beat to be commercial."

"Another thing," added John. "If it came out as a single, think how often we'd have to perform it. All that shouting would tear my throat to ribbons!"

The Beatles recorded two editions of their popular radio show on August 1. Also, the first issue of *The Beatles Book Monthly* went on sale. Published by Sean O'Mahony and edited by Johnny Dean, this official magazine presented a vast selection of photos of, articles about, and interviews with the boys.

After a seven-week absence the Beatles returned to Liverpool on the second for their last show at the Grafton.

A memorable era came to an end at the Cavern Club on August 3. After 274 shows, over two and a half years, the Beatles gave their final performance on the stage that had been their launching pad to revolutionizing the pop music world. Tickets had sold out thirty minutes after going on sale July 21.

Afterward, Brian Epstein promised Bob Wooler, the emcee, that the Beatles would return someday. They never did. The club that had played such an important role in the Beatles' success was simply too small to accommodate the large crowds they now attracted. During the next three years the boys would appear in their hometown only four times.

The next night the Beatles played the Queen's Theatre in Blackpool. All of the entrances were jammed with fans and the boys had to sneak through a builder's yard, walk across some scaffolds, and descend through a trapdoor in the theater's roof to get inside.

As audiences became more maniacal they created dangerous situations that could easily involve bodily harm to the lads. The worst part was

Above: "My Bonnie," now by Tony Sheridan and the Beatles, was re-released in England in June. *Facing page:* The second anniversary issue of *Mersey Beat* showed the Beatles in their soon-to-be-famous collarless suits.

getting them from the stage to their van. Neil Aspinall, the loyal road manager, had been doing his best to shield the boys, but hazards continued to intensify. Although they were enjoying a string of Number 1 hits, they were still a few months away from chauffeured limos and a platoon of policemen to protect them from crazed fans. A decision was made to give Aspinall an assistant, and that's when Mal Evans joined the team. A former bouncer at the Cavern, "Big Mal" became an essential part of the Beatles' lives and was very popular with everyone.

An interesting bill was presented on August 5 as the Beatles headlined a four-act show in Urmston. Among the groups was Brian Poole and the Tremelos, who had beat the Beatles out of a contract after the auditions at Decca Records in 1962.

The boys went to Jersey on the sixth for four shows at the Springfield Ballroom. On the eighth they flew thirty miles to Guernsey for a sellout show at Candie Auditorium, then rushed back to Jersey on the tenth for the last two shows of that engagement.

On August 12 the Beatles began a week at the Odeon Cinema in Llandudno, Wales. On the fourteenth they made a quick trip to Manchester to film a TV segment for "Scene at 6:30."

On August 18 they sang "She Loves You" and "I'll Get You" for the radio show "Thank Your Lucky Stars—Summer Spin."

A week at the Gaumont Theatre in Bournemouth began on the nineteenth. That night the Beatles and Brian Epstein gave a wild party for Billy J. Kramer's twentieth birthday.

During one performance at the Gaumont an over-eager fan tossed a five-inch metal pin toward the stage and nearly hit Paul's face. Epstein was getting worried.

Johnny Dean of *The Beatles Book Monthly* presented his view of a concert. "Anyone near a Beatles show knows that all they have to do is mention one of the Beatles' names to get an immediate reaction from the audience. As soon as they came on stage the screams immediately reached fever pitch and the sounds never really dropped until the boys were back in their dressing room forty minutes later.

"Standing at the side of the stage in Bournemouth was a bit like watching four people playing to a volcano. Everything they did brought great roars of approval and any extra movement or sound produced an immediate reaction which at

MERSEY BEAT 6d

Vol. 2. No. 52   JULY 18—AUGUST 1, 1963

HIT PARADE 'SCOUSERS'

Top left: THE BEATLES. Bottom left: THE SWINGING BLUE JEANS. Right: THE SEARCHERS.   —Photographs by GRAHAM SPENCER (MBX)

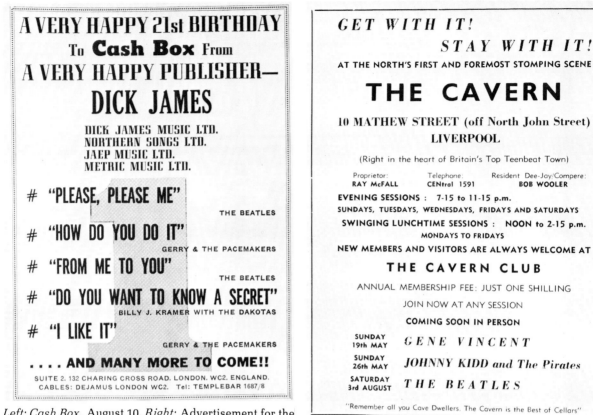

Left: Cash Box, August 10. *Right:* Advertisement for the Beatles' final Cavern performance, August 3, 1963.

times threatened to overwhelm them. The Beatles had made the transition from the small, crowded clubs where they used to play, to these enormous stages with consummate ease. They cope with a huge auditorium just as easily as they did at a small club. After their final song they hurry to their dressing room to an absolute pandemonium of screaming from the audience."

The Beatles took a break on the twenty-first and spent the morning and afternoon remixing new songs at Abbey Road.

"She Loves You"/"I'll Get You" (Parlophone R5055) was released August 23. It debuted on the *New Musical Express* chart seven days later at Number 2. The song was Number 1 for five weeks beginning September 7, then dipped as low as Number 4 for several weeks. It hit Number 1 again for two weeks on November 23 and last appeared on April 4, 1964, at Number 47.

The Beatles were in Blackpool's ABC Theatre on the twenty-fifth. The next day Paul McCartney lost his driving privileges. For his third speeding con-

viction, he was fined £25 and banned from driving for a year by the Wallasey Crown Court. The Beatles began a week at the Odeon Cinema in Southport that night.

On the morning of August 27 they gave a private performance in Southport for a BBC-TV crew who were filming a documentary called "The Mersey Sound." The producers had tried to film the boys during a show at the Odeon but their voices were overwhelmed by the screaming crowd.

Brian Matthew, deejay for the "Saturday Club," quipped: "If the Beatles made a disc of themselves snoring for two minutes, it'd go to Number One!"

"She Loves You" was released to rave reviews in Australia on August 29. Although "From Me to You" had been a Top 10 song there, the Beatles were not even close to matching the overseas success of Gerry and the Pacemakers, who had scored high in every market except the United States.

On September 1 the Beatles were on the "Big Night Out" television show and the next day "She Loves You" reached the half-million mark in sales—eight days after its release.

On the third the boys spent nine exhausting hours at London's BBC studios taping the final three editions of their radio show.

During September 4 through 7 they performed to excited fans in Worcester, Taunton, Luton, and Croydon.

The Beatles made another "Big Night Out" appearance and another "Saturday Club" appearance on the seventh, then wowed the crowd at Blackpool's ABC Theatre the next night.

The *Daily Mirror* for September 10 featured an article by Donald Zec headlined FOUR FRENZIED LITTLE LORD FAUNTLEROYS WHO ARE EARNING 5,000 POUNDS A WEEK! Though in the article, Zec wrote, "I doubt if one single Beatle is earning 5,000 pounds unless you include a hefty estimate of Lennon & McCartney writing royalties. The stone-age hair style boys are as nice a group of well-mannered music makers as you'll find perforating the eardrum anywhere."

One year to the day after recording "Love Me Do," the Beatles returned to the familiar studio on Abbey Road on the eleventh and spent two days recording additional songs for their next album.

As a special tribute to the beat sound that had swept the country, *Melody Maker* published a huge *Big Beat Boys* magazine on September 12. It was filled with stories of all the Merseyside music makers and had a cover photo of the Beatles.

On the thirteenth the boys performed at Public Hall in Preston. Afterward, Paul took a twenty-five-mile journey to Nelson and participated as a judge in a contest to select the new Imperial Miss of 1963.

Two days later the Beatles headlined the "Great Pop Prom," a twelve-act show at London's Royal Albert Hall. The affair was sponsored by three magazines to assist the Printers' Pension Corporation. Included on the bill were the Rolling Stones.

On September 16 "She Loves You"/"I'll Get You" (Swan 4152) was released in the United States. Gil Music had acquired the rights from EMI in August and planned to have the Beatles record station breaks for use on key radio stations.

On the nineteenth, Swan Records began a modest crusade against the serious school dropout problem among teenagers. Special labels with the advice "Don't Drop Out" were used on subsequent copies of "She Loves You," and Swan executives promised that the slogan would appear on all of their future single releases. Tony Mammarella of

Swan's promotional department said in *Cash Box:* "It will not sell any records for us, but it might be a good reminder to deejays and record buyers that dropping out of school is not the wise thing to do."

Also on the nineteenth, *Cash Box* picked "She Loves You" as the "Newcomer of the Week."

Since all work and no play can put you in a padded room, the Beatles began a two-week vacation on the same day that "She Loves You" appeared in American music stores.

George Harrison crossed the Atlantic to visit his sister in St. Louis, Missouri. "I've wanted to go there for years," said George, "but I could never afford it before. Also, this may be my last chance for a while, cause it may be ages before the Beatles can get two weeks free again. America's the country to visit. It's so big and so modern, and so swing-

Mersey Beat ad for Tommy Quickly's recording of "another smash hit from the sensational song writing team of John Lennon and Paul McCartney." (The issue is dated August 1–15, 1936!)

A BEAT MONTHLY PUBLICATION

The Beatles BOOK

London Office :
244 EDGWARE ROAD, LONDON, W2

POSTAL SUBSCRIPTION:
£1-1-0 per annum

AUGUST 1963

World Copyright Reserved

EDITOR: JOHNNY DEAN

Editorial

Hi!

I MUST BEGIN my first editorial for The Beatles Book by thanking all of you who wrote to me, or to The Beatles themselves, because it was your letters more than anything else, which helped to give GEORGE, JOHN, PAUL and RINGO their very own monthly magazine.

I, PERSONALLY, am very honoured to be their editor, because I think they're just about the greatest thing that ever happened to British pop music.

IN THIS FIRST ISSUE each of the boys, and their manager Brian Epstein, have a short introductory feature. Later on, we'll be giving you the full story on each of them in turn. But that will take quite a few editions of The Beatles Book.

ALSO IN No. 1 are the "firsts" of many regular features—The Official Beatles Fan Club Newsletter by Anne Collingham—This Month's Beatle Song—Beatle News—Letters from Beatle People—AND, of course, lots and lots of the best pics we can lay our hands on.

THE BEATLES are all wonderful performers and personalities and I'll always try and give each of them one quarter of the Book. In some issues this may not be possible and you will find that one of the boys hasn't got as many pics as the others. But, don't worry, because I'll make it up to him in the following edition.

IF YOU HAVE any comments or suggestions to make for YOUR Beatles Book don't forget to write them down and send them to me.

LETTERS to The Beatles, themselves, or applications to join the Fan Club, on the other hand, should always be sent direct to Monmouth Street, where the Fan Club lives.

I MUST JUST mention that in No. 2 we will be starting "A TALE OF FOUR BEATLES." This is the true story of their fantastic rise to success and something you won't want to miss. Plus all the goodies I've already mentioned.

See you soon.

Johnny Dean
Editor.

Beatle People rushing to get autographs when the boys and George Martin arrived at the recording studios to record their next single "She Loves You."

in' too. My brother Peter is coming with me. We shall spend most of the time in St. Louis and a few days in New York."

John and Cynthia Lennon decided to spend their time in Paris. "My reason for going there," said John, "is that I did the trip two years ago when I was near enough broke. I hitched most of the way and stayed in some pretty low dumps. Now I want to see what it's like being there with money in your pocket."

Paul and Ringo went to Greece. Paul joked that he went "to have all my teeth out" while Ringo was along "to get my toenails tattooed." Actually, Greece had been suggested as a great holiday spot by their producer, George Martin.

The Beatles came home on October 2. The next night Ringo went to the Southend Odeon to see a show starring the Everly Brothers, Bo Diddley, and the Rolling Stones.

After a live appearance on a new television show called "Ready, Steady, Go" on the fourth, the Beatles prepared for a minitour of Scotland October 5–7. They were mobbed at Glasgow Concert Hall on the fifth and performed for more than 3,000 wild spectators in Kirkcaldy and Dundee.

October 9 was John Lennon's twenty-third birthday but the hectic schedule continued with an appearance on the "Ken Dodd Show." That evening the BBC aired "The Mersey Sound" television documentary that had been produced in September.

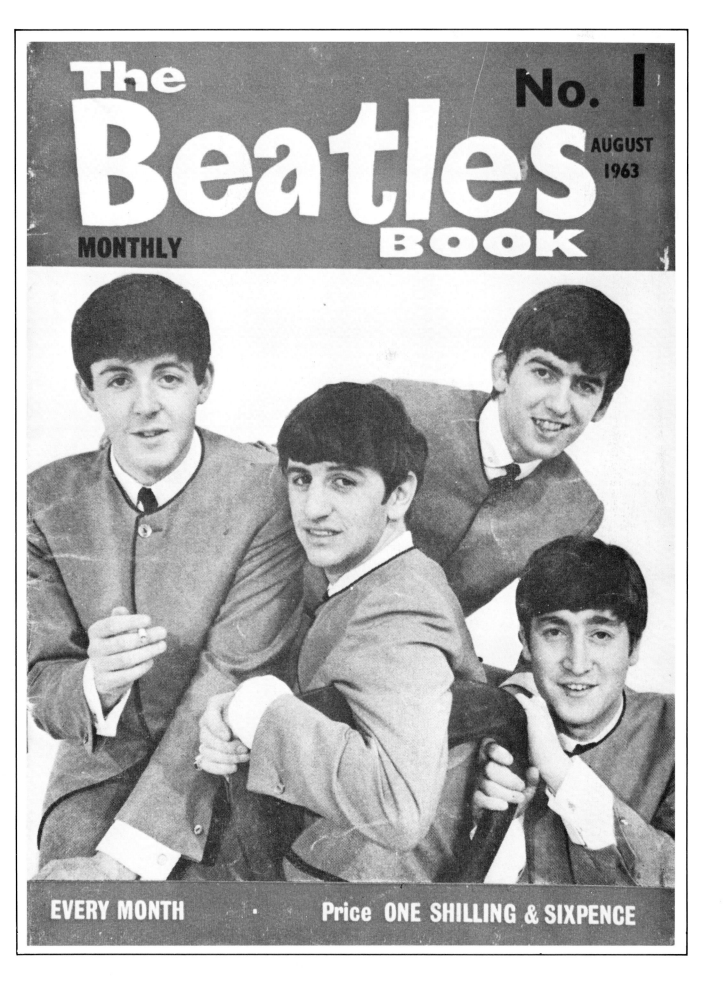

The Beatles won their first Gold Record on October 10, when it was officially confirmed that sales of "She Loves You" had exceeded one million. It was a very happy and proud moment. Three-quarters of the sales had been in England, with the remainder from around the world.

October 13 was the most significant day to date in the explosion of Beatles' fame. They were the stars on Britain's top-rated variety show, "Val Parnell's Sunday Night at the London Palladium," televised live nationwide. Fifteen million people saw the boys sing "I Want to Hold Your Hand," "This Boy," "All My Loving," "Money," and "Twist and Shout."

The next morning every national daily newspaper reported the spectacular show and one unknown Fleet Street headline writer coined the word "Beatlemania," which was instantly picked up by the entire media.

SIEGE OF THE BEATLES was the *Daily Herald* headline. The reporter told his readers: "Nearly 2,000 teenage girls, screaming 'We Want the Beatles' battled through a panting police cordon outside the London Palladium last night. The battle reached its climax minutes after the curtain came down at the close of ITV's Sunday Night at the

personally speaking

JOHN LENNON born 9th October, 1940, in Liverpool, is 5 ft. 11 in. tall, has brown eyes and brown hair, attended Quarry Bank High School in Liverpool, and Liverpool Art College.

He likes the colour black, steak and chips and jelly, admires the work of singers Carl Perkins, Chuck Berry, Ben E. King, The Shirelles, Larry Williams, Little Richard, The Miracles, Elvis Presley, Gene Vincent and Kay Starr. A long list of favourite film stars includes the names of Marlon Brando, Brigitte Bardot, Peter Sellers and Anthony Quinn, he likes clothes which are dark in colour—and suede and leather.

John Lennon plays harmonica, marraccas and "a bit of piano and banjo," and spends much of his spare time writing, playing records, and composing. He likes music, books, curries, painting, television and some modern jazz, and dislikes—thick heads and traditional jazz. His kind of girl must be blonde and intelligent, and for ambitions he lists "money and everything."

PAUL McCARTNEY born in Liverpool on 18th June, 1942, is 5 ft. 11 in. tall, has brown eyes, dark brown hair, and attended the Liverpool Institute. He likes the colour black, steak and chips, and follows the work of Ray Charles, Peggy Lee, Dinah Washington, Chuck Berry, Larry Williams, Little Richard, Carl Perkins and Fats Waller. His list of film stars also includes the names of Brando, Bardot, Peter Sellers and Anthony Quinn, and as far as clothes are concerned favours back polo necked sweaters, suits, leather and suede. He also plays "a bit of piano, drums, guitar and banjo," and enjoys music, reading and writing songs. He dislikes false and soft people, shaving, likes music, television, drums and cars and any type of girl—except soft ones. He, too, is clear on his ambition—"money, etc."

GEORGE HARRISON born 25th February, 1943, in Liverpool, is 5 ft. 11 ins., has hazel eyes and dark brown hair, and attended the Liverpool Institute. He likes the colours blue black, enjoys egg and chips, Whispering Paul McDowell, Carl Perkins and Eartha Kitt, and wants nothing more than to retire with lots of money. He likes casual clothes, Alfred Hitchcock, and goes for the girl who is blonde and smallish. In his spare time you will find George around either records, the guitar, or girls. He plays one-finger piano, likes driving and television, and dislikes having his hair cut and travelling on buses.

RINGO STARR born 7th July, 1940, in Liverpool is 5 ft. 8 in. tall, has blue eyes and brown hair. He went to St. Silas and Dingle Vale Secondary Modern School, likes the colour black steak and chips, Ray Charles and Dinah Washington, Paul Newman and Brigitte Bardot, and sleek suits and ties. Educated at the same school—and in the same class—as Billy Fury, Ringo lists girls, drums and cars as his hobbies, and says that his type of girl must be 5 ft. 5 in. blonde and well built. He dislikes onions, tomatoes, Chinese food, motor bikes and Donald Duck, and likes fast cars, mother and father—and anyone who likes him.

Program and tickets from the August "Beatles Show" (through p. 149). Val Davies went to all six of the Bournemouth shows, Monday through Saturday!

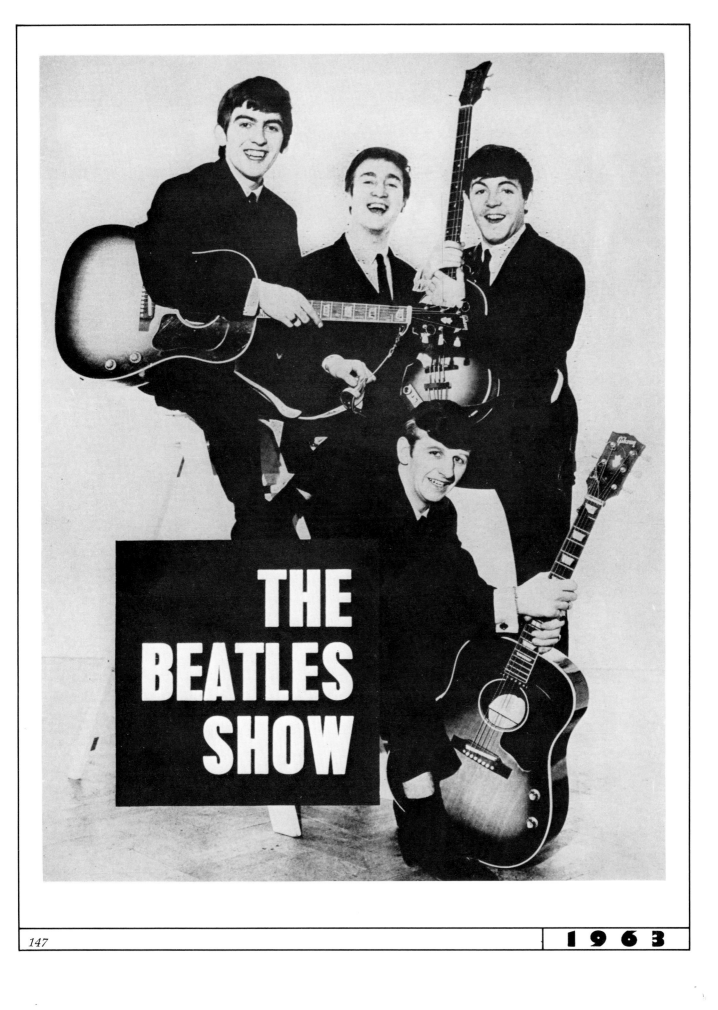

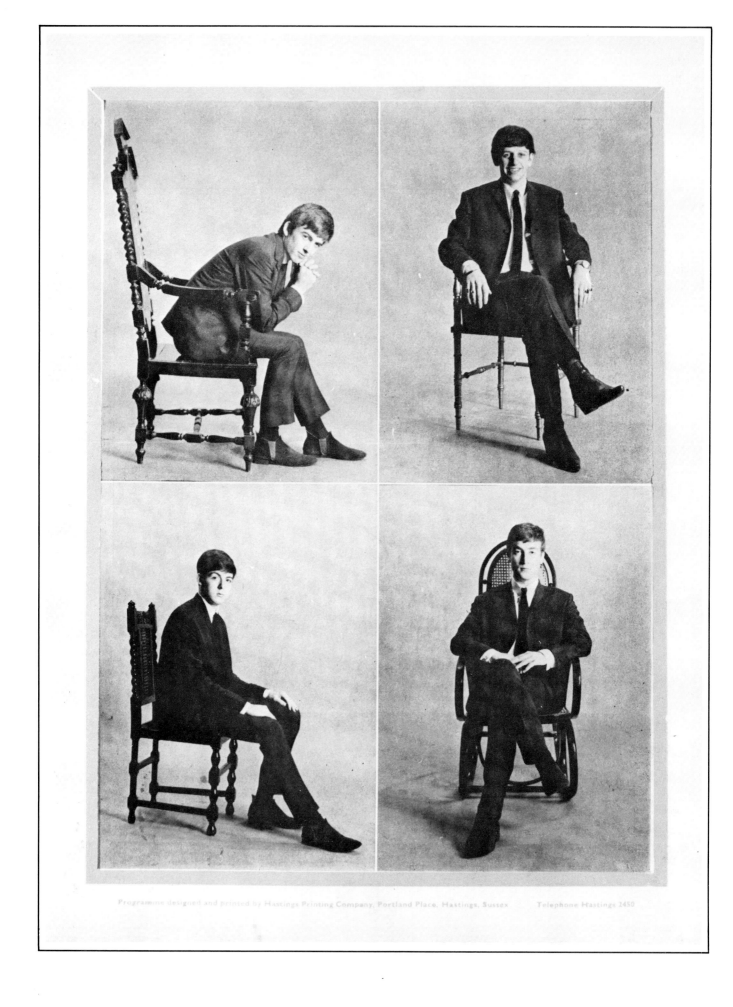

Programme designed and printed by Hastings Printing Company, Portland Place, Hastings, Sussex   Telephone Hastings 2450

Palladium. Since mid-morning, Liverpool's Beatles group . . . had been prisoners in the Palladium while the teenagers surged outside. Extra police stood at the gangways while more sealed off the stage door.

"But when the Beatles, with their bobbed haircuts, finished their twelve-minute act, the trouble really started. Screaming girls launched themselves against the police—sending helmets flying and constables reeling. Police vans sealed off the front of the theatre so that the Beatles could be smuggled out. The pop group dived down the theatre steps into a car. The teenagers charged forward and the Beatles' car went off into Oxford Street chased by the crowd.

"Stage-doorman George Cooper said: 'There's been nothing like it since American singer Johnnie Ray came here in 1955.' "

The Beatles had reached another peak—they were now England's biggest pop music stars. Tony Barrow, the Beatles' press agent, said the event was a publicist's dream. "Fifteen million viewers may have watched the actual Palladium show, but up to twice that number of people all over the nation saw the following morning's 'Beatlemania' stories. From that day on my job had changed. From spending six months ringing up newspapers and getting 'no' I now had every national reporter and feature writer chasing *me*. The birth of 'Beatlemania' went international, those amazing Palladium pictures making space in newspapers around the world. It was also revealed that the Beatles would appear on November 4 in the 1963 Royal Variety Performance at London's Prince of Wales Theatre. The papers started falling over themselves to include maximum coverage of the Beatles in almost every day's issues."

The Beatles appeared at Floral Hall in Southport on the fifteenth and the next day they recorded another "Easy Beat" show.

On October 17 they went to the Abbey Road studio and recorded both sides of their next single, "I Want to Hold Your Hand"/"This Boy," plus a special Christmas message for fan club members.

After a riot by crazed fans at the Pavilion Gardens in Buxton on the nineteenth, the boys filmed another "Thank Your Lucky Stars" episode the next day.

The Beatles completed the recording sessions for their next album at Abbey Road on October 23, then were off to Sweden for their first foreign tour since they went to Germany. They recorded a

radio show for "Pop '63" in Stockholm on the twenty-fourth.

During the five-day tour beginning October 25 the Beatles played to enthusiastic, screaming Swedes in Karlstad, Stockholm, Göteborg, Borås, and Eskilstuna. The event was splashed all over the British and Swedish press and television.

In Stockholm, forty policemen with nightsticks guarded the stage. Some fans eventually broke through the cordon and rushed onto the stage, knocking George to the floor. Order was quickly restored and no Beatle was injured. Additional police with dogs vainly tried to control the mob outside the theater.

On October 29 the boys recorded a segment for "Drop In," a Swedish television show.

The next morning the Beatles boarded an SAS Caravelle jetliner to London. They were mobbed

Like those of the three previous singles, the first-pressing labels of "She Loves You" had the title in the small-print style.

by thousands of screaming fans who, despite a heavy rain, turned Heathrow Airport into a scene similar to a shark-feeding frenzy. Fifty reporters and photographers from various newspapers plus a BBC camera crew were on hand to capture the arrival.

A car carrying Prime Minister Sir Alec Douglas-Home was delayed by the wild crowd, and Miss World was totally ignored by the press and public as she passed through the gate.

That evening, George Harrison took advantage of a day off and went to the Odeon in Lewisham for a concert starring Little Richard, the Everly Brothers, Bo Diddley, and the Rolling Stones. Little Richard was a friend from the Beatles' days in Hamburg, while the Everlys and Bo Diddley had influenced the boys for many years.

To avoid recognition, George donned an unfamiliar cap and turned up his coat collar. It worked, but he had to remove the cap to get backstage and visit his friends.

The Beatles began their fourth nationwide tour of the year on November 1. On opening night in Cheltenham the deafening crowd's high-pitched screams overshadowed the Beatles' amplified sounds. It was impossible for them to do a countdown and begin playing in unison because they were unable to hear what they were singing or playing.

The Beatles No. 1 (Parlophone GEP 8883), released on the first day of the autumn tour, debuted on the EP chart at Number 40 on November 9. It was on the charts for twelve weeks before last appearing at Number 48 on February 1, 1964. The EP contained two Lennon-McCartney songs, "I Saw Her Standing There" and "Misery," plus "Anna," penned by Arthur Alexander, and *"Chains,"* a Gerry Goffin–Carole King composition.

After appearing in Sheffield on the second, the Beatles went to Leeds. During this performance a portion of the show was taped for use in a court case involving the Performing Right Society.

The Beatles took a break on the fourth to appear in their most prestigious booking of their career—the Royal Variety Performance at the Prince of Wales Theatre in London. Beatlemania was the scene outside the theater as thousands of screaming fans were restrained by rows of constables. It was the only time that the arrival of members of the royal family was overshadowed by a band of rock 'n' roll musicians.

The Beatles were seventh on a nineteen-act bill to perform for the Queen Mother, Princess Margaret, and Lord Snowdon, who heard "She Loves You," "Till There Was You," "From Me to You," and "Twist and Shout."

The Beatles captured the royal audience as easily as they had won the Cavern crowds long ago, using, as well as music, the wit that remained a prominent part of the act. Prior to singing "Twist and Shout," John stepped to the mike and said, "For this number we'd like to ask your help. Will the people in the cheaper seats clap your hands? All the rest of you just rattle your jewelry."

On November 5, as the boys continued the tour in Slough, Brian Epstein was en route to America. In New York he visited Ed Sullivan and discussed having the Beatles appear on his successful television show.

Sullivan was astonished when Epstein asked for top billing, because the Beatles were virtually unknown in America. An agreement was eventually reached that gave the Beatles top billing in exchange for a substantial fee reduction. They were signed to appear live on February 9 and 16, and to tape a segment for use on the twenty-third. The fee for all of these appearances was only $10,000. Epstein gladly accepted and Sullivan agreed to pay round-trip airfare and hotel accommodations for the boys.

The Beatles were in Northampton on the sixth and gave their first performance in Ireland at Dublin's Adelphi Cinema the next day, followed by a show in Belfast.

Backstage at the Granada in East Ham on the ninth, George Martin announced that advance orders for their next single "I Want to Hold Your Hand," had nearly reached one million.

John had mixed emotions about the news. "I'm delighted," he said, "but how do we top that? It means the single will go straight to number one and burn itself out in a week. We may sell a million overnight but it means our stay at the top will be short and another group will take over from us long before Christmas."

Just prior to the release date, advance sales exceeded a million—the first time this had ever happened in Great Britain.

On November 10 the Beatles were in Birmingham and newspapers the next morning carried photos of the boys escaping from the Hippodrome disguised as constables.

The Portsmouth show for the eleventh was canceled due to illness. Thousands of fans mourned Paul McCartney's battle with gastric flu as the news media issued hourly bulletins updating his condition.

On the thirteenth "The Mersey Sound" docu-

Your SUNDAY ENTERTAINMENT AT THE ABC BLACKPOOL

EUROPE'S MOST LUXURIOUS THEATRE **ABC** BLACKPOOL PHONE 24233
PROPRIETORS: ASSOCIATED BRITISH CINEMAS LTD. MANAGING DIRECTOR D.J. GOODLATTE ASSISTANT MANAGING DIRECTOR W. CARTLIDGE RESIDENT MANAGER R J PARSONS

SUNDAY, SEPTEMBER 8th

1 SONS OF THE PILTDOWN MEN

2 TERRY YOUNG

3 JACK DOUGLAS

4 LEE LESLIE

5 **THE COUNTRYMEN**

INTERVAL

6 SONS OF THE PILTDOWN MEN

7 CHAS. M'DEVITT &
   SHIRLEY DOUGLAS

8 JACK DOUGLAS

9

The BEATLES

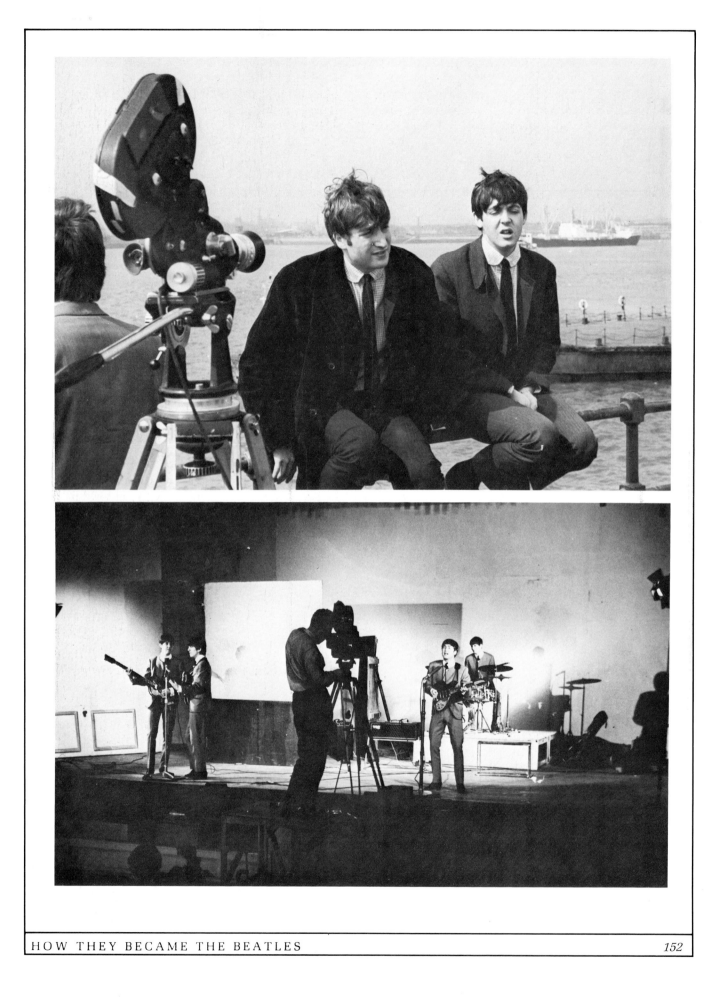

mentary was rerun on BBC-TV. The tour resumed in Plymouth, where high-pressure water hoses were used by police to control the rioting crowd.

The Beatles suddenly became a controversial subject in Parliament. Questions were asked regarding the thousands of policemen who were working overtime throughout the country at great personal risk while protecting the popular singers.

The boys played Exeter's ABC Cinema on the fourteenth and Bristol the next day. Beatlemania was spreading like wildfire and camera crews from America's three networks filmed parts of the Beatles performance in Bournemouth on November 16. Excerpts from these recordings were aired a week later in the United States.

It is my belief that *Introducing the Beatles* (VJLP 1062) was not officially released but that the album

Three behind-the-scenes photos from the filming of the BBC-TV documentary "The Mersey Sound." The show aired Wednesday, October 9.

was simply put into distribution in November 1963.

The July 22, 1963, release date given in all Beatles discographies is incorrect because the logo on the back of the first issued jackets—*VJ* in brackets—was not used until October 1963. Interviews with Randy Wood, former president of Vee Jay Records, substantiates this fact.

All Vee Jay albums—including later albums by famous artists such as the Four Seasons and blues singer Jimmy Reed—had liner notes and the song titles on the back of the jackets.

The first album covers for *Introducing the Beatles* in 1963 featured an advertisement listing twenty-five Vee Jay albums. There was no reference to the Beatles by name or a list of songs contained on the album.

When Vee Jay announced the albums for its Fall Release in June 1963, Randy Wood said: "A sample cover was made up with identical liner notes by Tony Barrow, just like the *Please Please Me* LP in England, with twelve songs instead of fourteen."

Wood called the printer and canceled the cover with the liner notes. Toward the end of the year a

Below: Cash Box review of "She Loves You," the Beatles' third American single. *Right:* Promo label of "She Loves You," September, before Swan began their Don't Drop Out campaign. *Facing page, left:* Commercial label from the first Swan pressing. This was the Beatles' third single in America that year. *Facing page, top right:* New promo label including the Don't Drop Out slogan, September.

new cover, advertising the twenty-five albums, was used instead.

In discussions regarding why the original cover with the liner notes was replaced, Randy Wood declined to say anything definite. When I offered certain suggestions, Wood smiled, as if to say, "Don't quote me, but you've got the idea."

The idea was startling.

Trans-Global, a music licensing firm in New York, had canceled Vee Jay's contract to release Beatles-covered masters on August 8, 1963, because of the nonpayment of royalties for two singles that Vee Jay had released earlier in the year. Vee Jay was informed that it no longer had the licensing rights for "Love Me Do" and "P.S. I Love You." The album containing those songs, however, had already been pressed and to destroy them would destroy Vee Jay Records. To avert financial

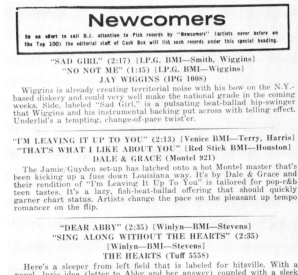

disaster, a back cover that did not list any songs on the disc was substituted.

Vee Jay's Fall Festival of albums in the September 14, 1963, issue of *Cash Box* was the last to feature any albums with the Vee Jay logo on the front cover.

In October, Vee Jay had introduced a new logo with the letters *VJ* in brackets. On November 16, 1963, a second and final full-page advertisement for Vee Jay's Fall Release appeared in *Cash Box* showing *Africa Calling* (VJLP 1061), plus five additional albums featuring the new VJ logo on the front covers.

The back cover of *Introducing the Beatles* shows the same five albums that were announced on November 16—with the new logo in the top right section—clearly negating the theory for a July 1963 release date.

The front cover of *Introducing the Beatles* shows the same Angus McBean photograph used on *The Beatles' Hits* Parlophone EP, but it is cropped and reversed.

On November 18, the Beatles were the guests of honor at a special ceremony at the EMI House in Manchester. The lads received a Silver LP each for *Please Please Me* and *With the Beatles,* presented by EMI chairman Sir Joseph Lockwood. The boys also accepted a small Silver EP and single from *Disc* editor Gerald Marks for *Twist and Shout* and "She Loves You."

Two days later, Pathé News filmed an eight-minute color newsreel showing the Beatles singing before the hysterical crowd at the Ardwick ABC Cinema in Manchester.

The hectic tour schedule for November 21–30 included Carlisle, Stockton, Newcastle, Hull, Cambridge, York, Lincoln, Huddersfield, and Sunderland.

The Beatles' second British album, *With the Beatles* (Parlophone PMC 1206/PCS 3045), was released in England on November 22, the day that John F. Kennedy was assassinated. The LP entered the chart at Number 1 on November 30 and their first album dropped to Number 2. *With the Beatles* held the top album spot for twenty-two weeks and was on the charts for forty-three weeks, with its final listing on September 19, 1964, at Number 10.

On November 23, "All I Want for Christmas Is a Beatle" (Fontana TF 427) by comedienne Dora Bryan went on sale. During her nightclub act at London's Adelphi Theatre, Bryan was joined by three colleagues wearing suits and Beatle wigs. As "The Cockroaches," they did a satirical tribute to the Fab Four. Some Beatles fans objected to having their idols treated in such an insulting manner, but the Beatles were very pleased.

"I love the record," said Paul in *The Beatles Book Monthly,* "and I think it's extremely funny. Let's face it, Dora is funny, isn't she? I went to see her show in London and it knocked me out."

George said, "I hope it's a big hit." Ringo also loved the song, while John said, "I enjoy people making fun of us. It makes a change from nasty comment."

On November 29, "I Want to Hold Your Hand"/This Boy" (Parlophone R5084), was released in England. It debuted on the singles chart on December 7 at Number 1 and held that coveted spot for four weeks. It last appeared on April 11, 1964, at Number 45.

During Brian Epstein's visit to America he called

on Capitol Records, which had previously turned down an option to release the group's records in the United States.

Capitol executives were quickly becoming aware of the Beatles' incredible success in England and other parts of the world. An agreement was signed for Capitol to issue "I Want to Hold Your Hand" early in January 1964. Numerous radio stations, however, were already playing a promotional copy obtained from England, and anxious teens were storming the record stores with demands for the song.

The massive increase in the Beatles' popularity created terrific pressure for press agent Tony Barrow, who also supervised the official fan club operation. Because of daily press releases and meetings with the media, he had no time for fan club activities. At first there were long delays in answering mail but the volume of incoming mail had grown to staggering proportions. Unopened sacks were piled on the staircases above Barrow's office. Something had to be done and Barrow desperately needed a solution to satisfy the legion of anxious fans. Finally, he came up with the idea of a Christmas record—a special message from the Beatles thanking all of their fans for their support. It would be an exclusive release for fan club members whose dues were paid.

Brian Epstein was not thrilled with the idea of

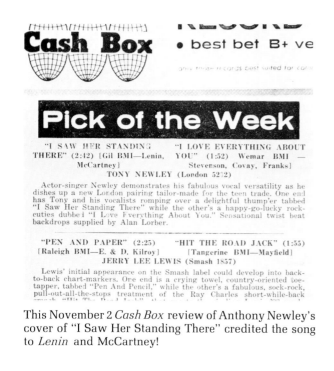

This November 2 *Cash Box* review of Anthony Newley's cover of "I Saw Her Standing There" credited the song to *Lenin* and McCartney!

spending money to produce a disc that offered no direct return in sales. Barrow finally convinced him that it would be a great public relations ploy and would create enough excitement among the 30,000 hard-core Beatles fans to ensure automatic sales of future records as well as sign new members.

The Beatles spent a half hour recording their messages and singing carols. John began by leading the boys through his version of "Good King Wenceslas." Then he made a short speech: "Hello. This is John speaking with his voice. We're all very happy to be able to talk to you like this on this little bit of plastic. This record reaches you at the end of a really gear year for us and it's all due to you. . . ."

After a reference to their Royal Variety Show performance, they whistled the national anthem, sang a few more carols, and ended with a crazy version of "Rudolph the Red-Nosed Ringo."

After editing the tape, Barrow ended up with a five-minute presentation that would fit on a single side of a seven-inch flexi-disc. He hoped it would keep discontented fan club members away from his door.

Successful people are never immune to criticism. The first newspaper to slam the Beatles was London's *Daily Telegraph,* which claimed that the mass hysteria was simply filling empty heads just as Hitler had done.

The *Daily Mirror* defended the popular singers. "You have to be a real sour square not to love the nutty, noisy, happy, handsome Beatles. If they don't sweep your blues away, brother, you're a lost cause. . . . The Beatles are wacky. They wear their hair like a mop, but it is washed. . . ."

The British Communist newspaper, *Daily Worker,* was not going to let such a controversial issue go by without comment. "The Mersey Sound is the voice of 80,000 crumbling houses and 30,000 people on the dole."

Sir Edward Boyle, the Conservative education minister, stated that "the Beatles have no future." A psychologist, explaining the Beatles brouhaha, announced that the boys were "relieving a sexual urge." Doctors had "reported" that many young girls had had orgasms at concerts by the Fabulous Four. The Beatles were even attacked but later defended by leaders of the Church of England.

Tony Barrow said from his press office at NEMS that "the Beatles seem to have achieved so much

Extremely rare stereophonic issue of the Beatles' first American album, released in November. Front and back.

The Beatles' second Parlophone album, *With the Beatles,* released November 22. Stereo (this page) and mono.

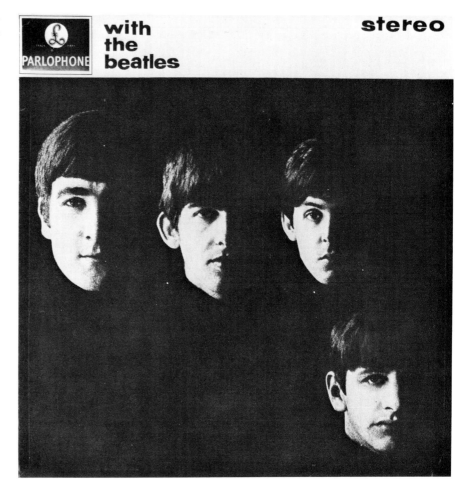

with the beatles

PARLOPHONE

stereo

during this first standout year that, short of getting themselves a fan club branch on the moon, I doubt if there are many more strengths for them to go on from or to!" But Barrow, thinking only of the boys' success in the United Kingdom, was curbing his imagination.

The Beatles appeared in Leicester on December 1. The next day, after taping a session at ATV's Boreham Wood for the "Morecambe and Wise Show," they sang at a charity event at London's Grosvenor House.

On the third they spent the morning autographing *With the Beatles* albums for a dozen lucky contest winners. That night they appeared in Portsmouth, then took a three-day break.

On the sixth the Beatles Fan Club flexi-disc was mailed to members. "Sincere Good Wishes for Christmas and the New Year from John, Paul, George and Ringo" appeared on the yellow cardboard foldout insert. The back had two photo-

graphs: the top one showed the boys at the fan club's national headquarters with staff members "Anne Collingham and Bettina Rose." (Actually, the girls pictured were Valerie Sumpter and Maureen Payne, two NEMS employees who stood in when faces were required for the fictitious Anne and Bettina.) The bottom photo showed their presentation before the Queen Mother at the Royal Variety Performance.

National Newsletter No. 2 was printed on the inside of the insert, which also contained the flexi-disc. The disc (LYN 492) was labeled "Not For Sale. Issued free of charge to fan club members in December 1963."

This particular fan club record is very rare because members had to be enrolled and their dues paid up by November 30, 1963, to receive it. Those who joined during December were ineligible.

The Beatles made television history on the seventh by taping two BBC shows during the Beatles

Northern Fan Club Convention at the Empire Theatre in Liverpool. One show, "It's the Beatles," was a special version of their stage act. The other show was an unusual edition of "Juke Box Jury" with all the Beatles as members of the panel judging new records. They decided that songs by Elvis, Steve Lawrence and Eydie Gorme, and Billy Fury would be hits, but gave thumbs-down to Paul Anka, Shirley Ellis, and Bobby Vinton. Both shows were aired that evening to 23 million viewers. Some critics were beginning to refer to the BBC as the Beatles Broadcasting Corporation.

After the taping sessions the boys ran fifty yards down Podsey Street and did two shows at the Odeon Cinema. The street had been closed by the police to prevent the boys from having to run a gauntlet of overenthusiastic fans,

December 8–13 the Beatles played to impassioned masses in Lewisham, Southend, Doncaster, Scarborough, Nottingham, and ended the autumn tour in Southampton.

On the fourteenth they played for the London Fan Club Convention at the Wimbledon Palais

Top right: The Beatles' fifth single, released in England November 29, would be the song to catapult them to fame in America early the following year. *Middle:* Pass for the Beatles' Record Roundabout appearance.

Bottom: "All I Want for Christmas Is a Beatle," by popular British star Dora Bryan, was the first Beatles-related novelty item. Released by Fontana on November 23.

ABOVE: THE BEATLES at the National Headquarters of The Official Fan Club with Joint Secretaries BETTINA ROSE (right) and ANNE COLLINGHAM (left).

BELOW: THE BEATLES are presented to The Queen Mother at this year's Royal Variety Performance (Monday 4 November : Prince of Wales Theatre).

The Beatles special flexi-disc Christmas message was mailed to fan club members on December 6. Only members paid up through November 1963 received the disc. Anyone who joined in December was out of luck.

Ballroom. Afterward, they lined up behind a long bar and answered questions while shaking hands with 3,000 fervid teens.

Tony Barrow said, "I joined Neil, Mal and several of our office people in helping to control the steady flow . . . consoling dozens of tearful girls, utterly overcome with the sheer ecstasy of coming face to face with a fave rave Beatle! I think more people passed out at that ordinary concert because the very personal contact with the Beatles was something few fans normally encounter."

CAPITOL GETS THE BEATLES FOR U.S. was the headline of the lead article in the December 14 issue of *Cash Box*. The story revealed that Beatles records would be marketed exclusively in America by Capitol in 1964. The first release would be "I Want to Hold Your Hand," followed by an album.

On December 15 the Beatles recorded another All-Liverpool Special for "Thank Your Lucky Stars."

Another "Saturday Club" was taped on the seventeenth, and the next day they did a personal two-hour radio special, "From Us to You."

Two days later they were on "Scene at 6:30." On the twenty-first they performed a preview of their Christmas Show in Bradford, and a final preview the next day in Liverpool.

The Christmas Show began on December 24 at London's Astoria Cinema. The extravaganza contained music and comedy from the Beatles, Billy J. Kramer and the Dakotas, Cilla Black, Tommy Quickly, and the Fourmost. There were two evening performances for sixteen nights. Tickets had gone on sale October 21. By November 16 all 100,000 tickets had been sold.

Brian Epstein arranged for the Beatles to fly home on the twenty-fourth and spend Christmas Day with their families. Paul, George, and Ringo stayed with their parents while John went to his Aunt Mimi's.

On December 26, "I Want to Hold Your Hand"/ "I Saw Her Standing There" (Capitol 5112) was rush-released in the United States as the Christmas Show resumed in London.

The December 28 issue of *Cash Box* was filled with articles about the Beatles, in addition to a mop-top with the Capitol logo and a bold title, THE BEATLES ARE COMING!

Capitol's Brown Meggs announced that the

"The Beatles Show" program, November/December 1963.

group's first Capitol album, *Meet the Beatles,* would be released in January instead of the original date in February.

In the same issue, United Artists revealed plans for a Beatles movie to be filmed in 1964. The producer, Walter Shenson, said that Alun Owen would write the script while John Lennon and Paul McCartney composed the score. Richard Lester would direct the as yet untitled film.

Jack Paar announced the Beatles would make their American debut via film on his television show on January 9.

Capitol Records hired hair stylist Gene Shacove to design a new coiffeur, patterned after the Beatles' famous hairdo. The first woman to wear the new style was actress Janet Leigh. A Beatles-cut press kit, with photos of Miss Leigh, was distributed to the beauty editors of all daily newspapers.

Additional merchandising gimmicks began to

Top: The Beatles rehearse to record their segment of the "Saturday Club," to be shown December 21. Rare photo of John wearing glasses. *Right:* The Beatles topped the *Mersey Beat* poll for the third time.

MERSEY BEAT

POPULARITY POLL 1963
BEATLES HAT-TRICK
THEY TOP POLL FOR THIRD TIME!

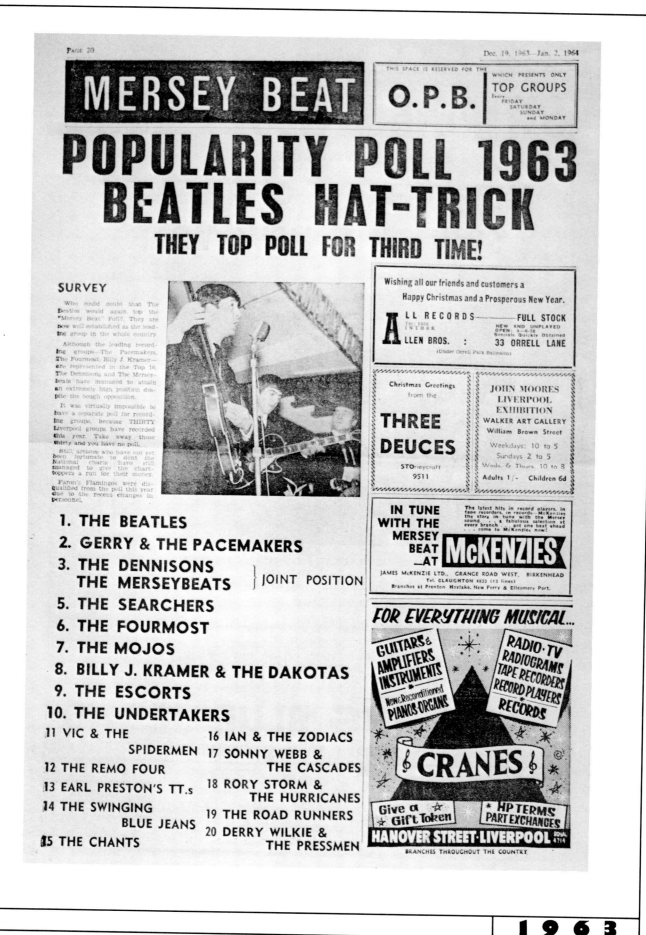

SURVEY

Who could doubt that The Beatles would again top the "Mersey Beat" Poll?. They are now well established as the leading group in the whole country.

Although the leading recording groups—The Pacemakers, The Fourmost, Billy J. Kramer—are represented in the Top 10, The Dennisons and The Merseybeats have managed to attain an extremely high position despite the tough opposition.

It was virtually impossible to have a separate poll for recording groups, because THIRTY Liverpool groups have recorded this year. Take away those thirty and you have no poll.

Still, artistes who have not yet been fortunate to dent the National charts have still managed to give the chart-toppers a run for their money.

Faron's Flamingos were disqualified from the poll this year due to the recent changes in personnel.

1. THE BEATLES
2. GERRY & THE PACEMAKERS
3. THE DENNISONS
   THE MERSEYBEATS } JOINT POSITION
5. THE SEARCHERS
6. THE FOURMOST
7. THE MOJOS
8. BILLY J. KRAMER & THE DAKOTAS
9. THE ESCORTS
10. THE UNDERTAKERS

11 VIC & THE SPIDERMEN
12 THE REMO FOUR
13 EARL PRESTON'S TT.s
14 THE SWINGING BLUE JEANS
15 THE CHANTS
16 IAN & THE ZODIACS
17 SONNY WEBB & THE CASCADES
18 RORY STORM & THE HURRICANES
19 THE ROAD RUNNERS
20 DERRY WILKIE & THE PRESSMEN

Capitol Gets The Beatles For U. S.

THE BEATLES

NEW YORK—The sound of The Beatles, which has coined the "Beatlemania" craze in England, will be marketed exclusively by Capitol Records in 1964.

Preceding the rock-market quartet's appearances on Capitol has been a tremendous barrage of publicity stemming from national magazine, newspaper and broadcasting coverage of its remarkable success in England.

Word reached the U.S. last week that the instrumentalists' latest single, "I Want To Hold Your Hand," which will be Capitol's first disking by the group, had received pre-release orders totalling more than 1 million copies in England.

Capitol will issue "Hand" in mid-Jan., to be followed by an LP in early Feb. The Beatles will make three appearances on Ed Sullivan's audience-in-the-millions Sunday night TV'er, the first in Feb.

"Hand" is one of a series of sensational singles and LP successes by the musicians, including the current number 1 English best-seller, "She Loves You," which "Hand" should replace next week, and the first two top sellers on both the LP and EP charts. Numbers 1 and 2 on the LP listing are "With The Beatles" and "Please Please Me," while the EP chart lists "Twist And Shout" and "The Beatles Hits." "She Loves You" was released in the U.S. awhile-back on the Swan label, but did not make-the-grade.

Their diskings are released through EMI's Parlophone label. EMI, of course, is a principal shareholder in Capitol Records.

Only a year ago, the four youths, aged 21-23, who are now the biggest entertainment attraction in England and the Continent, were knocking down about $15 a week in a small club in Liverpool, the hub of rock and roll in England. They had made a few records, but those had gone unnoticed among those of scores of similar groups. In order to earn more money, they went overseas to work. It was in one of Hamburg's rowdy and raucous strip joints, the Indra Club, that they were discovered by young English talent agent and promoter, Brian Epstein.

There followed in quick succession a recording contract with EMI, top-notch bookings in England, France, and Germany, TV shows, and a landslide of publicity—all under the guid-

come that has increased a hundredfold in the past year.

Onstage, the Beatles are as spectacular as their recent history. Their collective trademark is an immense mop of hair.

Beatlemania reached a peak last month when the group appeared at the annual Royal Command Performance. The Queen Mother found them "young, fresh, and vital."

Ernesto Lecuon

NEW YORK—Ernes called the George G and writer of such classics as "Malagu "The Breeze & I," Nov. 29 in the Cana age of 68.

Lecuona, dead of recently came to the to recuperate from a

Trained in serious i ist ala Gershwin, credited with bringin conga rhythms up to where they became ites in the 30's and

Like Gershwin, L his talents in both and pop music. "Ma duced in the U.S. in work which has been song, and "The Bre from a popular conc lucia." To both field love for native rh Gershwin had tried popular musical idio

The writing of " troduced by the wri Theater in New York with composer Maur most famous work, written in the same r guena."

Other popular com cuona, who also wrot stage and films, incl include "Say Si S Drums." He also tours throughout the

saturate the market. Beatles sling bags, stockings, sweaters, brooches, wigs, pendants, handkerchiefs, drums, jigsaw puzzles, pencils, and bedspreads were all popular items.

NEMS Enterprises was the copyright owner of the name Beatles and Brian Epstein personally approved all official products for licensees. The Beatles themselves never endorsed anything.

To avoid lawsuits many manufacturers of unauthorized merchandise spelled the boys' name "Beetles" and substituted four hairdos for actual photos of the Beatles.

Novelty records about the Beatles were still popping up. "Beatles Crazy" by Bill Clifton and "We Love the Beatles" by the Vernons Girls were already on the Top 50 music chart.

It had been quite a year. And Brian Epstein had been quite a taskmaster. The Beatles had survived twelve months of grueling concert tours, one-night stands, press interviews, autograph parties, recording sessions at EMI, and numerous radio and television shows.

Along the way the crowds had evolved from a few hundred excited teens to thousands of riotous disciples. It was sheer madness. Stardom had created an alien world of cramped dressing rooms and bedlam onstage, followed by a police-cordoned escape to a car that swiftly roared away from hysterical crowds. The Beatles were the most newsworthy subject for every media form throughout the United Kingdom.

Now they would conquer the world.

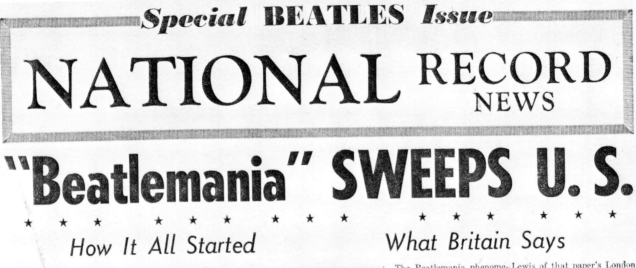

NATIONAL RECORD NEWS

"Beatlemania" SWEEPS U.S.

★ ★ ★ ★ ★ ★ ★ ★ ★ ★ ★ ★ ★ ★ ★

How It All Started

They wore black leather jackets, their hair was untidy and the only way one could tell them apart from characters in a Marlon Brando movie was that they had no motorcycles.

They were the Beatles, but no one knew it. In those days they called themselves a variety of things—The Quarrymen, Moon Dogs or The Moonshiners. It was early 1958, and they spent most of their time playing in the cellar of a friend's home in Liverpool for kicks.

CELLAR CLUB

If there was a turning point for the four young men who eventually went on to become the biggest recording group in England's history, it was probably in that cellar. Before that George Harrison, John Lennon and Paul McCatney wandered around with various groups and took any job available. Then they met Pete Best and his mother. She volunteered her cellar for their use and then she decided to turn the cellar into a club —The Casbah.

It wasn't long before all the

THE BEATLES, four young Englishmen, have become, in just one year, the hottest thing in the history of British show business. Their first American album, "Meet The Beatles," has just been issued in the United States by Capitol Records. The young quartet will come to America for the first time in February to make three appearances on the Ed Sullivan Show, beginning Feb. 9.

SHOW BIZ MIRACLE

"The sound of their music is one of the mos' persistent noises heard over England since the air raid sirens were dismantled. This year they have sold over 2.5 million records." That's what Newsweek magazine had to say about The Beatles, the show-business miracle. And that's what Newsweek said before their latest record was released in England Nov. 29. Titled "I Want to Hold Your Hand," the disk achieved the impossible: It had sold, via advance orders, over 1,000,000 copies before it was issued! Nobody, not even Elvis, has ever done that before. The record is the same one Capitol Records released here late in December and is also contain'd in The Beatles' first American album, called "Meet The Beatles." As a result of their

What Britain Says

The Beatlemania phenomenon that began in England last year and is now sweeping the United States, has created a wave of controversy so extensive that psychologists and sociologists are taking a hard clinical look at it. Many adults regard Beatlemania with horror, distaste, and even fear and find it easy to blame the Beatles for what they, the adults, feel is a lack of taste and control and a dangerous mass hysteria among young people.

CORBETT SAYS

Anthony Corbett, a noted English psychologist praised the Beatles as having provided "a desperately needed release for the inhibitions which exist in all of us."

GREAT NEED

Dixon Scott of the London Daily Mirror interviewed a well-known psychiatrist (unnamed because of medical ethics) in an attempt to get at the root of Beatlemania. "We are all chaotic and mixed-up inside," the psychiatrist told Scott. "We are anxious to have a greater freedom to live. We have a greater feeling of the need to express our-

Lewis of that paper's London bureau, examined the sociological implications of Beatlemania and came up with other theories.

"They (the Beatles) are working class and their roots and attitudes are firmly of the north of England. Because of their success, they can act as spokesmen for the new, noisy, anti-establishment generation which is becoming a force in British life," Lewis wrote.

"The Beatles are part of a strong-flowing reaction against the soft, middle-class south of England, which has controlled popular culture for so long."

Beatlemania has touched all corners of English life and all types of people.

Obviously, it has had an enormous effect on the young people of Great Britian who have been responsible for the majority of the 3,000,000 Beatles records sold in 1963. But Beatlemania hasn't stopped with youth. It has touched virtually everybody, high and low, rich and poor, scholars and the less educated; as the New York Times put it, "Beatlemania affects all so-

Which Beatles

Have the Phonies?

WHICH BEATLES HAVE THE PHONYS? Here are two pictures, each with four men. One picture is of the Beatles, the other is of four imposters who would have people think they are the Beatles. The question is: Which is the real group? If you guessed the one above, you're right. They are the Beatles, hair-do's and all. The types shown at right, who are masquerading as the famous English rock-and-roll singers are, in real life, some men from Capitol Records. In fact, they're some of the top men. In the usual order are Alan W. Livingston, President of Capitol, and three vice presidents—Bill Tallant, Stan Gortikov and Voyle Gilmore.

Fans Curtail Tours

Their popularity almost forced the Beatles to stop working last December. In the interest of their own safety, the phenomenally popular English rock-and-roll quartet had to cancel all "one-night stands." From now on, the group will appear only where their show can last several days.

According to their manager, Brian Epstein, the main reason for the move is the risk invoved in getting the foursome through the masses of teeange fans who gather at stage doors after their performances. The Beatles' clothing has been ripped to shreds several times and all four of the boys can display bruises as a result of plunging through crowds of over-eager fans.

Advance publicity from Capitol Records. *Left:* The "Special" *National Record News,* released to the press in December. *Above:* Inside was a photograph of the Capitol Records president and three vice-presidents, in Beatles wigs. *Right:* This image was plastered all over America in December 1963. The Beatles Are Coming! appeared on telephone poles, walls, billboards, windows—anywhere and everywhere it would be seen by an unsuspecting public.

"There can be nothing more important . . . can there?"

—*Brian Epstein to John Lennon,
on hearing that "I Want to Hold Your Hand"
was Number 1 in America*

The new year began with the Beatles dominating every music chart in Great Britain, and the same frantic show schedule they had survived during the previous twelve months.

"I Want to Hold Your Hand" was Number 1; "She Loves You," Number 2; the *Twist and Shout* EP, Number 17; *The Beatles' Hits* EP, Number 19; and *With the Beatles* LP, Number 20.

On January 3, a segment of their November show in Bournemouth was shown in America on "The Jack Paar Show."

On January 14, John, Paul, and George waved good-bye to several thousand fans at Heathrow and flew to Paris. A mere sixty teens welcomed them when they stepped from the plane at Le Bourget. It was immediately clear that they were not going to win any popularity contests in France. Ringo arrived the next day and was rushed to the hotel by champion race driver Stuart Turner, who had just returned from a rally in Monte Carlo. All of the publicity hoopla failed to raise one French eyebrow.

London newspaper editors and music promoters wondered why Brian Epstein had not selected a more favorable country for the Beatles' next marathon concert. France was an isolated territory for popular music and not the place to launch a new wave of Beatlemania. The answer was simple. Brian Epstein loved Paris and thought it would be challenging to invade the French market. (Although the Beatles would have found instant success in Germany, they were not allowed there because of legal problems involving several paternity claims arising from their earlier tours in Hamburg.)

On January 16, the Beatles launched a three-week engagement at the Olympia Theatre in Paris. Ten additional acts shared the bill, including American singer Trini Lopez. The Beatles' repertoire comprised "From Me to You," "Roll Over Beethoven," "She Loves You," "This Boy," "I Want to Hold Your Hand," "Boys," "Twist and Shout," and "Long Tall Sally."

The spectacular opening-night performance was anything but spectacular. In fact, it was nearly a disaster. As the boys played to an audience of tuxedos and evening gowns their amplifiers failed three times. The Paris elite was not impressed and offered a chilling reception. French newspapers added to the Beatles' misery with negative reviews and articles.

Suddenly a few British newspapers decided that

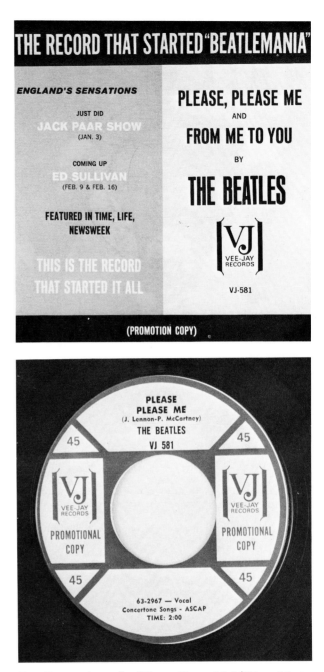

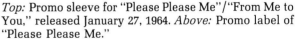

Top: Promo sleeve for "Please Please Me"/"From Me to You," released January 27, 1964. *Above:* Promo label of "Please Please Me."

unflattering articles and ribald cartoons about the Beatles would sell more papers than the constant success stories. It was suggested that the Fab Four was about to split up since they no longer traveled together. Articles were published regarding the sparse number of fans that welcomed the Beatles to Paris. When a Dave Clark Five record became

Number 1, Fleet Street reporters rejoiced in announcing that the Beatles had been toppled.

London reporter Vincent Mulchrone aptly summed up the Paris reaction in the *Daily Mail:* "Beatlemania is still, like Britain's entry into the Common Market, a problem the French prefer to put off for a while."

After the opening night, and discouraged by the equipment failures, audience rejection, and backstage chaos, the boys were in a somber mood. Then a telegram arrived. Their spirits soared. "I Want to Hold Your Hand" had skyrocketed to Number 1 in *Cash Box*. The Beatles instantly forgot about the French rebuff and began a celebration party that continued until dawn. They had finally reached the top of the singles chart in the most important record-selling country in the world. This was the one prize Brian Epstein had eagerly awaited. No artist or group from Britain had ever scored so high on American music charts and this was no fluke. "I Want to Hold Your Hand" had sold a quarter of a million copies in America three days after being released. It reached 1 million on January 10, and, though it hardly seems possible, by the thirteenth it was reportedly selling at the rate of 10,000 copies each hour in New York City alone.

While the British press continued to malign their most popular singing group, competition for Beatles coverage in America created a frenzy among every major news magazine and television network. Hordes of reporters and photographers flew to Paris to investigate this weird British phenomenon that was causing such a hullabaloo among teenagers in the United States. Brian Epstein was showered with offers from U.S. concert promoters.

On January 20, "I Want to Hold Your Hand" topped the charts in Australia and Ireland, and

THE BEATLES OPEN-END INTERVIEW

	SIDE ONE PRO 2548		TOTAL TIME: 6:08

DJ: I have the hit record "I Want To Hold Your Hand" by the "Beatles" coming up . . . before I play it, though, I'd like to read you a quote from the New York Times . . . it says: "The Beatles' impact on Britain has been greater than that of ANY OTHER exponent of popular music. There has been adulation before . . . but NO ONE has taken the national fancy as have the Beatles . . . 'Beatlemania,' as it is called, affects all social classes and all levels of intelligence." Well, with that in mind, we're not only going to feature the Beatles on RECORD, but you're going to MEET the boys right NOW . . . John Lennon, Paul McCartney, George Harrison and Ringo Starr . . . The "BEATLES" . . . welcome to the show, fellas.

All: Thank you, thank you very much . . . it's a pleasure to be here.

DJ: Say, John . . . how did you ever decide on a name like the BEATLES for the group?

John: Well, I had a vision when I was twelve . . . and I saw the man on a flaming pie and he said, "you're Beatles with an A," and we are! (Laugh)

DJ: (over laughs) Well, I ASKED for it I guess . . !

John: Well that's how it started anyway . . .

DJ: And how about your first RECORDING date?

George: We made our first record at the beginning of 1963 and we had a hit with that. But I think the whole bit really started when we did a Palladium show and then later we were asked to do the Royal Variety Command Performance, you know;

DJ: Uh huh . . .

George: and we met the Queen Mother and she started clapping . . . JOHN: and Princess Margaret too . . . GEORGE: Yeah and Princess Margaret.

DJ: How many records did you SELL last year, do you know?

Ringo: uh . . . well . . . the last count was six million, I think . . . JOHN: That's just Ringo's records (laugh) RINGO: The others don't sell (laugh).

DJ: Well, as a matter of FACT, I understand this record of yours is not only a hit HERE and in ENGLAND, but in OTHER countries as WELL!

George: Yes, well we've heard that our latest record "I Want To Hold Your Hand" came into the Australian top 20, right into number 1, which is very nice . . . And I think it's selling in Finland and Sweden and other places like that too!

DJ: (with authority) Ladies and Gentlemen . . . the BEATLES have now taken over the WORLD!

George: Well that's a nice thing to say, isn't it . . . RINGO: We were very lucky.

DJ: By the way . . . who's your BARBER . . . uh, you DO HAVE one, don't you?

George: No, it's a dirty rumor, we don't (chuckle) . . . PAUL: No, we cut it ourselves (laugh).

DJ: (laugh) Well, which one of you guys dreamed up this haircut idea, anyway?

Paul: I think it was my dad really, he said, "You know, Paul, it's a bit square" this . . . the haircut I had . . . you know, short back and sides. He said, "Why don't you get a 'Beatle Cut' son . . ." (laugh)

DJ: Say, I understand things get a little VIOLENT sometimes because your fans are quite exuberant, is this true?

Paul: Well, they get exuberant, you know, but we enjoy . . . we don't come to any harm 'cause the policemen are equally as exuberant, you see . . . The Police have a great time . . . ! (laughs).

DJ: (over laughs) I'll BET they do (chuckle) Now, what are your plans HERE for the STATES?

George: Well we're over here to do three Ed Sullivan TV shows and meet the Press . . . RINGO: And a bit of a rest on Miami Beach.

DJ: And I hear you're going to be making a MOVIE sometime soon . . .

George: Yeah, well when we get back to England from this current visit of America, we . . . to America . . . by America . . . Well we . . . you see we were making a film which we don't know the title of but, it's going to be a film just about us. JOHN: We don't know the script, and we know what songs are going to be in it. GEORGE: But it should be released in the States about the end of this year . . . sometime we hope. JOHN: With no title, and no songs and no script . . . (laughs).

DJ: (over laughs) Sounds like a winner ALREADY, you know!

John: (laughs) I give in! (laughs).

DJ: Well, maybe we'd better get to the RECORD right about here . . . Fellas, thanks very much for being on the show . . .

All: Pleasure to be here . . . Thank you . . . Bye Bye . . . Thank you very much.

DJ: (music sneaks in) And here's the record . . . "I WANT TO HOLD YOUR HAND," by our special guests . . . THE BEATLES!

MUSIC: UP TO END   "I WANT TO HOLD YOUR HAND"

Single #5112 The BEATLES   Produced by Jack Wagner

Label and sleeve of the Compact 33 single "Open-End Interview" for their first Capitol album, *Meet the Beatles.*

Meet the Beatles (Capitol ST2047) was released in America. Inevitably, the Beatles' success in America started providing work for the legal profession. In New York, U.S. District Court judge David N. Edelstein reserved a decision on a temporary restraining order obtained on January 16 by Ardmore-Beechwood Music (Capitol Records' U.K.-based music publishing subsidiary) against Vee Jay Records and its New York distributor regarding the use of "Love Me Do" and "P.S. I Love You" on Vee Jay's album, *Introducing the Beatles.*

The suit noted that Vee Jay was initially licensed by Trans-Global, a New York firm licensed to distribute EMI products. Capitol claimed that since EMI held the original Beatles contract, Trans-Global had canceled its contract with Vee Jay on August 8, 1963, because of nonpayment of royalties. Trans-Global had allegedly relinquished its rights to EMI, which subsequently had been acquired by Capitol Records.

Under the Capitol injunction, "Vee Jay, its agents, attorneys and servants" were prevented from selling or advertising records by the Beatles. Capitol attorney Sidney Zatz indicated that "steps would be taken" against dealers who persisted in selling Vee Jay Beatles records, though he did not elaborate.

Jay Lasker, executive vice president of Vee Jay, said his firm had stopped shipping Beatles products upon receipt of the restraining order. One album, ready for distribution but not released owing to the legal action, was *Jolly What! The Beatles & Frank Ifield on Stage* (VJ1085).

Vee Jay contended that it had a five-year contract with the Beatles and that it was not in default for failure to pay royalties. The legal department countered with a suit against Capitol and Swan to prevent them from selling Beatles products.

Above: Picture sleeve for the January black-label issue of "She Loves You"/"I'll Get You." *Right:* Very rare picture sleeve for "Can't Buy Me Love"/ "You Can't Do That," released March 16.

On January 25, "She Loves You" (Swan 4152) debuted in *Billboard* at Number 69. It was Number 1 for three weeks beginning March 21, and last appeared on May 2 at Number 36.

On January 27, "My Bonnie"/"The Saints" (MGM K13213) was released in America. The *Introducing the Beatles* LP was reissued with a black-and-white cover photo of the boys.

The Beatles went to EMI's Pathé-Marconi studios in Paris on the twenty-ninth and recorded German-language versions of "She Loves You" ("Sie Liebt Dich") and "I Want to Hold Your Hand" ("Komm, Gib Mir Deine Hand"). The songs would be released in West Germany to boost the Beatles' popularity. During this session they also recorded their next single, "Can't Buy Me Love." Contrary to most published accounts, the flip side, "You Can't Do That," was not recorded here.

On January 30, a new Vee Jay single, "Please Please Me"/"From Me to You" (VJ581) was released. The previous version (VJ498) was a big seller and the sleeve of the new issue had the same black-and-white photo featured on the cover of *Introducing the Beatles*. A special sleeve accompanied the white-and-blue deejay promo label proclaiming it as "The Record That Started Beatlemania."

"Sweet Georgia Brown"/"Nobody's Child" (Polydor NH 52-906) was released in England on the last day of January. More of the 1961 Hamburg recordings by Tony Sheridan and the Beatles (John, Paul, George, and Pete Best) were beginning to appear. Sheridan had redone the vocals to include contemporary references to the Beatles' hairstyle and their fan club.

A pair of Beatles singles and an album entered *Billboard*'s music charts on February 1. "Please Please Me" (VJ581) debuted at Number 68. It was Number 1 for two weeks starting March 21, and last appeared at Number 29 on April 25. "I Saw Her Standing There" (Capitol 5112) debuted at Number 117 and peaked at Number 14 on March 21. It last appeared on April 18 at Number 45. *Meet the Beatles* debuted on the album chart at Number 92 and was Number 1 for eleven weeks starting February 15. It last appeared at Number 121 on June 5, 1965. Early in February in America, "I Want to Hold Your Hand" and *Meet the Beatles* were certified RIAA Gold, and *The Beatles with Tony Sheridan and Their Guests* (MGM SE4215) was released. This album included four songs recorded during the 1961 Polydor sessions in Hamburg.

Notwithstanding all the gold records and chart-topping hits, Beatlemania *really* exploded during fifteen exhilarating days in February when the group invaded and conquered America. Numerous people openly took credit for the boys' triumphant tour. Among the more visible knaves were Jack Paar, Ed Sullivan, and New York disc jockey Murray the K.

The indisputable fact is that credit for the Beatles' incredible U.S. conquest was due to only four people—John, Paul, George, and Ringo. "I Want to Hold Your Hand" had sold a record-shattering 1.5 million copies in less than three weeks and became Number 1 just as Capitol Records' expansive publicity campaign, which included the nationwide display of 5 million "The Beatles Are Coming!" posters and publicity photos of Capitol's top brass wearing Beatles wigs, was getting under way.

On February 7, Pan American's Flight 101 landed at John F. Kennedy Airport. Sharing the first-class section with the Beatles were John's wife, Cynthia, Brian Epstein, Maureen Cleave of the London *Evening Standard,* and *Liverpool Echo* reporter George Harrison. American record producer Phil Spector sat in an aisle seat in front of Paul. In economy were Neil Aspinall, Mal Evans, photographers Leslie Bryce and Dezo Hoffman, and *Daily Express* reporter Harry Benson.

By now, the images from that day, pictures of a weeping, hysterical teenage mob crowding the runways, have become the ultimate symbol of Beatlemania. But as the Clipper *Defiance* taxied to the gate the Beatles thought they had arrived at the same time as the U.S. president or some other dignitary.

George was the first Beatle to emerge from the plane. He was followed by John, a grinning Paul, and Ringo with his overcoat buttoned up to the neck. It was only upon seeing the banners and signs that they realized that the screaming masses had come to see them.

Brian Sommerville, the Beatles' publicity chief, had his hands full coordinating the army of news crews. The din of 4,000 hysterical teens penetrated the building during the press conference in the airport's VIP lounge. As reporters shot rapid-fire questions, photographers' flashbulbs turned the room into a Fourth of July light show.

"Look at this camera, Ringo! Will you do it once more?"

"I haven't stopped doing it for the last time!" said Ringo.

This 1964 Vee Jay catalogue used a 1962 photo that prominently featured George's black eye.

"John, there is some doubt you can't sing."

"We need money first," said John.

"Are you going to have a haircut?"

"We had one yesterday."

"What do you think of Beethoven, Ringo?"

"I love him," replied Ringo. "Especially his poems."

"How do you account for your success?"

"We have a press agent."

Afterward a cordon of guards herded each Beatle to an individual limousine. The convoy raced away from the airport, along the expressways, down Fifth Avenue, and stopped at the luxurious Plaza Hotel.

Outside, the cold, windy weather did not deter hundreds of screaming fans from trying to crash police barricades. Soon the crowd grew to more than 5,000 and mounted police were called.

The Beatles' suite—the entire twelfth floor—soon acquired the appearance of a motion picture soundstage. Expensive furniture sagged beneath cameras, lights, and recorders plus sacks of fan mail.

One gate crasher ingratiated himself with the Beatles by virtue of his gift of gab and sheer tenacity. The intrepid intruder was Murray the K, a popular deejay at WINS Radio.

Murray began an on-the-air countdown as soon as the boys departed London. Upon their arrival at the Plaza, he phoned them for live interviews and started calling himself the Fifth Beatle. Murray later collected a beautiful bevy of girls, including the Ronettes, and charged into the Beatles' suite as if he were its tenant.

Brian Epstein and the entourage rightly considered the Beatles' upcoming appearance on "The Ed Sullivan Show" a special event. It was business as usual to Sullivan except for the screaming teenagers, whom he considered a nuisance. The CBS Television office on West Fifty-third Street was overwhelmed by 50,000 requests for tickets to the 700-seat studio. Colonel Tom Parker sent a "Good Luck" telegram from Elvis and himself.

On the night of February 9, 73 million people saw the Beatles sing "All My Loving," "Till There Was You," "She Loves You," "I Saw Her Standing There," and "I Want to Hold Your Hand."

The Beatles spent the next day with newspaper and radio reporters. That evening they enjoyed a night on the town, accompanied by Murray the K and the Ronettes. Waking to an icy, sleet-driven blizzard, the boys refused to fly to Washington, which left their travel agent with the hopeless task of acquiring train tickets one hour before departure time. Arrangements were made for a private car to be hooked to a Richmond, Fredericksburg, and Potomac train leaving New York's Penn Station.

At Union Station, 3,000 fans welcomed the boys to the nation's capital. During their one-day visit they occupied the entire seventh floor of the Shoreham Hotel.

On February 11 the Beatles performed their first concert in the United States. The huge Coliseum was used for many sports events and the boys were impressed with its size. The stage, surrounded by the audience, sat in the center of the auditorium. In addition to the technical difficulties of performing in the round, a truly unexpected hazard was present throughout the performance—jellybeans.

"They hurt," said George. "Some newspaper had dug out the old joke which we'd forgotten about, when John once said I'd eaten all his jelly babies. Everywhere we went I got them thrown at me. They don't have soft jelly babies in America but hard jellybeans like bullets."

Eight thousand fans screamed as the Beatles sang "Roll Over Beethoven," "From Me to You," "I Saw Her Standing There," "This Boy," "All My Loving," "I Wanna Be Your Man," "Please Please Me," "Till There Was You," "She Loves You," "I Want to Hold Your Hand," "Twist and Shout," and "Long Tall Sally."

Ringo was just as excited as the crowd. "What an audience! I could have played encores all night!" CBS filmed the entire show to be shown over closed-circuit television in March.

On February 12, stormy weather grounded all flights. The Beatles departed Washington by train and made their New York stage debut that evening.

Promoter Sid Berstein wanted to hold the concert in a large arena, but Brian Epstein had talked him into two half-hour shows in New York's prestigious Carnegie Hall. More than 360 of New York's finest were hired as bodyguards.

A *New York Times* review said, "Nearly 3,000 shrieking Beatle People held a concert last night.

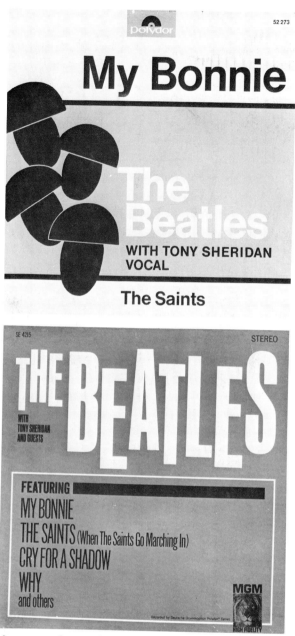

More repackages from the seemingly endless Tony Sheridan/Beat Brothers industry (through p. 179). *Top:* Picture sleeve of the German reissue, January. *Above:* Very rare stereo issue of the MGM LP of *My Bonnie.*

The Beatles were present as inaudible accompanists." (Actually, more than 6,000 shrieking fans attended Carnegie Hall's first rock concert.)

On February 13, the boys flew to Miami aboard a National Airlines plane whose captain wore a Beatles wig.

In spite of strict advance security planning,

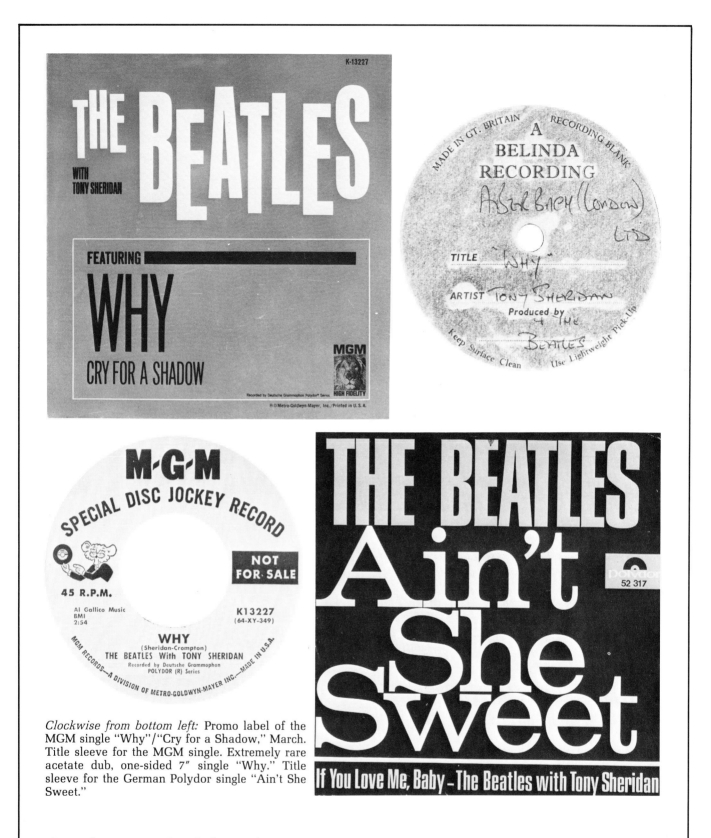

Clockwise from bottom left: Promo label of the MGM single "Why"/"Cry for a Shadow," March. Title sleeve for the MGM single. Extremely rare acetate dub, one-sided 7″ single "Why." Title sleeve for the German Polydor single "Ain't She Sweet."

chaos always arrived with the Beatles. Every police chief mistakenly believed he could handle the enormous crowds, until the boys actually appeared. Miami was no different. The frenzied masses effortlessly swept through the barricades. National Airlines officials were more alert and

The German sleeve for "Take Out Some Insurance," which used the title "If You Love Me, Baby."

were not going to let their famous passengers be crushed by an avalanche of well-meaning admirers. As the airplane stopped, the Beatles jumped to the ground and ran across the ramp to a limousine. A special squad of motorcycle police quickly guided the convoy away from the gate and raced along streets lined with Beatles worshipers, all the way to the Deauville Hotel.

On February 16, more than 70 million viewers saw the second Beatles performance on "The Ed Sullivan Show," this time broadcast live direct from the Deauville Hotel.

The Beatles with Tony Sheridan and Their Guests (MGM SE4215) debuted on *Billboard*'s album chart at Number 147 on February 15. It peaked at Number 68 on April 18, and last appeared on May 16 at Number 146.

On February 22, the Beatles returned to London on Pan Am Flight 121 and were greeted by thousands of faithful fans. Some had slept overnight at the airport. Security leaders realized the danger of allowing crowds onto the tarmac and made arrangements for all well-wishers to gather atop the three roof-level balconies of Heathrow's buildings.

As the Beatles waved and walked toward their car, a roar erupted amid banners saying "Welcome Home Boys." Prime Minister Sir Alec Douglas-Home declared that they were "our best exports and a useful contribution to the balance of payments." A Roman Catholic priest said they were "a menace," while Prince Philip considered them "good chaps." It was a glorious finale to their successful visit to America.

In America the taped Beatles performance was aired on "The Ed Sullivan Show" on the twenty-third.

Meanwhile, in the halls of justice, Capitol and Vee Jay lawyers called a truce. Capitol decided that *Introducing the Beatles* could be reissued provided that the two songs originally owned by Ardmore-Beechwood ("Love Me Do" and "P.S. I Love You") were removed from the existing album. Vee Jay executives agreed and replaced the songs with "Please Please Me" and "Ask Me Why." Vee Jay was back in the Beatles business and published a full-page ad in *Cash Box* announcing the reissue of *Introducing the Beatles* and *Jolly What! The Beatles & Frank Ifield on Stage;* the latter album went on sale in America on February 24. During February the Beatles were responsible for 60 percent of all records sold in the United States.

Above: Vee Jay's full-page ad, February 22, for the two new albums. *Above right:* White Capitol label from acetate proof of *The Beatles' Second Album. Right:* Cover of the Vee Jay 45 rpm EP released March 23.

Label and picture sleeve for the Tollie single.

On George Harrison's twenty-first birthday, February 25, the boys went to Abbey Road and recorded "You Can't Do That," the flip side of their next single, "Can't Buy Me Love." They also recorded several songs for their first movie.

Less than ten days after their return from the conquest of America, the Beatles were setting out to conquer a realm in which their skills were untested. They were understandably anxious; a failure could have been harmful to their future, and pop music fans were still notorious for their short attention span and general fickleness. Executives at United Artists were not worried. The black-and-white movie was a relatively low-budget production, and the producers were convinced that fans would race to theaters just as they raced to record stores and Beatles concerts. The producers were right.

Filming began on March 2 at Paddington Station and continued at Gatwick Airport on Friday the thirteenth. At Twickenham Studios, the Beatles spent time between scenes playing cards, at which Ringo was the big winner. To their irritation, card games were regularly interrupted by phone calls from Murray the K demanding yet another radio interview. They had not expected him to follow

them back to England. (It was during filming that George met Patti Boyd, a pretty blonde model-actress who played a schoolgirl in the train segments and whom he would later marry. In fact, all four boys had become quite romantically stable. John's wife, Cynthia, was with him in London, Ringo had been joined by his longtime Liverpool girl, Maureen Cox, and Paul was seriously involved with Jane Asher.)

During the final days of shooting, United Artists executives decided it was time for the movie to have a title. *Beatlemania* was instantly rejected, as was Paul's proposal, *What Little Old Man?* "A hard day's night" was an expression Ringo had once used to describe an exasperating concert. The phrase became the film's title by unanimous choice. On April 15, the Beatles recorded the title song.

While the Beatles were publicly unavailable for the duration of the filming, the seemingly infinite tidal wave of new releases was taking the world by storm. On March 5, the German-language version of "She Loves You"/"I Want to Hold Your Hand" (Odeon 22671) was released in West Germany. On March 14, two more songs hit the *Billboard* singles chart in the United States. "Twist and Shout" (Tollie 9001—Tollie was a subsidiary label of Vee Jay Records) debuted at Number 55, twelve days after going on sale. It peaked at Number 2 on April 4, remaining there for four weeks, and last appeared on May 23 at Number 41. "Roll Over Beethoven" (Capitol 72133) debuted at Number 122, climbed to Number 68 on April 4, and last appeared seven days later at Number 78. On March 20, "Can't Buy Me Love"/"You Can't Do That" (Parlophone 5114) was released in England and sold 1.5 million copies in seven days. On the twenty-fourth it was released in America (Capitol 5150), where advance sales exceeded 2 million. "Can't Buy Me Love" debuted in *Billboard* at Number 27 four days after going on sale, and was Number 1 for five weeks.

On March 23, Vee Jay issued a single and an EP. The single was "Do You Want to Know a Secret"/"Thank You Girl" (VJ587) and the EP *The Beatles* (VJEP1-903). "Do You Want to Know a Secret" was on *Billboard*'s chart for eleven weeks, peaking at Number 2. "Thank You Girl" spent six weeks on the chart. On March 27, the Beatles owned the top six positions on the singles chart in Australia and "Why"/"Cry for a Shadow" (MGM K13227) by Tony Sheridan and the Beatles was released in America. In fact, Polydor had gone all out to promote their Sheridan/Beatles material outside Europe. Press releases mystified fans with rumors that a tape of the first Beatles recording was locked in a vault. Of course, Sheridan received all royalties from the Polydor records, because the Beatles had been paid a flat session fee as backup artists in 1961.

Two more songs—"All My Loving" and "You Can't Do That"—entered *Billboard*'s singles chart on March 28. On April 4, the Beatles occupied the top five positions on record charts in Great Britain, Australia, and America.

As though that were not enough, on March 23, *In His Own Write,* a book of poetry by John Lennon, was published in England by Jonathan Cape. Literary critics considered the small volume a publicity stunt and predicted it would not sell. It went immediately to the top of the best-seller list.

Three days later, former Beatle Pete Best flew from London to New York to promote his contract with Decca Records and do a television appearance with the Pete Best Four.

It is surprising to consider now, but as early as the spring of 1964, the canonization of the Beatles was well under way. The Cavern became the subject of a weekly show on Radio Luxembourg simply because the Beatles had performed there. And Madame Tussaud's famous museum began exhibiting four wax Beatles.

The Beatles' domination of the American pop music charts raged unabated. "There's a Place" (Tollie 9001) debuted in *Billboard* on April 11 at Number 74. On April 13, *The Beatles' Second Album* (Capitol T2080) was awarded a Gold Record, just three days after its release. It remained on *Billboard*'s chart for fifty-five weeks.

John's book, *In His Own Write,* was released in America by Simon and Schuster on April 27. On the same day, "Love Me Do"/"P.S. I Love You" (Tollie 9008) went on sale. "Love Me Do" was on *Billboard*'s chart for fourteen weeks and was Number 1 for the week of May 30. "P.S. I Love You" debuted at Number 64 on May 9 and peaked at Number 10 on June 6.

On May 21 "Sie Liebt Dich"/"I'll Get You" (Swan 4182) was released in America. This German-language version of "She Loves You" debuted in *Billboard* on May 30 at Number 108 and last appeared on June 27 at its highest position of Number 97.

An interview by Ed Sullivan taped on the set of *A Hard Day's Night* the previous month was shown in America on May 24. It was followed by a filmed performance of "You Can't Do That," taken during their American tour.

John and George ended a vacation on May 26 and returned to London for a preview of *A Hard Day's Night.* Paul and Ringo arrived the next day, tanned and ready for work.

"Ain't She Sweet"/"If You Love Me Baby" (Polydor NH 52-317) went on sale in Britain on the twenty-ninth. This particular release caused plenty of excitement for Beatles fans because John sang lead vocal on "Ain't She Sweet."

The Beatles spent the first two days of June in the Abbey Road studio recording songs for the British issue of the soundtrack for *A Hard Day's Night.* These songs, not used in the movie, were "Anytime at All," "Things We Said Today," "When I Get Home," and "I'll Be Back."

On June 1, "Sweet Georgia Brown"/"Take Out Some Insurance" (ATCO 6302) was released in America and credited to the Beatles with Tony Sheridan.

On June 3, Ringo was rushed to London's Uni-

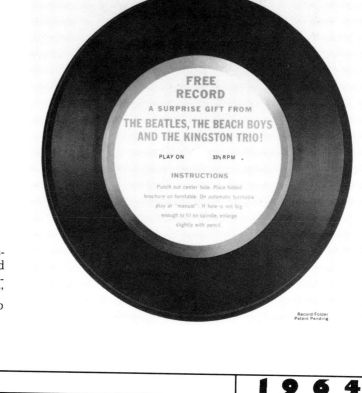

Above: An April newspaper supplement advertising the Capitol Records Club featured a cardboard disc. *Right:* The Beatles sang "Roll Over Beethoven," the Beach Boys sang "Little Deuce Coupe," and the Kingston Trio sang "When the Saints Go Marching In."

The Beatles' first commercial EP, released May 18.

versity Hospital, where his doctor diagnosed a severe case of tonsilitis. The doctor informed Brian Epstein that Ringo would not be available for at least a week, perhaps two. It could not have come at a worse time. The Beatles were scheduled to depart for their summer world tour, in which they would play thirty-two concerts in nineteen days. Epstein was in a quandary. He had to find a substitute drummer. Finding someone to join the Beatles for half a world tour was a special kind of problem. The stand-in would have to be experienced but not well known, and someone who could do the job without becoming a prima donna or claiming Beatles status in articles and interviews afterward.

"You can't expect the guy to keep his mouth shut all the time," Tony Barrow told Epstein.

"I want him to have as little as possible to say," ordered Epstein. "We don't want a drummer who

1964 was a big year for Beatles-related recordings—some by actual Beatles relations! (Through p. 189.)

Election year in America.

The task of finding a drummer who could measure up to the requirements set by John, Paul, George, and Brian seemed impossible but the first name that came up was Jimmy Nicol, who had recently played for Tommy Quickly, another singer Brian managed. Nicol was familiar with most of the Beatles songs since he had performed on a *Beatlemania* LP of anonymous cover versions of Beatles songs released on the Top Six label.

Less than twenty-four hours after Jimmy's audition, he and John, Paul, and George departed Heathrow Airport amid "Get Well Soon Ringo" signs. John, Paul, and George insisted that Jimmy not only perform as a drummer but take part in all events, including press interviews and photo sessions. Epstein reluctantly agreed.

Nine thousand fans screamed as the Beatles appeared in Copenhagen on June 4. Jimmy Nicol wore Ringo's gray suit while the others sported mohair. They flew to Amsterdam the next day, where the crowds threatened to create a security problem outside the Royal Hotel.

On the sixth they did two shows at the Blokker Cabbage Auction Hall to a sellout crowd of 7,000 fans. The next day they boarded a flight to Hong Kong, making fuel stops at Zurich, Beirut, Karachi, Calcutta, and Bangkok. At each airport, whenever a Beatle left the plane, the crowd exploded. More than 1,000 screaming fans greeted them in Hong Kong. It was no secret that Beatlemania had reached the Orient.

The Beatles did two shows on the ninth at the Princess Theatre in Kowloon. Neither performance was sold out, however, because of the unscrupulous dealing of the promoter, who charged 75 Hong Kong dollars—approximately equal to an average local workingman's weekly salary. Brian Epstein was not aware of the rip-off price.

Following a press conference in Sydney, the Beatles flew to Adelaide on the twelfth. The newspapers offered a glimpse of some unwelcome moments that the Beatles feared. While most papers showed the crowds screaming as the boys ran to their limousine, the Sydney papers reflected upon the boys' annoyance at fans who bombarded them with jellybeans.

Apart from the candy-tossing fans, the Chamber Music Quartet of Sydney rated the Beatles among the noisiest they ever heard. An acoustics expert at New South Wales University stated that the Beatles' crowds made more noise than a Boeing 707 jetliner at full power. "Normally, noise reach-

is star-struck. We just want a stand-in, that's all. And the less that's written about him, the better pleased I shall be."

ing the ground from a Boeing jet plane 2,000 feet up is between 90 and 100 decibels," said the expert. "When the Beatles appeared, the pure screams alone showed 112 decibels on the recording apparatus. For the next half hour the needle never fell below 100 and many times leapt higher."

The welcome in Adelaide eclipsed all previous affairs, including those in the United States. It was estimated that 300,000 fans lined the streets just to get a quick glimpse of the Beatles—a sight forever etched in Jimmy Nicol's memory. There were 50,000 ticket requests for the 12,000 seats in Centennial Hall.

The Beatles arrived in Melbourne on the fourteenth and were joined by Ringo and Brian Epstein that night. Jimmy Nicol's moment of fame ended and he returned to London. The day prior to his departure from Melbourne the *London Sunday Telegraph* published a smiling photo of him headlined BIG PLANS AHEAD FOR JIMMY NICOL. His manager, Bill Welling, said that the "fifth Beatle" got just the break he needed when he replaced Ringo in the early part of their Far East and Australian tour, and added: "We are hoping that fans will remember Jimmy Nicol rather than just as Ringo's replacement drummer." During Nicol's brief stint with the boys a record previously issued by Jimmy Nicol and the Shubdubs was again released with the note "Jimmy Nicol, now with The Beatles." The song, "Humpty Dumpty," became another forgettable disc associated with the Beatles, one that appealed only to serious record collectors.

On June 18—Paul's twenty-second birthday—they flew to Sydney and performed the first of six shows to 12,000 fans, the largest audience ever for a pop concert in that city.

The Beatles did shows at Wellington's Town Hall June 22–23 during a seven-day visit to New Zealand. Back in Australia on the twenty-sixth, 5,500 fans screamed during four shows in Brisbane, and then the summer tour was over. Despite the fact that more than £200,000 had been made in Australia, breaking all previous concert records, the Beatles never returned.

The last of the Tony Sheridan/Beatles recordings made in Hamburg during 1961 went on sale in America on July 6. "Ain't She Sweet"/"Nobody's Child" (ATCO 6308) debuted in *Billboard* at Number 90 on July 18 and reached Number 19 on August 22, before its last showing at Number 37 on September 12.

Also on July 6, the Beatles attended the world

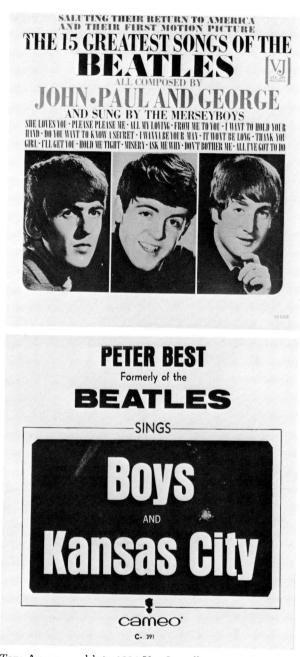

Top: An unusual late 1964 Vee Jay album. You have to read carefully to realize that the songs were recorded not by the Beatles but by the Merseyboys.

premiere of *A Hard Day's Night.* This charity affair at the London Pavilion benefited the Dockland Settlements and the Variety Club Heart Fund. Fans began arriving during the early morning. The crowd had swelled to 12,000 when the doors were opened to admit special guests. Hundreds of policemen wrestled with eager fans and Piccadilly Circus was closed to all motor traffic.

As the theater lights dimmed the boys anxiously awaited the reaction to their madcap movie. They really had nothing to worry about. The audience was ecstatic and gave a standing ovation. Reporters and photographers raced from the theater to cover the celebrity reception party at the Dorchester Hotel, where the big news was the presence of Princess Margaret and the Earl of Snowdon. The fact that they had attended the premiere itself was thought to be in regard for the charities involved. However, their arrival at the *party* proved that they were genuinely interested in the Beatles, which provided a most happy evening for Brian Epstein.

No one imagined that anything could top the spectacular events of the first showing, but the July 10 premiere in the Beatles' hometown did just that. Tony Barrow said, "The population of Liverpool in 1964 was said to be around three quarters of a million. It was estimated afterwards that over one in four Liverpudlians turned out that Friday evening to line the ten-mile route taken by the Beatles from Speke to the city center."

A stirring round of applause arose as the Beatles were led into the ballroom at Town Hall by the Lord Mayor.

"Liverpool has given the Beatles to the world!" shouted one official spokesman.

"And the world has lobbed us back at Liverpool," John said to those around him.

This day also marked the release in Great Britain of the single "A Hard Day's Night"/"Things We Said Today" (Parlophone R5160) and the movie soundtrack (Parlophone PMC1250/PCS3058), plus George Martin's instrumental album, *Off the Beatle Track* (Parlophone PCS3057).

A Hard Day's Night premiered in America on July 13, the same day "A Hard Day's Night"/"I Should Have Known Better" (Capitol 5222) went on sale. Both songs debuted in *Billboard* five days later. The A side was Number 1 for two weeks and remained on the charts until October 10. On July 18, *A Hard Day's Night* debuted in *Billboard*'s album chart at Number 12. It was Number 1 for fourteen weeks.

Capitol Records released two singles and one album on July 20: "I'll Cry Instead"/"I'm Happy Just to Dance with You" (Capitol 5234), "And I Love Her"/"If I Fell" (Capitol 5235), and the *Something New* LP (Capitol T2108). "I'll Cry Instead" debuted in *Billboard* on July 25 at Number 115 and

George Harrison's sister's first and only recording was perhaps the world's first "tell-all" disc.

Above: John Lennon's father, Freddie, composed and sang about his life in Liverpool. *Top right:* Mar Mar rushed this out while Nicol was filling in for Ringo. *Right:* Tower Records (a subsidiary of Capitol) issued this sing-along album late in the year.

peaked at Number 25 on August 29. It last appeared at Number 36 on September 12. "I'm Happy Just to Dance with You" hit the chart at Number 113 on July 25, peaked at Number 95 on August 1, and last appeared at Number 112 on September 5. "If I Fell" first appeared at Number 92 on August 1, climbed to Number 53 on September 5, and left the chart on September 26 at Number 59. "And I Love Her" debuted at Number 80 on July 25, reached Number 12 by September 5, and last appeared at Number 28 on September 28.

On July 23, a California superior court judge announced a significant decision that affected two giants of the recording industry. Capitol Records claimed that Vee Jay Records had violated its agreement made three months earlier regarding the album *Introducing the Beatles*. While visiting London on May 22, Jay Lasker, vice president of Vee Jay, had shown EMI executives a sample copy of the album in question. Repackaged, it also carried a new title, *Songs, Pictures and Stories of the Fabulous Beatles*.

Later that day, Jay Lasker received a hand-delivered letter from the president of EMI.

Dear Jay,
I confirm that this afternoon I telephoned

Walter Hofer to ask him to advise you that we feel that your proposal to release the Beatles album in the new package of which you showed me a sample this morning is in contravention of the settlement agreement signed between you and Trans-Global Music Co. Inc., a point which Walter appeared readily to appreciate.

I must therefore ask you to cancel immediately your plans in respect of this proposed re-sleeving.

Yours sincerely,
L. G. Wood

On June 5 Vee Jay Records received a registered letter from Capitol's legal department.

Gentlemen,
You have advised Capitol Records, Inc. that the master recordings by the Beatles of the license contract dated April 9, 1964 between Vee Jay Records, Inc. and Trans-Global Music Co. Inc., and Capitol Records, have been re-released as a long playing record and that such re-release differs from your long playing record VJLP No. 1062, titled Introducing the Beatles *in the following respect, a new*

This "slick" of the *Introducing the Beatles* cover was used as an exhibit in the Vee Jay/Capitol trial in July.

"magazine type" jacket has been substituted for the single jacket of VJLP 1062, there is new artwork on the cover of the jacket, new liner material and photographs for the expanded "liner," a new and different title in place of Introducing the Beatles, *and a new album number.*

Demand is made that you comply with your obligations under said settlement agreement by immediately removing from the market the re-designed album and notify Capitol that you have done so.

Vee Jay was given ten days to respond and did so on June 22 by petitioning the superior court of Los Angeles, California, for a judgment. The trial was held without a jury on July 15.

Lawyers representing Vee Jay Records argued that the April 9, 1964, license did not mention or prohibit Vee Jay from using any jacket to market phonograph records from the covered masters. Capitol objected, saying that the redesigned package constituted a breach of the license agreement.

Vee Jay offered Exhibit A, a contract dated April 9, 1964, in which Vee Jay entered into an agreement with Capitol Records and Trans-Global Music, Inc., to lease certain master recordings called covered masters. This contract would expire on October 15, 1964. Next came Exhibit B, a "slick" of the front and back cover of *Introducing the Beatles.* The back listed the twelve covered masters. This was followed by Exhibit C, a "slick" of the redesigned cover for *Songs, Pictures and Stories of the Fabulous Beatles.*

Judge Mervyn A. Aggeler listened to the arguments and studied the exhibits. Eight days later, July 23, he announced his decision:

The court finds in favor of Vee Jay Records on all the issues raised by Vee Jay and against Capitol Records on all issues raised in their cross-complaint.

Vee Jay Records has the unqualified right to advertise and promote the covered masters in any cover, jacket or package which Vee Jay Records, Inc., deems appropriate.

Vee Jay has the unqualified right to advertise, sell and promote the long playing album in the type of jacket (Songs, Pictures and Stories of the Fabulous Beatles), *a copy of which is attached to Vee Jay Records complaint, marked as Exhibit C.*

Capitol Records and Beechwood Music,

Top: White test-pressing label of *A Hard Day's Night.* Brian Epstein's handwriting is on the label. *Above:* Rare title sleeve for the single issue of "Ain't She Sweet"/ "Nobody's Child."

Inc., are permanently restrained from declaring that promotion of the long playing record Introducing the Beatles, *in the redesigned jacket, constitutes or will constitute a breach in contracts, the License Agreement and Mechanical License both dated April 9, 1964.*

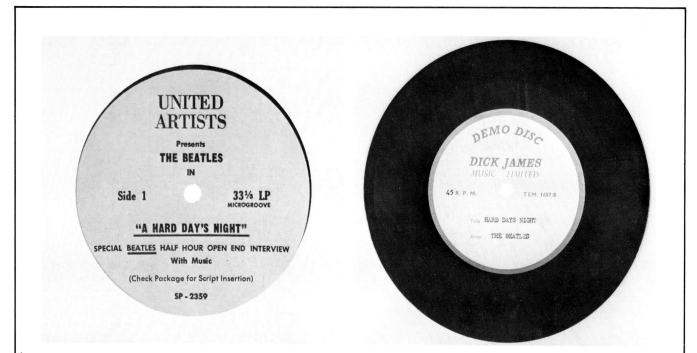

"A HARD DAY'S NIGHT"

OPEN END HALF HOUR WITH THE BEATLES

INTERVIEWER:	Well, Hello there, Beatles!!!
BEATLES:	Hello, it's certainly nice to be on your program. Certainly is. Certainly is. This is Paul speaking.
INTERVIEWER:	Paul who?
PAUL M:	Paul McCartney!
RINGO S:	This is Ringo Starr
GEORGE H:	George Harrison. (Together: "La, La, La, La!")
INTERVIEWER:	What happened to John?
PAUL M:	Well, actually he's gone down to the shipyard to have an estimate for a haircut.
RINGO S:	I don't know, he's supposed to be here. He's late, isn't he? What's happenin'. I don't know, don't ask me... Please don't ask me...
INTERVIEWER:	Well, I can't tell how thrilled we all are having the Beatles on our program, on a most auspicious occasion.... Your very first starring movie!
BEATLES:	"A Hard Day's Night." Thank you very much.... thank you.
INTERVIEWER:	Was it a "hard day's night," Ringo, making this first big one?
RINGO S:	Well, it was a hard two months... It took two months, actually, to make this film, but I think I found the biggest drag was when we were just sitting 'round doing nothing...
GEORGE H.	And getting up early
PAUL M.	That was one of those things. We had to get up about six o'clock in the morning, you know, sometimes, which is, Oh I'm sure it's not good for any one, that... It's very bad for your health.

The United Artists "open-end interview" LP—label (above left) and first page of script (left). *Above:* Demo disc of "A Hard Day's Night," one-sided 7″ single.

Also, Capitol Records and Beechwood Music were not allowed to cancel the April 9, 1964, contract, which would continue in effect until October 15, 1964. After that date Vee Jay would no longer be allowed to manufacture or sell any of the Beatles' covered masters in any form. Accordingly, Vee Jay did not waste any time in releasing *Songs, Pictures and Stories of the Fabulous Beatles* (VJLP1092) on July 25.

On August 2 the Beatles performed in Bournemouth, along with an unknown group from London called the Kinks.

On the eighth, *Something New* (Capitol ST2108) debuted on *Billboard*'s album chart at Number 125. It became Number 2 for nine weeks beginning August 22, and last appeared at Number 121 on May 15, 1965.

On the tenth, Vee Jay Records made an addition to their Oldies 45 line and released four Beatles singles. "Do You Want to Know a Secret"/"Thank You Girl" (OL149), "Please Please Me"/"From Me to You" (OL150), "Love Me Do"/"P.S. I Love You" (OL151), and "There's a Place"/"Twist and Shout" (OL152). These songs re-presented VJ581, 587, and Tollie 9008, 9001, previously released during the first quarter of 1964. A series of sleeves with humorous greetings were designed to sell the Oldies 45 line, known as teen fun cards, and were offered at no extra cost.

Vee Jay also released a peculiar album during August that appeared to be another collection of songs by the Beatles. *The 15 Greatest Songs of the Beatles* (VJLP1101) was quickly issued to salute the boys' return to America and their first movie. Huge photos of Paul, George, and John adorned the cover along with "All songs composed by John, Paul, and George," in bold type. There was a small notation that the songs on this recording were performed by the Merseyboys. The effort received little promotion and faded into obscurity with countless other Beatles-related items.

On August 16, the Beatles appeared at Blackpool's Opera House with a new rock band that would soon change its name to The Who.

At noon on the eighteenth the Beatles departed London and crossed the Atlantic to begin their "First American Tour." Although it was really their second visit to the United States, it would be their first concert tour across America. After brief stops in Winnipeg and Los Angeles, the boys were welcomed by 9,000 screaming fans at San Fran-cisco International Airport. The loyal flock had begun gathering around noon the previous day from all over the Bay Area. Some camped on the ground while others slept in the terminal. During the long vigil, Beatles signs were poised against the cyclone fence and local disc jockeys provided entertainment.

When the Beatles stepped from the plane the eager masses pushed through the fence and charged across the tarmac. Many fainted but others continued running and the Beatles were lucky to escape by seconds into their limousine.

The Beatles were relatively safe in their fifteenth-floor suite at the Hilton because the hotel was swarming with an army of policemen. Later, John and Ringo persuaded their press agent to help them get past the security guards. They went to a nightclub in Chinatown that was operated by their friend Billy Preston. The Beatles had first met Preston when he was a keyboard player with Little Richard's band during a show in Hamburg, and again in Liverpool in 1962. The musical paths of the Beatles and Preston would cross again in 1969 when he would play on their *Let It Be* album.

During the next thirty-four days the Beatles performed thirty-two shows at twenty-six concerts in twenty-four cities, and logged about sixty hours of flight time in their Lockheed Electra turboprop. The pace was frantic and the pressure unbearable due to constant traveling and interviews. Most of the time they did not know what city they were performing in.

The first concert was held on August 19 at the Cow Palace in San Francisco, where 16,000 wide-eyed teens barely heard the boys sing a dozen songs in thirty minutes. Many young girls were overwhelmed and required first aid.

The *San Francisco Examiner* reported: "Although it was publicized as music, all that was heard and seen of the Mersey Sound was something like a jet engine shrieking through a summer lightning storm because of the yelling fans. . . . The eerie scene of four young men with shaggy hairdos wiggling on the stage and moving their lips inaudibly was exaggerated by the flashes from a hundred cameras, like sheet lightning in the Midwest." This was a scene that became ordinary as the tour progressed.

On August 20 the Beatles created a riot in Las Vegas when security measures collapsed while the boys and their entourage were being delivered to the Sahara Hotel. A total of 16,000 fans saw two shows at the Convention Center.

At a show in Seattle for 14,720 screamers, local police had to recruit Navy volunteers from the audience to form a human barricade from the stage to the dressing room. Two sixteen-year-old girls were caught under a bed in the Beatles' hotel suite by a maid, who then found a third girl in the closet.

The Electra arrived in Canada on August 22, and the boys did one show at Vancouver's Empire Stadium. The opening acts included the Bill Black Combo, the Exciters, the Righteous Brothers, and Jackie DeShannon. Security was a joke as a mere 100 policemen tried to control 20,000 hysterical teens. The police actually had to fight their way into the crowd to rescue fans who would have been trampled by one another.

Afterward, the boys were rushed to the airport and took off for Los Angeles and the famous Hollywood Bowl, which was dubbed the Beatles Bowl by the fans. Nearly 18,000 saw the historic performance at the Bowl on the twenty-third. The concert was recorded by Capitol Records but was not released until thirteen years later. After doing twelve songs they were hustled into a small car that sped away while anxious fans kept their eyes glued on a black limousine decoy behind the Bowl.

On August 26, 7,000 fans attended the Beatles concert at the Red Rocks Amphitheatre in Denver.

The next day 14,000 saw the Beatles in Cincinnati. A television technician tried to measure the sound but gave up when his equipment reached its peak and broke. The 100 policemen assigned as security guards could only stand in the 115-degree heat and stare helplessly. They would have had better luck guarding the Beatles' dressing room during the show, because thieves were busy stealing cash and personal items there.

Beatlemania struck New York for a second time as the boys performed at the Forest Hills Tennis Stadium on August 28 and 29. More than 16,000 fans were bobbing and swaying and shrieking at each show. Thousands of teens had attended the New York premiere of *A Hard Day's Night* on August 11.

After the concert, a helicopter flew the Beatles back to their suite at the Delmonico Hotel, where another 3,000 fans waited and wailed.

On August 30, the Beatles gave a concert for 18,000 teens at the Convention Hall in Atlantic City, New Jersey, which one week earlier had hosted the Democratic Party's National Convention.

The Beatles performed for 13,000 shrieking fans in Philadelphia on September 2. The next day they thrilled 29,337 fans during two shows at the Indiana State Fair. Afterward they were spirited away for a quick press affair, where they learned that thirty girls had been treated for hysteria.

Touring with the Beatles was a hazardous occupation. Bess Coleman, a member of the official entourage, was mistaken for a fan by a policeman who tried to toss her over a fence as she followed the boys from the press conference. Reporters were pushed to the ground or accidentally struck in the face or ribs as police tried to protect the famous singers. Still, Ivor Davis, a reporter for the London *Daily Express,* told American newsmen that their task was much easier. "We have to do it every day. Your worries are over."

After one show for 11,500 fans in Milwaukee on September 4, the Beatles flew to Chicago, where 5,000 howling fans greeted them at Midway Airport. Beatlemania became bedlam during their performance at Chicago's International Amphitheatre on the fifth. The Beatles were the last act of a two-hour rock concert, but to their 15,000 faithful fans they were the *only* act. Girls hung precariously from balconies and stood on their seats and screamed like banshees.

The boys did two shows for 21,000 fans in Montreal on the eighth. Afterward they took off for Jacksonville, Florida, but their Electra was diverted to Key West to avoid an encounter with Hurricane Dora. Somehow, hundreds of excited teens were there to greet them when they made an unscheduled landing at 3:30 in the morning on the ninth. Hurricane Dora arrived on time in Jacksonville and caused so much damage that the Beatles had to wait two days before they could fly there. On September 11, they played for 20,000 teens, although an estimated 9,000 ticket holders were unable to get to the Gator Bowl because of the storm's destruction.

The Beatles flew to Boston for one show on September 12, followed by two performances for 28,000 in Baltimore on the thirteenth.

The next day Capitol Records released a promo

Cover and selected inside pages (through p. 199) from the souvenir program for the Liverpool premiere of *A Hard Day's Night.* Local merchants capitalized creatively on the success of the local heroes.

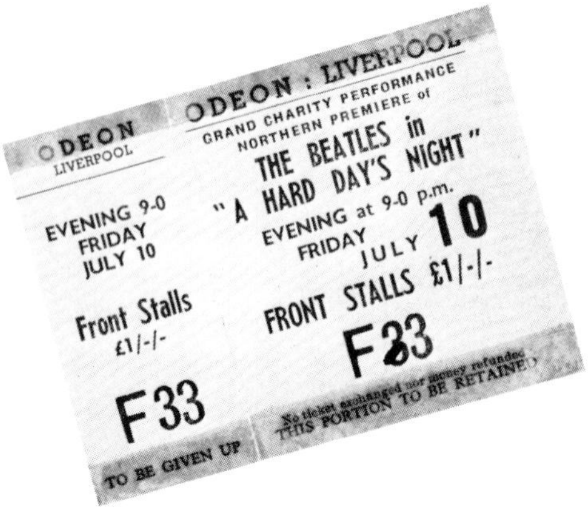
ODEON
LIVERPOOL
EVENING 9-0
FRIDAY
JULY 10
Front Stalls
£1/-/-
F33
TO BE GIVEN UP
ODEON : LIVERPOOL
GRAND CHARITY PERFORMANCE
NORTHERN PREMIERE of
THE BEATLES in
"A HARD DAY'S NIGHT"
EVENING at 9-0 p.m.
FRIDAY
JULY 10
FRONT STALLS £1/-/-
F33
No ticket exchanged nor money refunded
THIS PORTION TO BE RETAINED

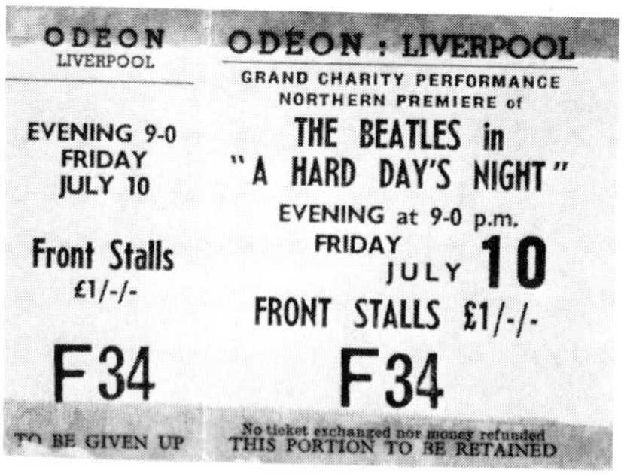
ODEON
LIVERPOOL
EVENING 9-0
FRIDAY
JULY 10
Front Stalls
£1/-/-
F34
TO BE GIVEN UP
ODEON : LIVERPOOL
GRAND CHARITY PERFORMANCE
NORTHERN PREMIERE of
THE BEATLES in
"A HARD DAY'S NIGHT"
EVENING at 9-0 p.m.
FRIDAY
JULY 10
FRONT STALLS £1/-/-
F34
No ticket exchanged nor money refunded
THIS PORTION TO BE RETAINED

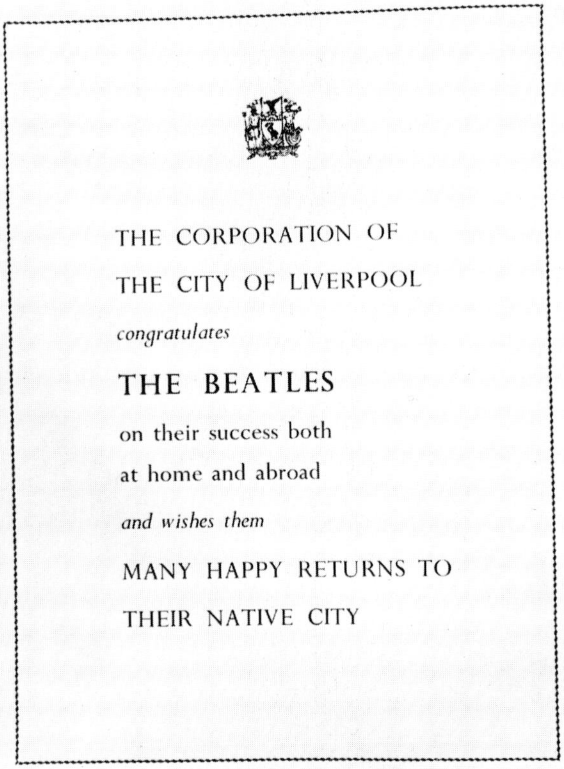
THE CORPORATION OF
THE CITY OF LIVERPOOL
congratulates
THE BEATLES
on their success both
at home and abroad
and wishes them
MANY HAPPY RETURNS TO
THEIR NATIVE CITY

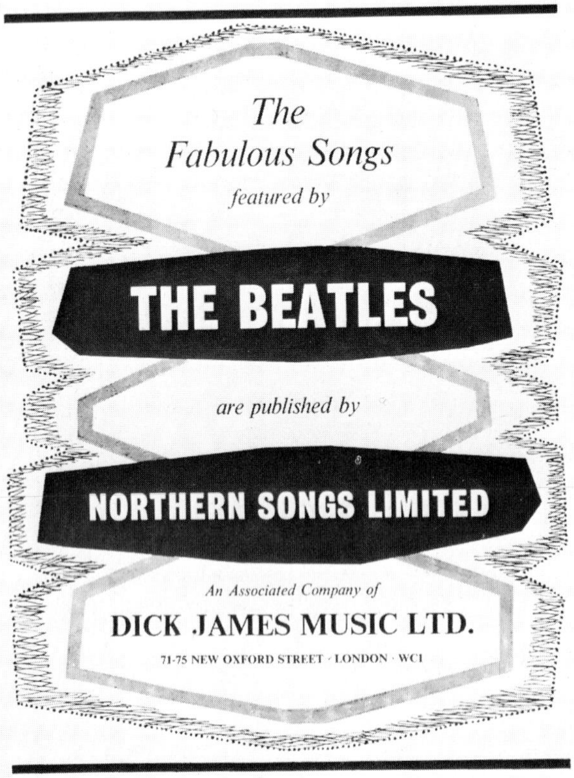
The
Fabulous Songs
featured by
THE BEATLES
are published by
NORTHERN SONGS LIMITED
An Associated Company of
DICK JAMES MUSIC LTD.
71-75 NEW OXFORD STREET · LONDON · WC1

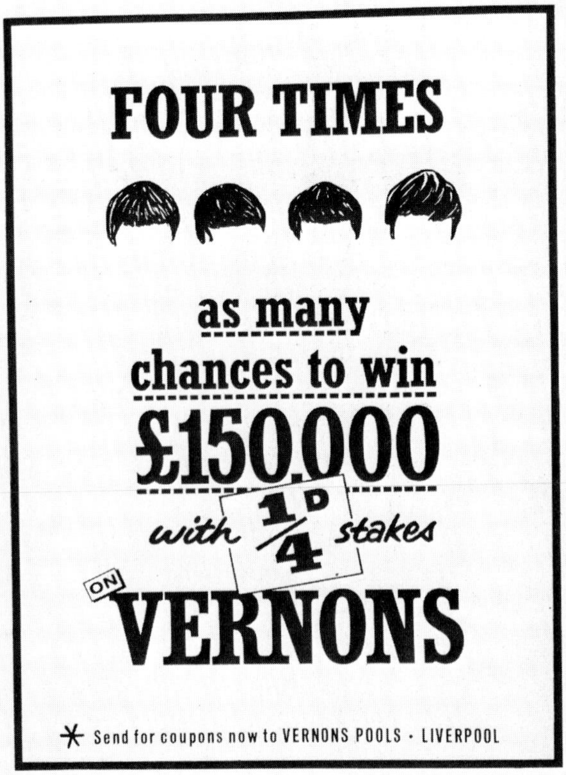
FOUR TIMES
as many
chances to win
£150,000
with 1/4D stakes
ON
VERNONS
* Send for coupons now to VERNONS POOLS · LIVERPOOL

tional EP, *The Beatles Introduce New Songs* (Capitol PRO2720). This disc had Paul and John introduce "I Don't Want to See You Again" by Peter and Gordon, and "It's for You" by Cilla Black.

Also on this day, 4,000 fans met the Beatles at Greater Pittsburgh Airport and followed their speeding motorcade to the Civic Arena. The *Pittsburgh Post-Gazette* said, "For the first time, Allegheny County Mounted Police . . . stood guard between the Beatles and their admirers. No President or presidential candidate has been accorded that police accolade."

Another rousing concert was held on the fifteenth in Cleveland and policemen had to stop the show when the crazed fans threatened to riot. The auditorium roared with protests when the music stopped and the Beatles reluctantly went to their dressing room. "This has never happened to us before—anywhere," John told a newsman from KYW Radio. "We have never had a show stopped. These policemen are a bunch of amateurs."

Eventually, the Beatles continued the show as many teenage girls sobbed in ecstasy. Although Cleveland officials were happy to see the Beatles'

airplane take off, authorities in New Orleans were not prepared for their arrival. It took more than 200 policemen and special guards nearly thirty minutes to restore order while 12,000 screaming fans reacted to the Beatles performance on September 16. The boys had been singing only fifteen minutes when the crowd began rushing across the field at City Park Stadium.

At two o'clock in the morning on the seventeenth, the Beatles stepped from their Electra and waved to a crowd of wet fans in Kansas City who had been waiting for hours in a rainstorm. This particular stop was not part of the scheduled tour and had been negotiated between Brian Epstein and millionaire sportsman Charles O. Finley, who desperately wanted the boys to perform in his town.

Charles Finley, owner of the Kansas City Athletics baseball team, made a special trip to see Epstein when the boys played in San Francisco. He offered Epstein $50,000, and then $100,000, for just one show. Epstein informed Finley that the only date available was September 17, a rest day for the boys. Finley was not about to be refused. He wrote another check for $150,000. Epstein told him to

wait a moment and went to the Beatles' room and interrupted their card game. He showed them the check and said it was entirely up to them. They went back to concentrating on their game for a moment, then John said, "We'll do whatever you want." The others simply nodded.

So on the evening of September 17, the Beatles appeared at the Municipal Stadium in Kansas City, Kansas. For this one show the Beatles earned $4,838 per minute—and this was only thirteen months since their last performance at the Cavern in Liverpool.

(The hotel manager in Kansas City sold all of the Beatles' bed sheets and pillowcases to a couple of Chicago businessmen who cut the material into three-inch squares and resold them for $10 each. "Merchandising" played a key role in many cities during this tour. In San Francisco the same thing had been accomplished with the unlaundered towels the Beatles had used at the Hilton.)

"An Evening with the Beatles" announced a special charity concert in New York City on September 20. This show, which aided United Cerebral Palsy, also was the final show of the American tour. More than 3,000 people paid $100 each to hear the boys sing, along with other acts at the Paramount Theatre. All of the artists, including the Beatles, performed free of charge.

On September 21, the Beatles left for London. In the month they had been in North America, they had been seen live in concert by more than 350,000 people.

"It was terrifying and terrific all at once," said Ringo. "Some nights I just sat there behind my drums and stared out across the sea of faces in front of the stage or the platform. It's the sheer size of everything in America that's frightening. But I must say that doing a show for such a huge audience gives you a marvelous buzz. There are so many voices available out there to do the screaming that it's one continuous sound."

The Beatles continued taping songs for their next album at Abbey Road on October 3, and the next day they recorded their next single, "I Feel Fine"/"She's a Woman."

On the fifth, *Ain't She Sweet* (ATCO SD33-169) was released in America. This album contained four Sheridan-Beatles songs from the 1961 Hamburg session previously issued in 1964 as ATCO singles.

On October 7 the Beatles were seen in America on ABC-TV's "Shindig." Two days later, Dick Clark presented an all Beatles program on "The New American Bandstand." This show included their latest recordings and film clips from *A Hard Day's Night,* plus interviews loaned by KRLA Radio in Los Angeles.

On October 9, John's twenty-fourth birthday, the Beatles began their first and only tour for the year in the United Kingdom. The schedule called for fifty-four shows at twenty-seven concert halls in twenty-five cities in thirty-three days.

Pandemonium greeted the Beatles on opening night at the Gaumont Cinema in Bradford, but the boys were startled by the contrast between doing a show in America and one in their homeland. Throughout the American tour they were performing to audiences of 15,000 to 20,000 at each show. The theaters in England, however, seldom held more than 1,500 to 2,000 seats. However, the fans were just as crazed and thrilled as their American counterparts and very grateful to have the famous quartet back home again.

Johnny Dean, editor of *The Beatles Book Monthly,* said, "Although I'd seen the boys perform many times over the previous two years I'd never seen them look slicker or more polished. But the marvelous thing about every Beatles performance was the way they enjoyed themselves so much."

In America, *Hear the Beatles Tell All* (VJPRO202) was released by Vee Jay in its final effort to cash in on the Beatles before relinquishing all rights to Capitol Records. Side 1 offered an interview with John by Jim Steck, while Side 2 had Dave Hull interviewing all four singers.

A quickly redesigned cover was printed for the *Jolly What!* album. It displayed the exact color illustration of the Beatles that appeared on the Tollie single sleeve. This new cover deleted the words *Jolly What!* and was retitled *The Beatles & Frank Ifield on Stage.* A limited quantity were distributed, to be bought by avid Beatles fans who had to have any record if the Beatles name appeared on the cover.

On October 18, the Beatles returned to Abbey Road to record eight numbers for their next album, as well as their 1964 Christmas message for their fan club.

On October 30, *Songs, Pictures and Stories of the Fabulous Beatles* debuted in *Billboard* at Number 121; it reached its peak on December 5 at

Number 63 before last appearing at Number 138 on January 9, 1965.

On November 4 and 5 two extended-play records went on sale in Great Britain in an attempt to cash in on as much success as the market would bear from the Beatles' movie. Extracts from *A Hard Day's Night* (Parlophone GEP8920 and GEP8924) were released with four tracks each, providing anxious teens with all of the songs the Beatles sang in the film.

On November 8, a special concert was presented at the Empire Theatre as the famous quartet played their hometown for the first time since December 22, 1963. Liverpudlians went crazy.

On November 13, "America"/"Since You Broke My Heart" (Parlophone R5197) by Rory Storm was released with Ringo on backing vocals when he was the drummer for the Hurricanes.

In America, on November 23, "I Feel Fine"/ "She's a Woman" (Capitol 5327), and the double album, *The Beatles Story* (Capitol ST1302222), went on sale. "I Feel Fine" debuted in *Billboard* on December 5 at Number 22 and was Number 1 for three weeks, beginning December 26, and last appeared at Number 40 on February 13, 1965. "She's a Woman" debuted on December 5 at Number 46 and peaked at Number 4 on the twenty-sixth before its final listing at Number 37 on January 30, 1965. *The Beatles Story* debuted on the album chart at Number 97 on December 12 and peaked at Number 7, beginning January 2, 1965, before its last showing at Number 108 on April 3, 1965.

On December 18, the official Beatles Fan Club mailed *Another Beatles Christmas Record* to its members. "Another Beatles Christmas Show" opened its twenty-day run on Christmas Eve at the Hammersmith Odeon in London. This extravaganza was produced by Peter Yolland, who had handled the first show. Along with the Beatles, the spectacular featured Freddie and the Dreamers, Jimmy Saville, Elkie Brooks, the Yardbirds, and Michael Haslam.

Tickets had gone on sale in September and 100,000 had been sold three months later. A complete sellout occurred by opening night for the forty scheduled shows. All box-office receipts for the December 29 performances were donated to the Brady Clubs and Settlement Charity in London's East End.

On December 31, EMI executive Joseph Lockwood hosted a party during which the Beatles learned that two of their albums had just been

Savage Records issued the Beatles' German recordings late in 1964 in this provocative package.

Left (top and bottom): Rare stereo issue of *The Beatles vs. The Four Seasons,* released by Vee Jay on October 1. *Above:* Acetate dub for *The Beatles Documentary* album on Capitol. *Above right:* The rarest Beatles album is the stereo issue of *The Beatles & Frank Ifield on Stage,* late 1964, a repackage of the *Jolly What!* album, which had been released February 26 of that year. *Far right:* White test-pressing label of Parlophone's *Beatles for Sale,* with Epstein's handwriting.

certified Gold in America—*The Beatles Story* and the newly released *Beatles '65.*

During the month the Beatles made the pages of newspapers and magazines throughout the world. They also made it into the pages of an obscure U.S. government publication entitled *International Commerce.* Neil C. Hurley, Jr., chairman of the National Export Expansion Council, detailed the value of the Beatles to the British exchequer via taxes on the millions they had earned on the recent American concert tour. The Beatles absorbed more U.S. money than exports of British automobiles. It was reported by EMI, who handled the Beatles' records in England, that there was a $30 million sales increase and the Beatles themselves earned sixty times the salary of the U.S. President. By December 1964, it was clear to everyone that

THE BEATLES & MURRAY THE 'K' AS IT HAPPENED

NEW YORK
MIAMI
LONDON
WASHINGTON

the Beatles had become a world commodity.

During the four years and seven months that began in May 1960, the Beatles were apprentices, learning their craft. From their musically and financially humble beginnings in small Liverpool clubs to graduating to the flamboyant nightclub scene in Hamburg, they persevered.

It was not an easy task. Personal conflicts and individual popularity became frustrating interrup-

tions, but the difficulties were overcome. The boys stuck together and allowed no one to discourage them.

Maturity, new creative insights, and individual growth would put a strain on their future lives, but in 1964 the Beatles gave the world a reason to come closer together through a common bond that was formed by fans and remains unshaken to this day.

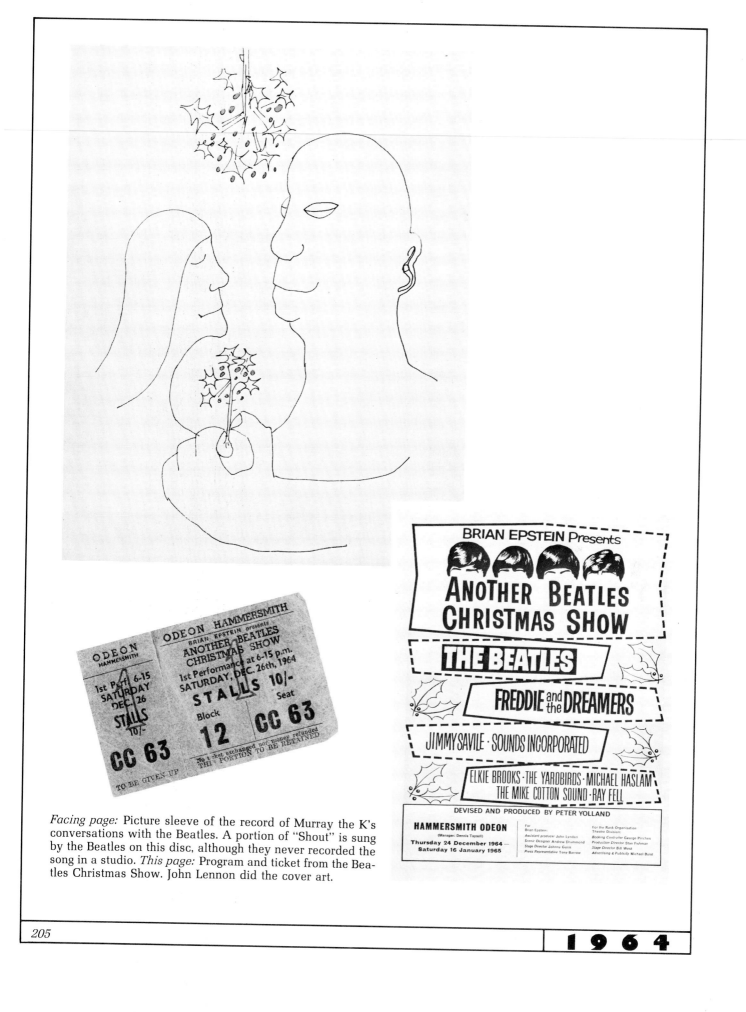

Facing page: Picture sleeve of the record of Murray the K's conversations with the Beatles. A portion of "Shout" is sung by the Beatles on this disc, although they never recorded the song in a studio. *This page:* Program and ticket from the Beatles Christmas Show. John Lennon did the cover art.

Above: The second British Christmas disc. It was never issued as a single in America. *Facing page, top:* Rare insert that accompanied the 1964 British Fan Club disc. *Right and far right:* The first American Fan Club fold-out cardboard disc contained the 1963 message.

Paul

George

Ringo

John

M
E
R
R
Y
C
H
R
I
S
T
M
A
S

The Beatle Bulletin
THE MAGAZINE OF THE OFFICIAL
NATIONAL BEATLES FAN CLUB

CHRISTMAS
ISSUE

December, *1964*

BEATLES (U.S.A.) LTD.
P.O. BOX 505, RADIO CITY STATION
NEW YORK, N.Y. 10019

BULK RATE
U.S. POSTAGE
PAID
NEW YORK, N.Y.
PERMIT NO. 788

Extremely rare U.S. poster.